Combating Educational Disadvantage

The 'New Labour' Government in Britain puts 'education, education, education' at the heart of its agenda, but is it doing enough to combat educational disadvantage?

This book sets the discussion of educational disadvantage within the socio-political context of the 1980s and 1990s, with its market philosophy in education, and brings together the contributions of leading writers and researchers of international standing.

The wide-ranging coverage of educational disadvantage in this book includes, in Part I, an examination of the educational problems experienced by particular 'at risk' groups: ethnic minority children; underachieving boys; looked-after children; poor school attenders; and children displaying disruptive behaviour in the classroom. Part II focuses on a variety of approaches to meeting the needs of disadvantaged children. A final chapter brings together common themes and issues, and relates these to the educational reforms of the present British Government.

Combating Educational Disadvantage provides an important source of authoritative discussion of various aspects of educational disadvantage, and will be highly relevant to educationalists, teachers and professional workers in educational support and allied services. It will also be of interest to those on undergraduate, postgraduate and higher degree courses in educational studies, including teacher training courses.

Theo Cox is an Honorary Departmental Research Fellow in the Department of Education of the University of Wales Swansea. His research interests have centred on educationally disadvantaged children, and he has written books and research articles on this topic. He is a Fellow of the British Psychological Society.

Combating Educational Disadvantage

Meeting the Needs of Vulnerable Children

Edited by Theo Cox

London and New York

First published 2000
by Falmer Press
11 New Fetter Lane, London EC4P 4EE

Simultaneously published in the USA and Canada
by Falmer Press
Garland Inc., 19 Union Square West, New York, NY10003

Falmer Press is an imprint of the Taylor & Francis Group

© 2000 selection and editorial matter Theo Cox; individual chapters,
the contributors

Typeset in Bembo by Taylor & Francis Books Ltd
Printed and bound in Great Britain by Biddles Ltd, Guildford and
King's Lynn

British Library Cataloguing in Publication Data
A catalogue record for this book is available from the British Library

Library of Congress Cataloging in Publication Data
Combating educational disadvantage : meeting the needs of vulnerable
children / edited by Theo Cox.
Includes bibliographical references and index.
1. Socially handicapped children – Education. 2. School improvement
programmes. 3. Educational change. 4. Education and state.
I. Cox, T. (Theodore)
LC4065.C66   1999
371.9–dc21   99-39563
CIP

ISBN 0–750–70901–4 (hbk)
ISBN 0–750–70900–6 (pbk)

Contents

Contents

16 Overview   **259**

List of Tables and Figures

Foreword

Ronald Davie

Edited books with chapter authors are sometimes a mixed blessing. However, some topics have many different facets, and the detail of those facets can be important to a consideration of the whole. In that case the contribution of specialist authors may help greatly to produce the kind of rounded picture which does justice to the topic. Educational disadvantage is one such case.

Since the end of the Second World War, in both the UK and USA, the issue of educational disadvantage has been a central one, albeit in varying degree. It came very much to the fore in the 1960s, highlighted in England and Wales by the Report of the Plowden Committee on Primary Education (in 1966). The end of that decade saw major initiatives designed to combat such disadvantage – notably, through 'early intervention', as with the establishment of Educational Priority Areas in Britain and the Head Start Program in the USA. Later, the nature of disadvantage was further explored in broader contexts, for example, the post-Head Start work and analyses by Bronfenbrenner and many others in the United States; the continuing stream of work arising out of the National Child Development Study data in the UK; and Rutter and Madge's commissioned review, also in the UK, on *Cycles of Disadvantage* in 1976.

However, by the late 1970s resistance was growing to at least one element in the equation, namely, the concept of social, cultural and even linguistic deprivation. The objection was that 'it devalues and denigrates working class culture, it labels children and may therefore activate a self-fulfilling prophecy'. (My summary of the situation at that time is in a chapter in *The School Years*, edited by John Coleman in 1979.)

Whether due to this sort of objection or for other reasons, the early intervention movement at least in the UK was struggling somewhat to maintain its momentum at that point. Further, the search to isolate factors in the home environment which could be leading to educational disadvantage was diluted by an emerging interest in the measurable effects of the school environment on educational progress. Rutter and his colleagues (*Fifteen Thousand Hours*, 1979) were probably pivotal in moving the focus of interest in the UK towards 'school improvement', and this focus is still clearly discernible today – well represented in some of the chapters which follow.

However, to portray the position as simply a shift of emphasis from home to school environmental factors over this period would be to oversimplify the situation. Not only has the importance of the early years re-emerged, but school improvement has moved from an educational issue to a political imperative – not least in respect of educationally disadvantaged children. Furthermore, other important dimensions have been added to the debate, including: the position of ethnic minority children; gender differences; the importance of inter-agency planning and co-operation in this field, especially for children in public care; and the need to have regard to children's perspectives, not only in considering the nature of 'disadvantage' itself but also in formulating solutions to combat it. All of these aspects are considered in chapters which follow.

One further factor, which the book also brings out well, is the impact of a 'market forces' ideology on the question of educational disadvantage. The past twenty years or so have seen this political ideology brought to bear on education, as on other public services. It was initially largely rejected by educationalists as incompatible with everything they stood for, and concerns continue to be expressed about the potentially adverse effects of school 'league tables', over-rigid assessment procedures, etc., particularly on our most vulnerable children. Gradually, the baby has been salvaged from the bathwater, and it is now perhaps possible to think the unthinkable, namely that the educationally disadvantaged may actually profit from an approach which sets out clearly to identify the nature and extent of their needs, attempts to quantify the cost of remedying the situation, sets targets for those involved and insists on delivery of agreed programmes.

One way of looking at the situation is that market forces have always operated, but that the wrong 'consumers' have held sway, namely, the professionals and administrators involved in education, together with a minority of articulate parents. The arguably more brash market forces which we see today could be said at least to have the virtues of transparency and accountability. Perhaps the educationally disadvantaged have something to gain from this. They do not have a great deal to lose.

1 Introduction

Theo Cox

Who Are the Disadvantaged?

There is now a vast literature on the causes, consequences and remedies for disadvantage, particularly in the USA but, increasingly in Britain, Europe and the various Organization for Economic Co-operation and Development (OECD) countries. There is a confusing variety of terms used as descriptors of disadvantage, such as deprivation (whether social, cultural or educational), inequality, at risk and, most recently, social exclusion. As Kellaghan et al. (1995) point out such terms are often used as if they were equivalent in meaning and this interchangeability may reflect the fact that educational disadvantage is a complex phenomenon resulting from the interaction of deep-seated economic, social and educational factors. This complexity is well represented in the present volume in which the contributing authors have chosen to discuss those aspects of disadvantage which are of particular concern to them.

A helpfully clear discussion of various definitions of disadvantage is provided by Natriello et al. (1990). After discussing the earlier use of terms such as 'culturally deprived' which aroused much controversy, they refer to the recent emergence of the term 'at risk', commenting that (perhaps like previous terms) it appears to mean different things to different observers. Despite this a general theme running through uses of this term is a future orientation, referring to students who may be more likely to experience problems at some point in the future, but with an emphasis on early identification before these problems become manifest. They further assert that, by defining the disadvantaged population as having characteristics that make it susceptible to certain environmental conditions, we can avoid the conflict over whether the problem is located in the students' families, community circumstances or their schools. On the negative side there is the risk that, while early identification can lead to appropriate educational or other provision being made for the students concerned, it also carries the danger of derogatory labelling and the creation of self-fulfilling prophecies resulting from lowered expectations of pupil performance. In another useful discussion of the concept of 'at risk' Evans (OECD, 1995) argues that it becomes an optimistic one if it moves the debate forward by recognizing the transactional nature of much learning. In the educational context this means that the right educational experiences over time can help to compensate for disadvantage and optimize the chances for success for all pupils.

Natriello et al. (op cit.) go on to offer a definition of educational disadvantage which borrows from earlier definitions but places it within an emerging understanding of education as a process that takes place both inside and outside of schools, i.e. within the family and the community as well as in formal education. Their definition is as follows:

> Students who are educationally disadvantaged have been exposed to insufficient educational experiences in at least one of these three domains. While the first awareness of the consequences of such experiences may surface in the schools where student performance is formally assessed, the source of the problem may rest with the school and/or with the family and the community in which the student is reared.
>
> (Natriello et al., 1990, p. 13)

The term 'at risk' was defined by the OECD in a recent review of research, policy and practice in the area of disadvantage as follows:

> The term 'at risk' refers to children and youth who are in danger of failing at school, or in making a successful transition to work. Educational, social and vocational failure are predicted by a range of factors, including: poverty, ethnic status, family circumstances, language, type of school, geography and community.
>
> Thus the term 'at risk' refers in a general sense to children and youth from disadvantaged backgrounds.
>
> (Day et al., 1997, p. 17)

This definition overlaps with that of Natriello et al. but is more comprehensive in scope and, as such, was communicated to all of the contributing authors of the present volume, although without any intention on the Editor's part of constraining their individual perspectives on disadvantage.

Although the term 'at risk', historically, has been used much more in the medical than an educational context in Britain it did actually feature strongly in the work of one of the units of the Schools Council Research and Development Project at University College Swansea (now the University of Wales Swansea). This unit developed a screening procedure for identifying those entrants to infant schools/departments who were at risk of educational handicap (Evans, 1978). Also, as Evans (1995) points out, when used in an educational context, the term 'at risk' is normally distinguished from the concept of special educational needs (SEN), although it is certainly true that some children with handicapping physical, sensory, cognitive or emotional disabilities may also experience educational disadvantages in addition. Regarding the estimated prevalence of educational risk in OECD countries Evans states that this ranges between 15 and 30 per cent of school age populations but he concludes that there is too much variability in the definition to enable a meaningful estimate to be made.

Risk Factors

As the definition of 'at risk' indicates there is a wide range of factors which can be implicated in this concept, particularly under the headings of family/ community and school factors.

Family and Community Factors

Schorr (1988) describes some of the major non-school risk factors as follows:

> growing up in persistent or concentrated poverty and in a family of low social class;
> being born unwanted or into a family with too many children born too close together;
> growing up with a parent who is unemployed, a teenager, a school drop-out, an illiterate, a parent who is impaired (as a result of alcoholism, drug addiction, or mental illness), and/or who is without social supports;
> growing up in a family or neighbourhood with such high levels of social disorganisation as to leave a young child unprotected from abuse and violence, and with little exposure to healthy role models;
> growing up outside one's family, especially in multiple foster care or institutional placements; and
> growing up with the sense that one has bleak prospects for good employment or a stable family life and little power to affect one's own destiny and that one is not valued by the outside world.

Schorr goes on to identify poverty as the greatest risk factor of all, relentlessly correlated with high rates of school age child bearing, school failure and violent crime, stating that:

> Virtually all of the other risk factors that make rotten outcomes more likely are found disproportionately among poor children: bad health in infancy and childhood, being abused or neglected, not having a decent place to live, and lacking access to services that protect against the effects of these conditions.

> (Schorr, 1988, p. xxiii)

While, like educational disadvantage, the concept of poverty is both relative and complex, there is good evidence that it is a persistent and world-wide problem, both in developing and in industrialized countries. A recent report published for the United Nations Development Programme (UNDP, 1998) states that over 100 million people are 'income poor' in OECD countries (i.e. having less than 50 per cent of the median disposable income), at least 37 million are without jobs and unemployment among youth (age 15–24 years) has reached unprecedented heights. Among 17 industrial countries in the OECD for which data are presented, the UK, Ireland and the USA are revealed as having the highest poverty index, a composite measure taking account of life expectancy, literacy, poverty and long-term unemployment. Mortimore and Whitty, in the present volume (Chapter 10), point to the increase in the proportion of children living in poverty in Britain and Carl Grant and LaVonne Williams (Chapter 14) describe the continuing substantial prevalence of poverty across the USA.

As with poverty, however defined, low social class (or low socio-economic status) has been consistently linked with poor educational achievement and prospects (see Silver and Silver, 1991; Halsey et al., 1980, and also Chapter 10 in this volume). A recent striking example of this association appeared in a report of research carried out by MacCallum into social class and national curriculum Key Stage 2 performance in English, maths and science in all 32 of the LEAs in Greater London (TES, 1997). His analysis of these results showed a clear trend for schools serving areas with higher proportions of low socio-economic status households to perform less well than schools serving more socially advantaged catchment areas. He claimed that almost 80 per cent of the differences (variance) in pupil performance in the London LEAs could be attributed to social class (i.e. the occupational status of the head of household), and only 20 per cent could be attributed to other variables, including school differences, which were independent of social class.[1] A parallel study by the same author, analysing the GCSE results of pupils in the same boroughs yielded a similar, though slightly less pronounced pattern of findings (MacCallum, 1996). Both of these sets of findings are in line with other strong evidence that family circumstances, including social class, parental interest in and attitudes to education, account for significantly more of the variation in children's measured school achievement than school factors (see Chapter 10). Recent evidence has also emerged about the importance of peer group pressure on pupil performance (see Chapter 9).

Although such analyses of the association between poverty and social class and educational performance have produced highly consistent and compelling results, they do not tell us how these factors actually operate within the family context of adult–child interaction. On this question Evans (OECD, 1995) quotes Stodolsky and Lesser (1967) who argued that we need to go beyond definitions of 'at risk', based upon such factors as social class, ethnicity and poverty, towards definitions which incorporate environmental circumstances which bear upon developmental process and which vary within and across social class and ethnic lines. As Evans puts it, the search is on for explanatory factors which have a direct bearing upon learning and which, in turn, can be manipulated to good effect. In the present volume Lucey and Walkerdine (Chapter 3), and Gregory (Chapter 7) throw some light on how parental attitudes and values towards education inform their home literacy practices and their expectations of their children's academic performance, which, in turn, affect the patterns of their children's learning. Elsewhere Wells (1986) and Tizard and Hughes (1984) have identified patterns of adult–child language interaction which appear to be most conducive to the educational development of young children in the home (and school) setting.

School Factors

In MacCallum's analysis of the Key Stage 2 performance of children in the London LEAs described earlier (TES, 1997) it was found that the 11-year-old children in about half of the LEAs were performing better in the tests than would have been expected, given their predominant social complexion, and the children in the remaining half were, with one exception, doing worse than expected. It is this variability in pupil performance across schools with similar social intakes which has underlain the drive by the present British Government and its predecessors to find reliable 'value-added' measures of school performance which will allow a fair comparison of the academic results across schools, allowing for differences in pupil intake.

The range of educational disadvantages experienced by pupils in poorer performing schools is well described in OFSTED's (1993) report on access and achievement in urban education. This was based on a survey of schools and institutions in seven highly disadvantaged urban areas in England, covering the range of pre-school provision to adult education/training. It showed that, overall, the pupils in these areas were poorly served by the educational system. In many cases under-achievement in the basic skills of these pupils which had been apparent in their early primary school years had not been reversed subsequently. Curriculum planning in the schools lacked challenge and pupil participation, there were poor standards in the planning of teaching and the assessment monitoring and evaluation of pupils' learning was weak in many schools. Pupils not doing well in GCSE examinations had few opportunities for post-16 study and there was a lack of co-ordination between post-16 providers, with little priority given to low attainers at 16. The report concluded that the quality and standards of much of the work in the schools were inadequate and disturbing, although there was some good quality work in each sector.

As discussed in Chapter 9 children's attitudes to learning and to education are linked with their motivation to learn and, at least indirectly, with their actual school attainments. Such attitudes appear to be strongly influenced by their home backgrounds, including parental interest in and attitude to their children's education, but also by school factors such as their teachers' expectations of them and the prevailing peer group attitudes to learning and to school. Where a pupil is in a school context of low teacher expectation and an anti-school culture among the peer group, they will experience formidable impediments to learning.

Risk Factors in Combination

Many other factors, in addition to the major ones already discussed, can increase the risk of children experiencing educational failure. Some of these are listed by Evans (OECD, 1995) on the basis of reports from the various OECD countries. They include other family factors such as one-parent families and breakdown in home-school relations, and community factors such as a lack of community support, the non-availability and non-use of leisure facilities, and the lack of political resources. Additional factors include poor knowledge of the majority language, and gender, linked with under-achievement in either girls or boys within the context of particular cultures. (See Chapter 3 for a discussion of gender issues in relation to working-class boys.) Surprisingly neither racism nor ethnicity are included in this listing although the disadvantages associated with these particular factors are well discussed by Sally Tomlinson in Chapter 2 of this volume.

As Mortimore and Whitty point out in this volume (Chapter 10) the risk factors are frequently found in combination and can act in an interactive and cumulative fashion. As Carl Grant and LaVonne Williams also describes in this volume (Chapter 14) social factors such as poverty, racism and discrimination, and conflicting home-school values may combine to impinge significantly upon a child's educational development. Similarly Sonia Jackson describes (Chapter 5) how the problems experienced by looked-after children, in common with other children from severely disadvantaged homes, are compounded by the discrimination they experience within the educational system. Rutter (1980) found that the presence of more than one risk factor in an individual case increased the chances of an unfortunate outcome in a multiplicative fashion. Thus children experiencing only one risk factor were no more likely to suffer serious consequences than those with no risk factors, but if two or three risk factors were present the chances of an adverse outcome increased four times: in the case of four risk factors the chances increased tenfold. Where poverty is present however, as discussed earlier in this chapter, there is a strong likelihood that it will combine with other factors in a detrimental fashion for the child. It is this multiplicative and interactive nature of risk factors that gives the concept of educational disadvantage its complexity.

The damaging effects of combined risk factors upon children's educational careers and life prospects have been well described in studies emanating from the National Child Development Study (NCDS) (see Wedge and Prosser, 1973;

Essen and Wedge, 1982), and also the Swansea Compensatory Education Project (Chazan et al.,1976, 1977; Chazan and Williams, 1978). A longitudinal study of a sample of children attending deprived area schools in England and Wales, as part of the Swansea Project, showed the widening gap in school achieve-ment between the disadvantaged and more advantaged groups in the research sample (Cox, 1983; Cox and Jones, 1983; Cox and Morgan, 1985). As Kathy Sylva describes in Chapter 8, long-term longitudinal studies of disadvantaged children carried out in the USA, in the evaluation of the efficacy of early childhood intervention programmes, have clearly demonstrated the damaging affects of early disadvantage upon the later and adult life experiences and opportunities of many of the children not receiving such intervention. There is also some evidence that disadvantage experienced early in life may be more damaging than that experienced later. Rutter (1984), for example, concluded that early circumstances can have some enduring effects which are not attributable simply to continuing environmental disadvantages (see also Pilling, 1990).

Combating Disadvantage

In Chapter 10 of this volume Mortimore and Whitty provide a succinct summary of the main approaches to ameliorating the effects of poverty on educational opportunities, namely meritocracy, compensatory mechanisms and intervention projects, and in Chapters 8 and 14 respectively Kathy Sylva and Carl Grant and LaVonne Willams describe some examples of successful intervention programmes. A very comprehensive and lucidly analytical account of the history and impact of compensatory and intervention projects up to the beginning of the present decade, mainly in the USA and Britain, is provided by Silver and Silver (1991). They describe how massive federal state funding for Head Start, Follow Through and other major intervention programmes in the USA was originally legislated for by the government of President Johnson in the 'War on Poverty' and has continued ever since, despite changes in the socio-economic climate and a major shift away from priority attention to issues of poverty and disadvantage, except where these were synonymous with race and related issues. They contrast the scale and continuity of this federal provision for anti-poverty educational measures in the USA with the much more modest, small scale and ad hoc approaches funded by successive British governments following the publication of the Plowden Report in 1967, which advocated the targeting of funds and resources into Education Priority Areas (EPAs).

Silver and Silver argue that, following the election of Margaret Thatcher in 1979, there was a much more decisive break with the liberal policies of the governments (both Labour and Conservative) of the previous two decades, than occurred in America. In Britain there occurred what they describe as massive shifts in educational priorities during the following decade in the context of international economic competition, new technologies and moves towards political and social values of a different order. Educational hopes lay in prospects for economic expansion which did not occur. As Ronald Davie points out in his Foreword to this volume, the loss of momentum in Britain's drive to combat disadvantage was partly also due to the growing awareness of the importance of such issues as gender and ethnicity and also the growth of the school improvement movement.

The impact upon disadvantaged children of the educational policies of the Thatcher and Major Governments in Britain is well described in the present volume by Peter Mortimore and Geoff Whitty (Chapter 10), and by Anne Sofer (Chapter 11), who assert that they refused to acknowledge the relationship between social disadvantage and educational achievement. In their view the disadvantages experienced by these children were largely compounded by the 'market led' policies adopted, which aimed to improve educational standards all round in the belief that this would be the most effective way of benefiting all children, including the disadvantaged. A fuller summary of the evidence for the impact of open enrolment and other educational policies on the educational prospects of disadvantaged children is provided by Whitty et al. (1998).

Despite these radical changes in government priorities intervention projects designed to help disadvantaged children and their families and communities continued in Britain, particularly through the efforts of LEAs and voluntary agencies, although, as Anne Sofer points out in Chapter 11, the scope for LEA support was considerably reduced by government budgetary measures. A good account of the range and scope of intervention projects in Scotland, led by the regional authorities, is provided by Nisbet and Watt (1994).

Beyond the USA and Britain there have been a wide variety of compensatory action and intervention projects targeted on educationally at risk groups, funded from public, private or voluntary sources. Those projects taking place in the OECD countries (including some in the USA and Britain) are described in an OECD (1995) report. In addition a range of European initiatives are described in a publication produced by the recently formed European Educational Research Association (EERA) Research Network on Children At Risk and Urban Education (see Day et al., 1997). The governments of several countries, including France, Ireland and Holland have adopted the approach of identifying and designating certain educational priority areas as the focus of action and resourcing to combat poverty and disadvantage.

In these schemes there is an increasing emphasis upon the integration of the contributing services as '... a way to provide more effective holistic, client oriented and preventative support to families and to children who are at risk of failing in school and the transition to work' (OECD, 1996, p. 3). In the voluntary sector the Bernard van Leer Foundation is a major source of funding and commissioning projects focusing upon disadvantaged children up to age 7 years. For the period 1996–2001 projects in 40 countries throughout the world are being funded, including Third World countries as well as developed industrialized nations (Bernard van Leer Foundation, 1997).

Educational Policies of the New Labour Government in Britain

The 'New Labour' Government was elected in Britain in May 1997 bringing to its task a political philosophy which combined 'a strong commitment to enterprise with social justice' (Tony Blair speaking in the *World at One* BBC Radio programme on 12 November 1998). In the educational field this philosophy has led the Government to retain some aspects of the market-led policies enacted by the previous Conservative Government, including open enrolment and school performance tables, while rejecting other measures such as the further selection of school intakes by general ability (but see Chapter 2) and the nursery voucher scheme. Indeed, those features of educational policy identified by Anne Sofer in this volume (Chapter 11) as characterizing the Thatcher Government's approach, including its strong central direction, have been largely retained, although modified in some respects. Nevertheless it seems clear that, while sharing the previous government's concern to raise national educational standards, the new Government is also powerfully driven by a desire to eradicate or at least ameliorate social, economic and educational disadvantage.

The principles guiding its educational policies are stated in its Education White Paper (DfEE, 1997). The first of these is that education is its 'Number One Priority' and, as such, will receive a guaranteed increased proportion of the national income during the life of the present parliament and beyond. The importance of raising educational standards, especially in the basic skills of literacy and numeracy, are affirmed, leading the Government to set up its Standards and Effectiveness Unit to help to achieve this aim. Other initiatives here include the reduction of class sizes for 5 to 7-year-olds, National Literacy and National Numeracy Projects (in England), target setting for both schools and LEAs and the focusing of OFSTED inspections upon weaker or underperforming schools. A further principle expresses the Government's wish to work in partnership with all those committed to raising standards, including businesses and parents.

Government Policies for the Disadvantaged

To date the Government has enacted a number of measures which are either targeted directly on disadvantaged groups or likely to benefit them in particular. On the wider front these include its New Deal scheme to help the young unemployed and its provision of financial support towards the cost of child care for single parents seeking employment. Its range of educationally oriented measures include a Family Literacy Initiative, operating in conjunction with the Basic Skills Agency, and its recently introduced Sure Start Programme which aims to provide integrated services for children under 4 and their families in deprived areas, including child care, early education and family support, including parenting. The latter is described as being part of the Government's strategy to draw together ministries to tackle problems with multiple causes. The Sure Start Programme also forms part of the Government's drive to improve the availability and quality of early years education, with nursery/pre-school provision currently being made available to all 4-year-olds whose parents want it, and ultimately, to all 3-year-olds as well. Other measures include the National Childcare Strategy and the designation of a chain of Early Excellence Centres throughout the country to provide good models of practice and training.

Two other major measures focusing on the disadvantaged are the establishment of Education Action Zones and of the Social Exclusion Unit. The Education Action Zones (EAZ) are now being set up in areas of deprivation, both urban and rural. They operate through 'Action Forums' which include LEAs and constituent schools, and representatives of parents, local business and the community. Each Forum draws up an action programme which includes targets for each particular school and for the zone as a whole. To date 25 zones have been selected by the DfEE through a competitive application process and more zones are scheduled in the coming years. The Government conceives the EAZs as 'testbeds for innovation', with flexibility of approach within a partnership framework. Each zone will receive £1 million a year for three years, of which one quarter should come from private sponsors (DfEE Press Release, 23 June 1998).[2]

The Social Exclusion Unit was set up by the Government as an inter-departmental agency in order to tackle truancy, homelessness and the poorest neighbourhoods. It aims to cut truancy and school exclusions by a third by the year 2002 through a series of measures. On the wider front the Government recently launched a three-year 'New Deal for Communities Programme' which, according to the *Guardian* (16 September 1998) was underpinned by a devastating report from the Unit on the deteriorating state of 'two nation Britain'. This initiative forms part of a national strategy for neighbourhood renewal under the title 'Bringing Britain Together'. The New Deal for Communities Programme is starting in seventeen 'Pathfinder Districts' which will receive funds to develop and implement local, community-based plans to include jobs, health and housing which are aimed at turning depressed areas around. These programmes will also aim to improve the education and employment prospects of children and young people at risk of social exclusion by giving them integrated help, including the Sure Start Programme, by finding better ways of motivating them to learn in school, and by providing older pupils with better alternatives to the attractions of drink and drugs. Other Government initiatives targeting at risk secondary school pupils include Study Support schemes for out-of-hours learning (see MacBeath's account of these in Chapter 15 of this volume), and work-related schemes for those who failed to achieve in school or those wishing to improve their skills in later life through the 'Lifelong Learning' Programme.

The Structure of this Book

Following the Introduction the book has two parts. Part I, entitled 'Vulnerable Groups' focuses upon a number of groups of children and young people who are highly at risk educationally. These are ethnic minorities (Sally Tomlinson, Chapter 2), under-achieving boys (Helen Lucey and Valerie Walkerdine, Chapter 3), poor primary school attenders (Tim Carroll, Chapter 4), looked-after children (Sonia Jackson, Chapter 5) and children behaving in disruptive ways in school (Maurice Chazan, Chapter 6). These authors also put forward their views on the educational and other measures needed to ameliorate the problems described.

In Part II of the book, entitled 'Meeting the Needs of the Disadvantaged', the emphasis shifts, relatively, from description and analysis of how the various disadvantages experienced by certain children interact to impair their educational and life prospects, to a fuller consideration of strategies and forms of educational or other provisions designed to ameliorate these damaging effects. As in Part I the chapters here are written from a variety of professional and research perspectives. In the first (Chapter 7) Eve Gregory provides an account of how certain family literacy practices relate to traditional school literacy programmes. Kathy Sylva discusses the need for high quality early education programmes (Chapter 8) and the present writer describes the attitudes and views of disadvantaged pupils on school and learning and how they might be improved (Chapter 9). The three following chapters discuss the respective contributions towards meeting the educational needs of disadvantaged children and their families of schools (Peter Mortimore and Geoff Whitty, Chapter 10), LEAs (Anne Sofer, Chapter 11) and school psychological services (Irvine Gersch et al., Chapter 12).

While most of the chapters are mainly set within the context of British education that by Peter Evans (Chapter 13) is written from an international (OECD) perspective and discusses the need for the co-ordination of educational and other services designed to combat disadvantage. This is followed by a chapter by Carl Grant and LaVonne Williams (Chapter 14) on the educational and related problems facing poor coloured children and young people in the USA and some promising educational programmes designed to tackle them. After this John MacBeath makes the case for integrating school learning within a much wider co-ordinated framework in order to equip children for lifelong learning (Chapter 15).

The invited authors contributing to this book were asked to address, as far as possible, the theme of the impact upon disadvantaged children of the previous government's market-oriented educational reforms to the educational system of England and Wales, and the likely impact of the New Labour Government's educational policies and approaches in this respect. As would be expected this theme has emerged more prominently in some chapters than others, depending upon the particular topic.

The final chapter of the book draws together common themes and issues concerning the education of disadvantaged children and discusses these with particular reference to the policies of the present Government.

Acknowledgements

The editor would like to thank the other authors in this book for their willingness to contribute to it. He would also like to express his appreciation of the interest and encouragement, throughout the course of planning the book, of Professor John Nisbet of the Centre for Educational Research at the University of Aberdeen, and also of Emeritus Professor Maurice Chazan.

Thanks are also due to Madeleine Rogerson and staff of the Education Department Library of the University of Wales Swansea for their assistance in locating and obtaining various publications, and to Steven Kennewell and David Hendley, in the Department of Education of the University, for their help in dealing with the computer word processing problems that arose from time to time.

Notes

1   Although, in the material submitted by MacCallum to the *Times Educational Supplement*, the writer pointed out that the factors which contribute to pupils' academic performance are more complex than can be indicated by this type of (correlational) research.
2   For the second tranche of the EAZs the Government's funding formula changed. At the time of writing only £500,000 of the £750,000 will be automatically awarded to each Zone, while payment of the remaining £250,000 will be dependent upon each Zone gaining matching (pound for pound) funding from private investment.

References

Bernard van Leer Foundation (1997) *Annual Report*, The Hague, Bernard van Leer Foundation.

Chazan, M. and Williams, P. (eds) (1978) *Deprivation and the Infant School*, Oxford, Basil Blackwell.

Chazan, M., Cox, T., Jackson, S. and Laing, A.F. (1977) *Studies of Infant School Children II: Deprivation and development*, Oxford, Basil Blackwell.

Chazan, M., Laing, A., Cox, T., Jackson, S. and Lloyd, G. (1976) *Studies of Infant School Children, I: Deprivation and school progress*, Oxford, Basil Blackwell.

Cox, T. (1983) 'Cumulative deficit in culturally disadvantaged children', *British Journal of Educational Psychology* 53, pp. 317–326.

Cox, T. and Jones, G. (1983) *Disadvantaged 11-Year-Olds*, Oxford, Pergamon Press.

Cox, T. and Morgan, K. (1985) 'The career aspirations and occupational interests of culturally disadvantaged children', *British Journal of Guidance and Counselling* 13, pp. 191–203.

Day, C., van Veen, D. and Walraven, G. (eds) (1997) *Children and Youth at Risk and Urban Education*, Research, Policy and Practice, Belgium, EERA and Garant Publishers.

Department for Education and Employment (DfEE) (1997) *Excellence in Schools* (Education White Paper), London, The Stationery Office.

Essen, J. and Wedge, P. (1982) *Continuities in Childhood Disadvantage*, London, Heinemann Educational.

Evans, P. (1995) 'Children and youth "at risk"', in Organization for Economic Co-operation and Development (OECD), *Our Children at Risk*, Paris, OECD.

Evans, R. (1978) 'The identification of children "at risk" of educational handicap', in Chazan, M. and Williams, P. (eds) *Deprivation and the Infant School*, Oxford, Basil Blackwell.

Halsey, A.H., Heath, A.F. and Ridge, J.M. (1980) *Origins and Destinations*, Oxford, Clarendon Press.

Kellaghan, T., Weir, S., hUallacháin, S. Ó. and Morgan, M. (1995) *Educational Disadvantage in Ireland. Combat Agency Research Report Number 20*, Dublin, Department of Education.

MacCallum, I. (1996) 'The chosen ones?', *Education*, 19 January 1996, 1, pp. 2–13.

Natriello, G., McDill, E.L. and Pallas, A.M. (1990) *Schooling Disadvantaged Children: Racing against catastrophe*, New York, Teachers College Press.

Nisbet, J. and Watt, J. (1994) *Educational Disadvantage in Scotland. A 1990s Perspective*, Edinburgh, Scottish Community Education Council.

Office for Standards in Education (OFSTED) (1993) *Access and Achievement in Urban Education*, a Report from the Office of Her Majesty's Chief Inspector of Schools, London, HMSO.

Organization for Economic Co-operation and Development (OECD) (1995) *Our Children at Risk*, Paris, OECD.

Organization for Economic Co-operation and Development (OECD) (1996) *Successful Services for Children and Families at Risk*, Paris, OECD.

Pilling, D. (1990) *Escape form Disadvantage*, London, Falmer.

Rutter, M. (1980) *Changing Youth in a Changing Society: Patterns of adolescent development and disorder*, Cambridge, MA, Harvard University Press.

Rutter, M. (1984) 'Continuities and discontinuities in socioemotional development: empirical and conceptual perspectives', in Emde, R.N. and Harmon, R.J. (eds) *Continuities and Discontinuities in Development*, New York, Plenum.

Schorr, L.B. (1988) *Within Our Reach. Breaking the Cycle of Disadvantage*, London, Doubleday.

Silver, H. and Silver, P. (1991) *An Educational War on Poverty: American and British policy making 1960–1980*, Cambridge, Cambridge University Press.

Stodolsky, S. and Lesser, J. (1973) 'Learning patterns in the disadvantaged', *Harvard Educational Review* 37, pp. 546–593.

Times Educational Supplement (TES) (1997) 18 April, p. 2.

Tizard, B. and Hughes, M. (1984) *Young Children's Learning: Talking and thinking at home and at school*, London, Fontana.

Theo Cox

United Nations Development Programme (UNDP) (1998) *Human Development Report 1998*, Oxford, Oxford University Press.

Wedge, P. and Prosser, H. (1973) *Born to Fail?*, London, Arrow Books in association with the National Children's Bureau.

Wells, G. (1986) *The Meaning Makers*, London, Heinemann.

Whitty, G., Power, S. and Halpin, D. (1998) *Devolution and Choice in Education. The School the State and the Market*, Buckinghamshire, Open University Press.

Part I
Vulnerable Groups

2 Ethnic Minorities and Education: New Disadvantages

Sally Tomlinson

In post-industrial plural societies education systems continue to be key institutions for the incorporation of minorities into the economy and the civil society and also places of continued tension. From the early 1960s the children of migrants entering the UK from the Asian sub-continent, the Caribbean and other former colonial countries were greatly disadvantaged as they entered the school system. The effects of disadvantage, which resulted in educational underperformance, have been well-documented. From the 1960s to the 1980s educational policy and practice changed slowly to accommodate minority pupils, and despite a good deal of xenophobia and lack of understanding, educational equity for minorities began to be regarded as important. Some minority young people began to achieve educational success particularly as a small 'black' and Asian middle class emerged. However, in the 1990s new forms of inequality and new disadvantages are emerging as the education systems respond to market forces and the government seeks to lever up educational achievements for everyone.

This chapter documents the effects of markets in education on ethnic minorities in terms of their social class and urban location, the emergence of the 'desirable' school pupil and the way in which some schools seek to exclude the 'undesirable' which disproportionately affects minority pupils, the increasing concentration of minorities in urban schools which run the risk of acquiring the 'failing school' label, and the reaction of the majority society as minorities do become more successful educationally.

Introduction

In post-industrial, post-colonial societies in the late twentieth century ethnic minority groups continue to experience problems in negotiating a position that will guarantee opportunity, equality and respect. Education systems remain key institutions for the incorporation of racial and ethnic minorities into the economy and the civil society, but are also sites for continued exclusion and new disadvantages. In Britain a key issue, still unresolved after forty years, concerns the levels of education required for minorities to participate fully in the society – 'whether ethnic minority children will achieve educational credentials that will provide them with employment opportunities and occupational and social mobility within the society' (Tomlinson, 1983, p. 3). An associated issue, also unresolved, is how far minority cultures can be accorded recognition and respect within schools.

Minorities entering their children into the education systems of post-industrial countries rapidly became aware that the systems were designed to select children on the basis (or supposed basis) of meritocratic educational achievements which led to superior or inferior occupational roles, and they expected equal treatment. They also became rapidly aware of the increased importance of educational credentials in the modern world and the higher level of qualifications demanded for any kind of employment. While there has undoubtedly been considerable success by minorities 'in reversing the initial downward mobility produced by migration and racial discrimination in the early years of settlement in Britain' (Modood, 1998, p. 70) the failure of the education system to deliver equal access and educational success to many minority children remains a source of considerable tension.

This chapter discusses some of the continuing inequalities and disadvantages experienced by minority children, and goes on to discuss new forms of disadvantage that are emerging. These are particularly associated with the effects of the creation of education markets, based on parental 'choice' and new forms of funding. While the creation of a market-driven education system was initially adopted in New Zealand (Waslander and Thrupp, 1995) and has become part of the school reform agenda in the USA (Fuller and Ellmore, 1996) it is Britain that is now globally regarded as 'having broken with tradition and moved boldly towards a choice-based system of public education' (Chubb and Moe, 1992, p. 45). New disadvantages discussed in this chapter concern the social class and urban location of minorities in an education market, school selection of 'desirable customers', the appearance of 'failing schools' largely attended by minority children, the effects of devolved budgets, and racial and ethnic segregation resulting from 'choice'. A final section discusses whether there are aspects of markets that enhance opportunities for minorities, and what the majority reaction is to minority success. There is certainly some evidence that, since markets create winners and losers, if minorities are successful in competitive education situations the majority will respond with an increased xenophobia (Wimmer, 1997).

Minorities in Pre-Market Education in Britain

From the early 1950s, migrants from the Caribbean, the Asian sub-continent, East Asia and West Africa, East Africa, Cyprus and other existing or former colonial countries, came to Britain expecting to improve the education and life chances of their children (see Tables 2.1 and 2.2, for the ethnic group composition of the UK, and birthplace of children). Whatever their socio-economic position, the educational values and aspirations of minority parents have clearly accorded with the aspirations and expectations of the UK middle classes. They have consistently indicated their belief that good educational qualifications are essential if their children were to become equal citizens with equal rights and chances (see Department of Education and Science [DES] 1985a; Vincent, 1995).

Table 2.1 Ethnic group composition of Great Britain, 1991

	Numbers	*%*
White	51,834,900	94.5
Ethnic Minorities	3,006,500	5.5
Black	885,400	1.6
Caribbean	499,100	0.9
African	207,500	0.4
Other	178,800	0.3
South Asian	1,476,900	2.7
Indian	840,800	1.5
Pakistani	475,800	0.9
Bangladeshi	160,300	0.3
Chinese/Others	644,300	1.2
Chinese	157,300	0.3
Other Asian	196,700	0.4
Others	290,100	0.5

Source: Adapted from 1991 Census statistical paper no 1. Centre for Research in Ethnic Relations, University of Warwick.

Table 2.2 Children born in the UK by ethnic group, 1991

	%
White	96
Black Caribbean	96
Black African	64
Black Other	97
Indian	93
Pakistani	89
Bangladeshi	65
Chinese	80
Other Asian	62
Other	86
Total	92

Source: 1991 Census data (Office for National Statistics).

From the 1960s through to the 1980s, the children of ethnic minority parents entered a school system in which overt selection was gradually disappearing and comprehensive schooling was becoming the norm. School admissions policies were co-ordinated by local education authorities, and, once selection at age 11 for grammar schools had been phased out in most authorities, students mainly attended a neighbourhood school. Central and local government were, at least notionally, committed to widening access to a broad secondary education for all social groups (DES, 1985b). Educational policy and practice changed slowly to accommodate minority students and despite a good deal of xenophobia and racism, liberal policy makers, educationists and the minorities themselves, exerted sufficient pressure to ensure the principles of social justice and equity in education began to be regarded as important. The policy aims for a multicultural Britain articulated by Roy Jenkins when he was Home Secretary in 1968 have never been formally abandoned by government. These were that there should be 'not a flattening process of uniformity, but cultural diversity, coupled with equal opportunity, in an atmosphere of mutual tolerance' (Rex, 1996, p. 32). Although these aims were proving remarkably difficult to achieve, by the 1980s schools and teachers had become more accommodating to the incorporation of minority children and their educational attainments were slowly improving (Gillborn and Gipps, 1996; Modood 1998; Blackstone et al., 1998).

Continuing Disadvantages

Research and literature from the early 1960s documented in some detail the disadvantages experienced by ethnic minority children within the British education system (see Kirp, 1979; Taylor, 1981, 1985, 1988; Tomlinson, 1983; Troyna, 1987). Initial disadvantages were associated with issues of English language teaching; low educational attainments; an inappropriate curriculum; selective systems that worked against minorities; lack of funding; and teachers who, if not overtly racist, held low expectations of the capabilities of children from former colonial countries, and had no training or awareness of minority educational issues. In particular, both research and commissioned reports noted the failure to produce national policies that would assist the incorporation and successful education of minority children. Kirp, an American academic, noted in 1979 that educational policy was characterized by racial inexplicitness, and by attempts to embed issues concerning race and ethnicity in 'some broad policy context such as educational disadvantage' (Kirp, 1979, p. 40).

There were certainly continual attempts by central government during the 1970s to define the problems experienced by minority children as part of a wider issue of disadvantage. A DES response to a House of Commons report on race and education produced in 1973 was that:

While the Government believes that it is necessary to make more formal arrangements for ... the education of immigrants and education for a multiracial society, they also see a need to provide for all those suffering from disadvantage.

(DES, 1974, p. 5)

By 1978 it was official policy to subsume minority issues under those of the disadvantaged. A Home Office report in 1978 noted that:

The Government's basic analysis is that a good deal of the disadvantage that minorities suffer is shared by less well-off members of the indigenous population and that their most fundamental needs – jobs, housing, education, health – are essentially the same as those of the general population.

(Home Office, 1978)

While this analysis had some merit, especially as poverty, inequality and economic disadvantage began to affect larger numbers within the majority society (OFSTED, 1993), subsequent events during the 1980s and 1990s demonstrated that minorities continued to experience disadvantages and discrimination considerably in excess of that experienced by indigenous populations – with specific minority groups particularly affected.

Literature from the mid-1980s documenting the situation of minority children and young people in the UK education system has been more sophisticated than earlier literature which tended to use crude blanket descriptions of country of origin – West Indian, Asian and UK, or simply 'white', being the common terms. From the mid-1980s, researchers and writers began to take more care to differentiate between specific countries of origin; rural or urban background; heritage languages spoken; and to take account of gender, social class, disability, location and experiences in the UK, school conditions, local labour market situations and so on (e.g. Tomlinson, 1992; Drew, 1995; Gillborn and Gipps, 1996; Vernon, 1996) and there is a much greater appreciation of the way factors combine to create or alleviate disadvantage.

However there are persisting themes in the literature on school achievement, documenting in particular the difficulties some Afro-Caribbean students (especially boys), some Pakistani students (especially girls) and Bangladeshi students experience in their school career (see Gillborn and Gipps, 1996). There is also continuing documentation of the use of special education, suspension and exclusions from mainstream education and, specifically, as to how the latter affects Afro-Caribbean boys (DfE, 1992). The continuing inappropriateness of the school curriculum for all young people growing up in a multi-ethnic society has continued to receive some limited attention (King and Reiss, 1993) and there has been more concentration on the post-school careers of minority students in further and higher education, training schemes and the labour market (e.g. Shaw, 1994; Macrae et al., 1997; Drew, 1995). But the continuing disadvantages and associated inequalities which affect minority children must be analysed within the context of the post-1988 education market.

The Education Market Post-1988

From 1988, in England and Wales a new framework for funding, administering and monitoring all aspects of education has developed. Funding has been devolved to school level, school budgets are determined by student numbers, a diversity of schools has been encouraged and selection of pupils by schools has re-emerged. At the same time, there has been a centralizing of control of the curriculum and its assessment. An educational market has been created, based on parental 'choice' of school. Competition between schools is fuelled by the annual publication of the raw scores of public examination and national curriculum assessment results, and schools are rewarded by a funding formula for the numbers of pupils they attract. In this educational climate, values of competition, individualism and separation have become important, social and racial justice and equity less so.

The intention of the education market was to change the balance of power from 'producers' to 'consumers' of education; choice and competition were to ensure that good schools prospered, while weaker schools closed. The vision driving this ideology was a nineteenth-century liberal individualism in which ostensibly free consumers embrace the laws of the market and the values of self-interest and personal and familial profit. In Britain in the 1980s this was supplemented by a moral authoritarianism and nostalgic imperialism. The curriculum was centralized via the 1988 Education Reform Act into a 'national' curriculum which quite explicitly excluded reference to the multi-cultural and anti-racist initiatives which had developed during the 1970s and 1980s. There were direct political attempts to influence the development of subject content, particularly English and history, in a monocultural and anglo-centric direction.

Governments around the world have embraced the school choice movements with varying degrees of enthusiasm and a variety of approaches to choice are in operation globally (OECD, 1994). However, Chubb and Moe (1992), authors of an influential text on markets and US schools have argued that there has been an international welcome for greater choice and account-ability in schooling, and that education markets have many advantages over central control and its associated bureaucracy. In fact the kind of educational market developed in Britain has increased central control via a national curriculum, national assessment and school inspection, and passed much of the bureaucratic function necessary to run public education down to teachers. A vast new bureaucracy, the Office for Standards in Education, has become established, paying teams of private inspectors, whose reports are made public.

Choice and Class

A major result of choice policies globally has been to increase social class segregation in schools. 'Sometimes this is because more privileged groups are more active in choosing desired schools. Sometimes it is because such schools are in more prosperous neighbourhoods whose residents continue to get privileged access to them' (OECD, 1994, p. 7). In the UK the research carried out by Ball and his colleagues indicates that social class differences enable privileged 'choosers' to discriminate between schools, evaluate teachers and avoid schools with negative characteristics. These privileged parents have the required cultural capital and the educational knowledge to enable them to emerge as winners in local school markets. The privileged 'choosers' are largely white middle-class parents (Ball et al., 1996). 'Semi-skilled choosers' – to use the terminology of Ball et al. – are mainly working-class parents who want to engage with the market but who do not have the skills and knowledge to maximize their children's advantages. 'Disconnected choosers' are almost entirely working-class, lack car ownership, and are attached to their local area. They settle for the nearest or a local comprehensive school (Gewirtz et al., 1995, p. 183).

Research by Noden and West and colleagues also indicates that non-white families were less likely to attend schools with higher examination performance, despite their expressed preferences and high aspirations for their children (Noden et al., 1998). In their study, middle-class black parents preferred schools with low proportions of other black students.

There is a small, emerging middle class among minority groups, particularly Indians and East African Asians. More Asian students are successful in reaching higher education (Modood, 1993), and there is documented business success in new economic areas (Ram and Deakins, 1996). There is also a decline in racial disadvantage in the labour market (Iganski and Payne, 1996) with minority group males having begun to move out of manual employment proportionately with their white peers. It is also the case, however, that ethnic minority men and women are twice as likely to be unemployed as whites, and to be concentrated in urban areas where full-time employment opportunities are scarce. Ethnic minorities in the UK are still predominantly part of the lower socio-economic groups with all the well-documented disadvantages of these groups. Given that education markets have been shown to favour the middle classes, the class position of ethnic minorities in the UK is undoubtedly continuing to disadvantage them in choice of school.

In addition, the competitive market situation in the UK and in other countries does encourage schools to reject socially and educationally vulnerable students and to orientate themselves to meeting the perceived needs of the middle classes.

Choice and Location

Over the past thirty years the settlement of minorities in particular urban areas of the UK has been consolidated and where minority parents live does dramatically affect the possibility of their 'choice' of school, and the research so far does suggest that social class of parents and their geographical location are closely interconnected. The 1991 Census showed that 60 per cent of Afro-Caribbeans and Indians live in the Greater London area or the West Midlands. Pakistani, Chinese and other Asian groups are more strongly represented in northern towns and Bangladeshis in East London. Some cities were settled by specific migrant groups – for example East African Asians in Leicester. Despite some rural and suburban settlement, 'the concentration of minorities in the most urbanized parts of Britain is clearly apparent' (Centre for Research in Ethnic Relations, 1992, p. 5). Ethnic minorities make up a quarter of the population of Inner London, and the younger age profile of minorities ensures that the school- and college-age minority population is very high in some boroughs.

While there has been 'gentrification' of some inner-city areas, with whites moving back into renovated housing, the areas most minorities live in have all the indices of disadvantage. In Tower Hamlets in 1991, for example, 47 per cent of students were of ethnic minority origin, mainly Bangladeshi, and spoke English as a second language. At that time 75 per cent of Bangladeshi men in the area were unskilled or semi-skilled (Tomlinson, 1992).

The urban schools most ethnic minority students moved into from the 1960s to the 1990s, although nominally comprehensive, were intended for the working class and had never been intended to prepare students for higher level academic work. Indeed, most were re-named secondary modern schools which, post-war, had initially been forbidden to enter students for public examinations (Simon, 1991). In a thorough survey of 1,560 comprehensive schools and colleges carried out in 1994 by Benn and Chitty, 519 institutions took in more than one ethnic group. There were distinct social class differences between schools with black and other minority students and those without. 'Their working-class intakes were much higher and their middle-class intakes lower than survey averages. Thus, 81 per cent of schools with West Indian groups had predominantly working-class intakes, as did 71 per cent of schools with Indians, 76 per cent with Chinese and 72 per cent with Irish concentrations' (Benn and Chitty, 1996, p. 175). The under-resourcing, high staff turnover, and low expectations of teachers in urban schools have been well documented as creating disadvantages for minority students (Rutter and Madge, 1976; Tomlinson, 1983).

However, where families of ethnic minority origin were concerned, there was certainly no urgency to alleviate disadvantage. A situation arose in the 1980s in Tower Hamlets where several thousand Bangladeshi children were without even a school place, a problem that the local education authority and central government allowed to continue despite legal challenge and which would never have been tolerated in a white area (Tomlinson, 1992).

As the legislation supporting the education market has begun to take effect, location has become a disadvantage affecting minority students. Urban schools in communities with high levels of deprivation continue to serve families from lower socio-economic groups, high proportions of ethnic minorities, adults with low educational levels and poor housing and transport (OFSTED, 1993; House of Commons Education Committee, 1995). A report by the education committee of the House of Commons examining performance in city schools noted the effects of the market

> which can propel a school on a downward slope, creating a poor reputa-
> tion, leading to a flight of more mobile better off parents, which in turn
> creates empty places which are filled by pupils excluded from other
> schools.
>
> (House of Commons Education Committee, 1995, p. liv)

Failing Schools

Nevertheless, there is now a targeting of schools described as 'failing' and a public pillorying of urban schools considered to be offering inadequate education to students (Beckett, 1994). Under the 1992 Education (Schools) Act 'special measures' can be taken when a school is deemed, under the new inspection system, to be failing. The special measures include the suspension of a delegated budget and the intervention of the local education authority. If there is no immediate improvement, the Secretary of State is empowered to send an Education Association into the school to take it over or recommend closure. Further legislation via the 1998 *School Standards and Framework Act* has increased Central Government powers of intervention.

Some 700 'failing' schools have been identified since 1993 (DfE, 1993). They have been concentrated in deprived urban areas with high proportions of minority students (OFSTED/DfEE, 1996). A school which closed after the appointment of an Education Association, Hackney Downs in the London Borough of Hackney, had 80 per cent of the students from ethnic minority backgrounds, half of them speaking English as a second language, and 70 per cent qualifying for free school meals (Tomlinson, 1998).

The press coverage of failing or closed schools has been negative and derisory, and responsibility for school problems has been chiefly assigned to schools, teachers, students and parents, rather than to historical, structural, economic or political factors. Market reforms exacerbate the difficulties of schools attended by minorities in already deprived urban areas by taking money and resources from them. The schools are then blamed for the diffi-culties that inevitably ensue. The 'failing schools' legislation is proving a new way of scapegoating and disadvantaging minority students in urban schools.

Choice and Segregation

While there is clear evidence in a number of countries that education markets encourage social class segregation by school (OECD, 1994), there is also evidence that ethnic and racial segregation is exacerbated by parental choice. In the UK it appears that choice is offering white parents a legitimate means of avoiding schools with high intakes of ethnic minority students. From the 1960s, government intentions fuelled by assimilationist ideologies were aimed at preventing the concentration of ethnic minorities in urban schools and to 'spread the children' (DES, 1965). White parental pressure influenced dispersal policies and both parents and government took the view that migrant and bilingual children could lower standards in schools (Power, 1967). Dispersal policies proved impossible to sustain and residential segregation, as minorities clustered in particular areas, ensured that schools in those areas became 'high minority'.

Debates during the 1970s centred on the undesirability of ghetto schools (Dhondy, 1974; Rex and Tomlinson, 1979) and overt white parental rejection of schools attended by ethnic minority students was officially frowned upon. However, during the early 1980s further evidence demonstrated that middle and working-class parents felt a stigma at having their children educated alongside minority children (Richards, 1983; Lane, 1988) and in the later 1980s white parental antagonisms to ethnically mixed schools were given media publicity, encouraged by a year-long dispute in Dewsbury, where twenty-two parents refused to send their children to a school attended by pupils of predominantly Asian origins and educated their children separately until they were allocated to another school (Naylor, 1989; Tomlinson, 1990a, p. 65).

The Dewsbury dispute had a major significance for the possibility of increased racial segregation in urban schools, particularly as white parents used religious arguments – they wanted a 'Christian environment' – but a Harris poll carried out in 1987 reported that, while 40 per cent of white parents favoured a school of their 'own race', in multiracial areas this dropped to 22 per cent. In 1988 it was possible to suggest that, 'contrary to well-publicized cases of white hostility at individual schools, white parents may be becoming more tolerant of their children being educated alongside minority group children' (Tomlinson, 1990a, p. 67). However, the passage of the 1988 Education Act signalled a conciliation towards 'racial' segregation. Opposition peers in the House of Lords, in conjunction with the legal section of the Commission for Racial Equality, sought to amend the requirements on open admission and parental choice, arguing that these policies could lead to racial segregation by school. Their amendment was withdrawn after a government minister denied that parents would give an openly racist reason for choosing a school (Tomlinson, 1990b). The minister was quickly proved wrong. In Cleveland LEA a parent was at the time taking legal action concerning the transfer of her daughter from a multiracial school on racial grounds, a request which was granted and which prompted a series of further white parental demands for similar transfers. The government had certainly considered the possibility that giving parents more choice in the market could lead to increased racial segregation. Lady Hooper, a Minister of State for Education, concluded in an interview on television reported in the *Times Educational Supplement* of 10 November 1987 that 'racial segregation may be a price to be paid for giving some parents more opportunity to choose' (Tomlinson, 1988).

In the research carried out by Ball and his colleagues between 1993 and 1995 it was noted that 'there is a racial dimension to the segregatory effect of the market, and "racially informed choosing" does take place' (Gewirtz et al., 1995, p. 165). While the privileged choosers are skilled at arguing their concerns over the ethnic mix of the school, other choosers are less reticent. A white working-class parent excluded one school from consideration with the following comment:

> it's all nig-nogs isn't it? It's all Asians and it's a known fact they hold ours back... the kiddies while they're at home speak Punjabi or whatever it is, and when they come to school they can't understand a bloody word ... there's no way he's (son) going there.
>
> (Gewirtz et al., 1995, p. 49)

White parents, who before the market reforms were offering covert reasons for school preference, which would not violate the 1976 Race Relations Act, are now overtly able to choose schools with few or no ethnic minority students. The market in the UK does encourage ethnic segregation.

'Desirable Customers'

The effect of the education market is to enhance the segregation of the predominantly white middle class from minority groups and from the white working class. Choice is allowing schools, whether centrally or locally funded, to become more selective and choose their pupils. In the schools market place some students are regarded as 'valuable commodities' or desirable customers, others are undesirable customers. Students who are valued above others are those with a high measured ability level, who are motivated and have supportive parents.

There are various ways in which schools are choosing their desirable customers and discouraging or excluding the undesirable. The corollary of this is that schools which lose out in the market for the motivated, able student and take in the less motivated, less able or troublesome students may then be regarded as a 'sink' or 'failing' schools.

Overt selection by 'ability' or aptitude, is permitted in the remaining grammar schools, in some specialist schools, and up to 10 per cent in other schools under 1998 legislation.[1] Streaming (tracking) and setting within schools, is now openly advocated. Voluntary-aided religious schools continue, as they have done since the 1944 Education Act, to select pupils largely by religious affiliation, which has worked against minorities from different religious backgrounds.

Ethnic minority students have never done well in situations of selection. In the 1970s Rex and Tomlinson found that less than 1 per cent of their minority respondents had attended selective schools (1979) and in the late 1980s Walford and Miller found that in the new City Technology College 'there had been no Asian children in the first year intake and only a small number of Afro-Caribbeans' (Walford and Miller, 1991, p. 105). In school interviews, minority parents have often been at a disadvantage, particularly second language speakers and those unfamiliar with educational processes.

The market *also* works to encourage schools to get rid of students who disrupt the smooth running of the school or who interfere with the credentialling of other students. In the UK, referral for special education has always provided one way in which minority students, particularly black students, can be removed from the mainstream (Tomlinson, 1981). Black students were four times over-represented in the stigmatized category of 'educationally subnormal' and as 'emotionally and behaviourally disturbed'. However, moving students out of mainstream schooling via special education procedures has always been a lengthy process. In a market situation where desirable customers are required quicker ways of removing the undesirable are needed. In the 1990s, the use of straight exclusion as a way of rapidly removing troublesome students has increased and black students are disproportionately represented among the excluded. In 1992, black Afro-Caribbean students constituted 2 per cent of the school population but over 8 per cent of those excluded from school (DfE, 1992). (See also Chapters 6 and 12.)

In Nottingham in 1991 one in ten Afro-Caribbean students were involved in exclusion procedures compared to one in fifty white or Asian students. Gillborn, who has researched black exclusions and relevant literature, has concluded that 'exclusions from school operate in a racist manner: they deny a disproportionate number of black students access to mainstream education' and that, as marketization of education has become more established, the rates of exclusion have risen (see Gillborn, 1995, p. 36–38).

Social class, race and ethnicity, special educational needs and behaviour problems have become filters through which the desirability or undesirability of particular students is understood. On most counts, minority students, particularly black Afro-Caribbean, are less likely to be regarded as desirable students by the majority of schools.

Funding

As a pre-condition for an education market, schools were given control of their own budgets. Post-1988, local education authorities were required to devolve most of the education funding they received to schools. The effects of this on ethnic minority students and on equal opportunities do not appear to be very positive. By 1993 some 85 per cent of what is known as the 'Potential Schools Budget' had been removed from local education authorities and handed over to school governing bodies (Troyna, 1995). It is the governing bodies who, under local management of schools (LMS), have the power to decide how the budget is spent. Governing bodies now make decisions about the staffing and other resource priorities in their schools.

The money allocated to schools known as the Aggregated Schools Budget is based on the age and number of students the school can attract, although a small part of the budget is allocated on the basis of other factors. These include social deprivation and special educational needs, but local authorities are prevented from developing preferential funding policies which would help create more equal opportunities on the basis of social class or ethnicity.

Studies of the effects of funding decisions to date confirm that without a specific focus on equal opportunities and social justice principles LMS can actually bring about a redistribution of resources from urban schools to rural and suburban schools. In their study of the Avon local authority, Guy and Mentor found that the new funding was 'disproportionately damaging to inner urban schools' (1992, p. 165). Troyna noted that crude measures of social deprivation work against the equitable distribution of resources to schools (Troyna, 1995, p. 153). For example, a major index of deprivation is the take-up of free school meals, not the eligibility, but many ethnic minority pupils do not take up their entitlement to free school meals.

Minority students are further disadvantaged by new funding mechanisms because local education authorities now have very little money available to support the range of activities developed during the 1970s and 1980s to assist ethnic minority students. Multicultural education centres have been closed down and local authority multicultural advisers have lost their jobs (Richardson, 1992). Money given by the Home Office under Section 11 of the 1966 Local Government Act for the special needs of ethnic minorities became discretionary. It could not be used to fund minority language teaching or race equality provision in general. From 1990 local education authorities had to bid competitively for these grants to assist students 'where linguistic and cultural barriers prevent such pupils gaining full access to main-stream education provision' (Brehony, 1995, p. 169). In urban areas local education authorities were required to bid under a Single Regeneration Budget for inner city areas and the needs of minority students competed with other urban needs.

In November 1998 the Government announced that a new Ethnic Minority Pupil Achievement Grant would be available to schools, distributed by the Department for Education and Employment, not the Home Office. While this grant was welcomed by teachers and the teacher unions, there was still concern that, as schools would have discretion to spend the money, former Section 11 staff could lose their jobs (*Times Educational Supplement*, 1998).

The social class and ethnic composition of governing bodies of schools has become an issue for research and comment now that they have more powers to make decisions concerning the finances, staffing and resourcing of their schools (Deem, 1989; Keys and Fernandes, 1990; Brehony, 1995). Not surprisingly the research indicates that the majority of school governors are male, white and have professional or managerial backgrounds. Women are under-represented, and although there has been an absolute increase in the numbers of black and Asian school governors, they are still under-represented and are concentrated in certain areas (Geddes, 1993). White governors of schools, if not openly hostile to ethnic minorities often 'show very little understanding of the educational issues which coalesce around ethnicity' (Brehony, 1995, p. 173).

Despite the promise of more power to school decision-makers, school governing bodies are restricted; they assist in what Weiler (1990) termed an 'efficiency' model of decentralized educational governance. They make decisions about funds which are often too small to allow all students an adequate education and this affects minority students disproportionately.

Winners and Losers?

Markets create winners and losers, and it is still an open question as to how far some minority students and families are winners. There is some evidence to indicate that black and Asian middle-class parents are, where possible, taking advantage of choice and making similar choices to white middle-class parents. A report in the *New Statesman* (McHardy, 9 February 1996) suggested that 'black and white parents alike are doing their best to get their children out of inner-city schools'. The report documented the case of the black politician, Bernie Grant, who with other black professionals, are able to choose suburban local authority schools or private schools for their children. The (now abolished) assisted places scheme, through which children from poorer families were able to attend private schools, initially had considerable interest from minority communities (Edwards et al., 1989). However, the small numbers of families who were successful in the scheme appeared to be middle-class Asians (Edwards et al., 1989, p. 117). Education markets may be able to enhance the life chances of middle-class minorities, leading to the situation described by William Wilson in the USA whereby 'Talented and educated blacks, like talented and educated whites, will continue to enjoy the advantages and privileges of their class status' (Wilson, 1979, p. 153). However, Wilson, in a recent comparison of cities in the USA and Europe, concluded that government market reforms in housing and education has encouraged segregation by race and class in urban areas in Britain (Wilson, 1996), given that, as noted above, most minorities are concentrated in lower socio-economic groups. Initially, minority parents supported what appeared to be new opportunities to influence schools' decision-making and budgeting as school governors. But as Brehony (1995) and others have shown, 'the promise of power for consumers has remained just a promise for black and Asian governors' (p. 172). Minority parents, in common with other parents, are also discovering that the rhetoric of 'choice' and 'diversity' does not match the actual reality whereby they and their children are selected or rejected by schools.

Improvement in the educational performance of minority students was set in train well before the impact of market forces. Schools, teachers, teacher educators and local education authorities had become more responsive to the needs of minorities during the 1970s and 1980s and there were political initiatives from both main parties to encourage this (Tomlinson, 1990a). One result of improved performance was that more minority students began to enter higher education (Modood, 1993). A report by the UK Higher Education Funding Council in 1996 noted that ethnic minorities are now well-represented in higher education, especially Asian and black African groups, although Afro-Caribbean men and Pakistani and Bangladeshi women are still under-represented, minorities study part-time courses more than whites, and 60 per cent of all minority students study in the 'new' universities − former urban polytechnics (HEFCE, 1996, p. 17).

Minority students have always stayed in education at further education post-16 colleges in greater numbers than white students, a trend which has intensified in the 1990s (Shaw, 1994). Market competition introduced after 1992 between colleges has encouraged some colleges to 'niche market'. Macrae and her colleagues found that some urban colleges deliberately aim to attract minority students, refugees and asylum seekers − students regarded as less desirable elsewhere (Macrae et al., 1997). Whether this is an advantage or disadvantage for students is debatable. It is good that minority students stay on in education and acquire qualifications, but it is a negative consequence of the market if they are 'guided' towards less prestigious urban colleges.

However, even limited educational success on the part of minority groups does not necessarily lead to expressions of admiration from the majority society and instead can increase xenophobia and racism. Wimmer, using a Weberian perspective, has attempted to explain increases in xenophobia and racism as expressions of an ultra-nationalist ideology; in particular, down-wardly mobile groups perceive people from outside their 'imagined community' as illegitimate competition for the collective goods the state has promised them (Wimmer, 1997). In Britain in the 1990s, there is no consensus as to how the civic incorporation of those perceived as 'outsiders' should take place and whether those regarded as racially or ethnically different will be regarded as equal citizens with a genuine choice of cultural affiliation. The educational success of any one minority group or individual is more likely to be resented by the increasing numbers in the majority population who are, or who fear, becoming downwardly mobile. Education has become a competitively sought after positional good, and from the point of view of the white majority, the fewer competitors the better. At the same time, the increasing concentration of minorities in urban schools (and failing schools) perpetuates the xenophobic reaction that the very presence of minorities lowers standards in schools.

Future Developments

As described in Chapter 1 the New Labour Government, which took office in April 1997, immediately set in train a number of initiatives designed to combat low educational achievement and poor employment prospects among young people living in disadvantaged circumstances. Until the announcement of the replaced Section 11 Grant the assumption, as in the 1970s, was that measures to benefit all disadvantaged groups would benefit minorities. The language of disadvantage changed to that of social exclusion and, as the social and economic consequences of the increased exclusion of particular groups became well documented, 'inclusion into one nation' became a central rhetorical theme. Prime Minister Blair opened the government Social Exclusion Unit, asserting that 'At the heart of all our work is Britain rebuilt as a nation in which each citizen is valued ... no-one is excluded, and we make it our purpose to tackle social division and inequality' (Blair, 1997). The staff of the Social Exclusion Unit included two Afro-Caribbean members, a former probation officer and a former Director of a charity aimed at reducing youth crime. Major issues the Unit focused on initially were school truancy, school exclusions, particularly of Afro-Caribbean youth, and crime-ridden housing estates. In September 1998 the first of 25 Education Action Zones (EAZs) began to operate. While not specifically aimed at locations with large numbers of ethnic minority children, those EAZs starting up in areas of London, Manchester and other Northern towns did include significant numbers of minority young people.

The new initiatives put forward by the new government to combat exclusion and disadvantage have been accorded a similar tentative welcome as that offered to Educational Priority Areas in the 1960s, and job training schemes in the 1970s and 1980s. Individual children will undoubtedly benefit but, until the choice policies described above are modified, it is unlikely that the structural situation of minorities living in disadvantaged areas and circumstances will change.

Conclusion

In Britain the market system in education and the choice policy does appear to create new disadvantages for ethnic minority students and their parents which outweigh advantages. Disadvantages do not necessarily accrue from ethnic or race-specific policies, they are the result of an absence of reference to minorities or minority issues as the legislation which created the education market passed through parliament. It must have been apparent to policy-makers that the socio-economic position and urban location of most minorities would inhibit their ability to 'choose' schools, and the effects of funding and resources moving away from urban schools attended by minority students would affect their education. As this chapter has discussed, it was apparent and acknowledged that the 'choice' legislation would increase ethnic and white school segregation. Minority students now bear additional market burdens. Many of them are likely to be regarded as undesirable, attending 'failing' schools, and schools with severely reduced budgets. Afro-Caribbean students are faring particularly badly in the market. Overall, a conclusion must be that the market in education could become a more sharply-focused mechanism for disadvantage, segregating most minority students in under-funded and under-staffed schools in urban areas, while a small number of minority students, defined by class position, develop an advantaged position, but may still not be recognized by the majority society as legitimate achievers.

Note

1   Although the New Labour Government has ruled out the introduction of any further selection of pupils by ability, except for 'fair banding' (see DfEE, 1998a), it has allowed such selection to continue in the remaining grammar schools, and also partial selection by ability or aptitude in other schools where it existed up to the school year 1997–1998, subject to the possibility of change by parental consent, or through an appeal to the new Admissions Adjudicators (DfEE, 1998b).

References

Ball, S.J., Bowe, R. and Gewirtz, S. (1996) 'School choice, social class and the realisation of social advantage in education', *Journal of Education Policy* 11, 1, pp. 75–88.

Beckett, A. (1994) 'Scenes from the classroom war', *The Independent on Sunday*, 27 November 1994, pp. 48–50.

Benn, C. and Chitty, C. (1996) *Thirty Years On: Is comprehensive education alive and well or struggling to survive?*, London, David Fulton.

Blackstone, T., Parekh, B. and Sanders, P. (1998) *Race Relations in Britain: A developing agenda*, London, Routledge.

Blair, T. (1997) *Speech at the Opening of the Social Exclusion Unit*, London, December 1997.

Brehony, K. (1995) 'School governors, "race" and racism' in Tomlinson, S. and Craft, M. (eds) *Ethnic Relations and Schooling*, London, Athlone Press.

Centre for Research in Ethnic Relations (1992) *Ethnic Minorities in Great Britain: Settlement patterns* (1991) Census Statistical Paper No. 1, Warwick, CRER.

Chubb, J. and Moe, T. (1992) *A Lesson in School Reform from Great Britain*, Washington, DC, Brookings Institute.

Deem, R. (1989) 'The new school governing bodies – are race and gender on the agenda?', *Gender and Education*, pp. 247–260.

Department of Education and Science (DES) (1965) *The Education of Immigrants*, Circular 7/65, London, HMSO.

Department of Education and Science (DES) (1974) *Educational Disadvantage and the Needs of Immigrants*, London, HMSO.

Department of Education and Science (DES) (1985a) *Education For All*, London, HMSO (report of an Enquiry chaired by Lord Swann).

Department of Education and Science (DES) (1985b) *Better Schools*, London, HMSO.

Department for Education (DfE) (1992) *Exclusions From School*, London, DfE.

Department for Education (DfE) (1993) *Schools Requiring Special Measures*, Circular 17/93, DfE.

Department for Education and Employment (DfEE) (1998a) School Admissions. Code of Practice (Consultative Draft), London, DfEE.

Department for Education and Employment (DfEE) (1998b) School Admissions. Interim Guidance. Circular Number 12/98, London, DfEE.

Dhondy, F. (1974) 'The black explosion in schools', *Race Today*, February, pp. 43–48.

Drew, D. (1995) *Race, Education and Work: The statistics of inequality*, Avebury, Aldershot.

Edwards, T., Fitz, J., Whitty, G. (1989) *The State and Private Education*, Lewes, Falmer Press

Fuller, B. and Ellmore, R.F. (1996) *Who Chooses? and Who Loses?*, New York, Teachers College Press.

Geddes, A. (1993) 'Asian and Afro-Caribbean representation in elected local government in England and Wales', *New Community* 20, 1, pp. 43–57.

Gewirtz, S., Ball, S.J. and Bowe, R. (1995) *Markets, Choice and Equity in Education*, Buckinghamshire, Open University Press.

Gillborn, D. (1995) *Racism and Antiracism in Real Schools*, Buckingham, Open University Press.

Gillborn, D. and Gipps, C. (1996) *A Review of Recent Research on Achievement by Minority Ethnic Pupils*, London, Office for Standards in Education/Institute of Education.

Guy, W. and Mentor, I. (1992) 'Local management: who benefits?' in Gill, B., Mayor, D. and Blair, M. (eds) *Racism and Education – structures and strategies*, London, Sage.

Higher Education Funding Council (1996) *Widening Access to Higher Education: A report by the HEFCE Advisory Group on access and participation*, Bristol, HEFCE.

Home Office (1978) *Proposals for replacing Section 11 of the Local Government Act – a consultative document*, London, HMSO.

House of Commons Education Committee (1995) *Third Report: Performance in City Schools*, London, HMSO, 2 vols.

Iganski, P. and Payne, G. (1996) 'Declining racial disadvantage in the British labour market', *Ethnic and Racial Studies* 1, pp. 113–134.

Keys, W. and Fernandes, C. (1990) *A Survey of School Governing Bodies*, Slough, NFER, Nelson

King, A. and Reiss, M. (1993) *The Multicultural Dimension of the National Curriculum*, London, Falmer Press.

Kirp, D. (1979) *Doing Good by Doing Little: Race and schooling in Britain*, Berkeley, CA, University of California Press.

Lane, D (1988) 'The Commission for Racial Equality: the first five years', *New Community* 14, 1/2, pp. 12–16.

Macrae, S., Maguire, M. and Ball, S.J. (1997) 'Competition, choice and hierarchy in a post-16 education and training market' in Tomlinson, S. (ed) *Education 14–19: Critical Perspectives*, London, Athlone Press.

McHardy, A. (1996) 'White flight, black heat', *New Statesman and Society*, 9 February, pp. 14–15.

Modood, T. (1993) 'The number of ethnic minority students in British Higher Education, Some grounds for optimism', *Oxford Review of Education* 19, 2, pp. 167–182.

Modood, T. (1998) 'Ethnic diversity and racial disadvantage in employment', in Blackstone, T., Parekh, B. and Sanders, P. (eds) *Race Relations in Britain: A Developing Agenda*, London, Routledge.

Naylor, F. (1989) *Dewsbury: The school above the pub*, London, The Claridge Press.

Noden, P., West, A., David, M. and Edge, A. (1998) 'Choices and destinations at transfer to secondary schools in London', *Journal of Educational Policy* 13, 2, pp. 221–236.

Organization for Economic Co-operation and Development (OECD) (1994) *School: A Matter of Choice*, Centre for Educational Research and Innovation, Paris, OECD.

Office for Standards in Education (OFSTED) (1993) *Access and Achievement in Urban Education*, London, HMSO.

Office for Standards in Education (OFSTED)/Department for Education and Employment (DfEE) (1996) *The Improvement of Failing Schools: UK Policy and Practice 1993–95* (compiled for an OECD seminar, November 1995), London, Office for Standards in Education.

Power, J. (1967) *Immigrants in School – A Survey of Administrative Practice*, London, Councils and Education Press.

Ram, M. and Deakins, D. (1996) 'Afro-Caribbeans in business', *New Community* 22, 1, pp. 67–84.

Rex, J. (1996) *Ethnic Minorities in the Modern Nation-State*, London, Macmillan.

Rex, J. and Tomlinson, S. (1979) *Colonial Immigrants in a British City*, London, Routledge.

Richards, K.J. (1983) 'A contribution to the multicultural education debate', *New Community* 10, 2, pp. 222–225.

Richardson, R. (1992) 'Race policies and programmes under attack – two case studies for the 1990s' in Gill, B., Mayor, D. and Blair, M. (eds) *Racism and Education: Structures and strategies*, London, Sage.

Rutter, M. and Madge, N. (1976) *Cycles of Disadvantage*, London, Heinemann.

Shaw, C. (1994) *Changing Lives 2*, London, Policy Studies Institute.

Simon, B. (1991) *Education and the Social Order*, London, Lawrence & Wishart.

Taylor, M. (1981) *Caught Between*, Slough, NFER.

Taylor, M. (1985) *The Best of Both Worlds?* Slough, NFER.

Taylor, M. (1988) *Worlds Apart?* Slough, NFER.

Times Educational Supplement (TES) (1998) 13 November, p. 5.

Tomlinson, S. (1981) *Educational Subnormality – A study in decision-making*, London, Routledge.

Tomlinson, S. (1983) *Ethnic Minorities in British Schools: A review of the literature 1960–1982*, London, Heinemann.

Tomlinson, S. (1988) 'Education and training', *New Community* 15, 1, pp. 103–109.

Tomlinson, S. (1990a) *Multicultural Education in White Schools*, London, Batsford.

Tomlinson, S. (1990b) 'Education and training', *New Community* 16, 3, pp. 441–446.

Tomlinson, S. (1992) 'Disadvantaging the disadvantaged: Bangladeshis and education in Tower Hamlets', *British Journal of Sociology of Education* 13, 2, pp. 437–446.

Tomlinson, S. (1998) 'A tale of one city: the case of Hackney Downs', in Slee, R., Weiner, G. and Tomlinson, S. (eds) *School Effectiveness for Whom?*, London, Falmer Press.

Troyna, B. (1987) *Racial Inequality in Education*, London, Tavistock.

Troyna, B. (1995) 'The local management of schools and race equality' in Tomlinson, S. and Craft, M. (eds) *Ethnic Relations and Schooling*, London, Athlone Press.

Vernon A. (1996) 'A stranger in many camps: the experience of black and ethnic minority women' in Morris, J. (ed.) *Encounters with Strangers: Feminism and disability*, London, Women's Press.

Vincent, C. (1995) 'School, Community and Ethnic Minority Parents' in Tomlinson, S. and Craft, M. (eds) *Ethnic Relations and Schooling*, London, Athlone Press.

Walford, G. and Miller, H. (1991) *City Technology Colleges*, Buckingham, Open University Press.

Waslander, S. and Thrupp, M. (1995) 'Choice, competition and segregation: an empirical analysis of the New Zealand secondary school market', *Journal of Educational Policy* 10, 1, pp. 1–26.

Weiler, H. (1990) 'Decentralisation in educational governance: an exercise in contradiction' in Granheim, M., Kogan, M. and Lundgren, U. (eds) *Evaluation as Policy-Making*, London, Jessica King.

Wilson, W.J. (1979) *The Declining Significance of Race*, Chicago, University of Chicago Press.

Wilson, W.J. (1996) 'Are ghetto trends emerging in Europe?', Lecture at London School of Economics, London, 27 June.

Wimmer, A. (1997) 'Explaining xenophobia and racism: a critical review of current research approaches', *Ethnic and Racial Studies* 2, 1, pp. 17–42.

3 Boys' Underachievement: Social Class and Changing Masculinities

Helen Lucey and Valerie Walkerdine

Current discussions of the educational underachievement of boys have tended to operate as though all boys were failing and all girls succeeding: a universalism that suppresses deep and enduring class differences between boys and girls and seriously undermines equal opportunities policy and practice. This chapter seeks to explore more fully the complex intersections of educational performance, masculinity and more general processes of social class reproduction in the family and at school and to place this in a context of immense economic change. Using data from a school-based study of literacy performance in one London borough and drawing on findings from a longitudinal study of middle-class and working-class young women, we refute the notion that underachievement is a problem for all boys in the 1990s and examine the social and emotional processes through which some, mainly working-class boys continue to fail, while other, mainly middle-class boys, maintain their educational success.

By the spring and summer of 1997 the concern over boys' apparent decline in educational performance which had been steadily growing since the beginning of the 1990s reached panic-status. The 'problem' of boys had become a full-scale crisis with almost daily media reports[1] as well as a proposed series of dramatic New Labour policy innovations to counteract it.[2] Particular worries about boys' relatively poor reading skills and performance in English have served to place literacy firmly at the centre of this panic, as both the source of the problem and the site of intervention. However, debates around gendered performance have shifted dramatically over the last few years; in the 1970s, in the wake of second wave feminism[3] a great deal of concern was expressed about the relative underachievement of girls, especially in maths and science subjects (Sutherland, 1983; Walkerdine, 1988, 1989; Whyte, 1986). Now, over twenty years later, in a very changed economic and social climate, concern is about the low performance of boys in a context in which girls are viewed as doing very well (Sammons, 1995).

In this chapter, we will explore the complex story of boys' underachievement as it has emerged in the 1990s. We suggest that a tunnel-visioned focus on gender not only does a disservice to feminism's project of equal opportunities for girls but has led to a serious neglect of other, powerfully interconnecting factors, especially social class, race and ethnicity in the context of massive social and economic change. Specific anxieties about boys and literacy have tended to produce universal truths (such as boys' 'anti-reading' or 'laddish' cultures), truths which seek to describe and explain all boys, but which consistently glaze over crucial class differences. We ask, how is it that middle-class boys maintain their high performance despite what seem on the surface to be such anti-school feelings and behaviours? Conversely, why is it that (relatively) high-achieving working-class children with parents who are viewed as doing 'all the right things' so routinely 'fail' educationally? Central to our argument is an exploration of the ways in which educational success or failure is not only differently constituted for working and middle-class children and their families, but is at the very heart of what it means, not only to be a boy or a girl, but to be reproduced as working class or middle class.

Confusing Data

Available data does point to significant gender differences in girls' favour up to GCSE and especially in English, where the performance gap between boys and girls is widest (EOC OFSTED, 1996; DfEE, 1997a). But the picture is by no means clear. All too often simplistic, statistical interpretations which concentrate entirely on gender differences serve to shore up a universal notion of boys' underachievement and present a picture which powerfully obscures and confuses enduring inequalities in attainment (Plummer, 1998). A more critical examination of the data reveals that the gender gap is nowhere near as severe as the class gap (Smith and Noble, 1995; Reid, 1994). The boys who are doing well and those who are doing poorly do not, generally speaking, come from the same constituency.

In our research on gender differences in literacy [4] an analysis of Key Stage 2 Literacy scores for all primary schools in the borough revealed that out of 12 schools whose pupil intake was mainly from professional middle-class families, 11 of these were in the top 20 performing schools. In 4 out of the top 5 scoring schools (all middle class) boys were doing better. In the lowest achieving schools (most of which had a majority black and white working class intake as well as significant proportions of families recently arrived in the UK), girls do achieve higher results in literacy than boys, but we should not be fooled into thinking that they are doing well: they are simply performing a little better than boys in what is essentially poor performance. Research carried out by the Child Poverty Action Group (1997) found that while there was an increase in 'poor' pupils achieving GCSE grades A–C, this increase has been far exceeded by schools in more prosperous areas. In 1996, the Chief Inspector of Schools for England defined the problems in falling standards of literacy as 'the failure of boys and in particular white working-class boys' (C. Woodhead quoted in *Times Educational Supplement*, 1997), although this declaration glosses over concerns about the levels of achievement of African Caribbean boys (Gilborn and Gipps, 1996). While headlines scream out that girls are doing better than boys at every level there is contradictory evidence to show that white middle-class boys continue to outperform girls at A level, in both mathematics and English (Murphy and Elwood, 1998). Significantly, in our study, classroom observations revealed that the literacy policy and practices of the two schools as well as the classroom practices of the target classes were remarkably similar. The main differences observed were in terms of the socio-economic and cultural location of the pupils and their families.

The confusion surrounding the interpretation of such data has led to a great deal of concern and uncertainty. In our study we found that amongst teachers, there was a general assumption that boys were achieving less than girls, even in the more middle-class school where this was not supported by boys' actual performance.[4] This perception is especially problematic for teachers in working-class schools, who are on one level aware that problems of under-achievement are not confined to boys alone, but on another level have been influenced by the panic over boys' performance and so are very keen on initiatives which target boys specifically. This contributes to teacher anxiety and loss of confidence about the teaching of literacy, particularly in an educational climate which equates educational standards with performance and little else.

Furthermore, while boys' underachievement in literacy is being presented as an entirely new phenomenon, educationalists have known about boys' tardiness at reading for many years (Douglas et al., 1968), but this has not until now been deemed worthy of interest or action (Cohen, 1996; Eldridge, 1997; Mahony, 1997). How then do we understand the dramatic emergence of this concern at this particular historical moment? It is in the context of a massive decline in male, manual employment across Europe, North America and Australasia, alongside a collapse in the youth labour market that the educational performance of working-class boys, especially in relation to literacy, takes on a special significance. First of all though, let us briefly look at some contemporary explanations of why boys are lagging behind in literacy.

School and Reading is for Girls

Central to this debate are various facets of the concept of 'feminization'. This enters as an explanation of girls' greater linguistic abilities from the very early years (Shaw, 1995; Swann, 1992). Early literacy education in schools is identified as problematic for boys because of the feminized environment of the primary school in which girls 'flourish' whilst boys are 'set off on a rockier subconscious road' (Shaw, op cit., p. 76). The OFSTED report 'Boys and English' (1993) suggests that this early feminizing influence can result in the formation of unhelpful or damaging attitudes towards English in adolescent boys (see also Millard, 1997).[5]

The knowledges associated with literacy and English are themselves regarded as somehow 'female' and as such are ones that girls will naturally do well in while boys will just as naturally be put off. An emphasis in the classroom on practices which require the student to be introspective, self-disclosing, empathic and able to creatively describe emotions may be incompatible with what boys understand to be an acceptable masculine identity (Shaw, op cit.; Davies, 1993). How to dissolve the rigid gender boundaries around reading is the focus of various strands of research including how to encourage and help boys develop as critical readers by, for instance, placing more value on the materials which boys choose to read for themselves (Hall and Coles, 1997). Alloway and Gilbert (1997) argue that many boys have literacy skills which are not recognized in the classroom, but are ones that are potentially powerful in the communication technologies of the future. Some research has focused on the lack of suitable role models for boys (Wragg, 1997a) and the promotion of such models has become part of proposed initiatives to break the notion that reading is only something that girls and women do. For instance in 1997 the National Literacy Trust ran a poster campaign showing famous football players reading novels. We can see then how literacy has become heavily implicated not only in educational performance, but in the very formation and expression of masculine and feminine identities.

Educational Success and Middle-Class Masculinity

There is a confusing twist in current popular accounts of 'resistance' and masculinity in relation to panics over boys and literacy. Government refers to the need for strategies to tackle anti-school 'laddish' cultures which are held responsible for boys' poor performance. Once again class differences are simply glazed over, as if all boys are doing badly, as if all 'laddish' cultures have the same genesis or, crucially, the same effects and consequences for all boys. The tendency towards such universal 'truths' only serves to obscure and confuse rather than clarify, particularly when they clash with other, equally powerful 'truths'. For example, while the feminization of the primary school, together with the essentially feminine nature of reading is at times used to explain all boys' relatively poor performance, it is the masculinity of working-class boys, not middle-class boys, which is viewed as far more rejecting of the feminine culture of school in general and literacy in particular.

At this point we would argue strongly that a discussion of masculinity, in the context of educational achievement, must be examined alongside considerations of social class – especially the reproduction of class position. First, we found in our study that middle-class and working-class boys exhibited a remarkably similar range of stereotypically 'masculine' behaviours. However, despite the middle-class boys also having defences against the more feminine aspects of schooling, they were still doing far better than the working-class boys and girls in every subject. How and why?

To understand this apparent contradiction it is crucial to recognize the centrality of educational success in the construction of middle-class hegemonic masculinity. So it was that even 'laddish' middle-class boys were able to take up another, contrasting subject position within the classroom – that of the studious boy.[6] Teachers of the middle-class boys explain their seemingly unproblematic take-up of two opposing subject positions by citing a combination of the high achieving environment of the school, parents' own educational achievements and expectations of high performance for their children as well as less rigidly gendered practices in the home.

> There's a lot of professional partners where both are working and the dads take their turn at seeing to the house and bringing the children in and vice versa. They're in professions where they are writing and the children see the need to write I think.
>
> (Teacher in middle-class school)

> I think they're seeing a lot of examples of writing and reading that's just part of the family situation [...] and there isn't 'this is what girls do and this is what men do'.
>
> (Teacher in middle-class school)

We would take the teachers' observations further and argue that being 'studious' is entirely compatible with middle-class boys' constructions of themselves as masculine. These boys come from families where to go to university and become a professional is an established pathway and one which their parents are confident their children will also follow.

HL:	How would you like to see Michael's education progress?
White, middle-class mother:	A levels and university. (*laughs*) It sounds like I've got it all planned out doesn't it? But, yes, I suppose that's what I expect ... um ... that's what he's more than capable of.
White, middle-class father:	Well we've spoken to him about university. I mean, he knows what it is – his mother's doing a post-graduate course at the moment ... he knows how important it is.

Tracey Reynolds (1998) notes that in the UK, black people are viewed as a homogeneous group, as automatically working class, therefore preventing class differences from emerging.[7] While we do not have the scope here for a full analysis of the subtle differences within groups designated middle class or working class, it is important to say that this commitment to a rigidly circumscribed educational pathway amongst various kinds of middle-class professional families was undisturbed by race and ethnicity.

HL:	How would you like to see Hassan's education progress?
British Pakistani middle-class mother:	Yeah, well, he's got an attitude problem with his work ... can't concentrate and is quite lazy ... but I want him to go to university, and his dad. It'll be harder for him than his brother. He needs pushing.

Nor are these expectations of academic success only the case for middle-class boys; middle-class girls are now required to join the race for places in professions previously occupied by their brothers. We argue more fully elsewhere (Lucey et al., forthcoming) that there is an overwhelming drive for the middle classes to defend themselves against failure and ensure the reproduction of their class position, life-chances, lifestyle and so on.[8] For this, a particular kind of educational trajectory and increasingly, a certain level of success within that trajectory is absolutely essential in order to join a profession and guard against downward social mobility (Reay, 1998a). So it may be the case that some middle-class boys are slightly behind middle-class girls and it may also be the case that they are not as interested in reading in the same way that girls seem to be, but this is completely irrelevant to the production of their success. Furthermore, the more troublesome aspects of masculinity must not be allowed to interfere with this reproductive process. We wish to stress therefore that educational failure is simply not an option for the middle-class children, boys or girls (Lucey et al., op cit.).

Working-Class Success?

How do the complex connections between masculinity, class and educational achievement get played out for working-class boys? Our starting point for examining this must also be the familial and social context in which school achievement is located. Successful progression through the examination system and onto higher education was certainly not a feature of the families of the working-class children in the study, nor indeed, of the wider community of which they were a part.

When considering the emotional well-being of children, it is taken as a commonsense 'truth' that they are most able to thrive when they feel themselves to be 'the same' as everybody else and to not stand out in any negative way. Being viewed as 'different' (and the grounds for this difference can be entirely spurious) is recognized in the literature on bullying for example, as the cause of much misery, even long-lasting psychological damage for those children (Tattum and Herbert, 1997) (see also Chapter 12). Let us for a moment examine the more emotional meanings of academic success for working-class children in this light. While achieving academic success in order to follow a well-trodden (though increasingly competitive) path towards university and a professional career is a necessary part of middle-class subjectivity, for most working-class boys (and girls) doing well at school is to be profoundly *different* from the overwhelming majority of boys and girls, men and women in their families and social milieu. While working-class parents want their children to do well at school and feel immense pride when they do, we suggest that the hopes and aspirations of working-class children and their parents inevitably become intertwined with the pain of difference, separation and therefore loss (Lucey et al., op cit.).

It is feminist academics, themselves from working-class families, who have begun to shed light on some of the painful consequences and costs of such success (Mahony and Zmroczek, 1997; Walkerdine, 1990; Steedman, 1986). A constantly recurring theme in these analyses is the ways in which a transformation of the self, from accent and language to values had to be achieved in order to 'do well' at school and university (Clancy, 1997). Reay points out that 'the positive connotations invested in terms such as transformation and change mask an inherent negativity often overlooked in discussions of meritocracy' (Reay, 1997, p. 19).

This connection is one which has escaped the imagination of successive policy makers, who fail to see the transformation of identity that maintaining high school performance requires for most working-class children. Most seriously, educationalists are left without an adequate framework in which to understand and work with the disabling responses such as ambivalence and 'resistance' which many working-class children develop as defences against the prospect of such difference. Such a framework must however, be able to incorporate the complexities of the unconscious and appreciate it not only as an abstract theory but as a driving force, able to produce real, material effects. Only then can it's 'creative significance' to 'our practices as teachers and researchers' be fully realized (Raphael, 1995).

In relation to boys, it is clear from this and previous research that to be both academically successful and acceptably masculine requires a considerable amount of careful negotiation on the part of working-class boys (Mac an Ghaill, 1994). Other research has found that, amongst economically disadvantaged Year 6 children, 'posh' as a powerfully stigmatizing term of abuse was confusingly intertwined with 'cleverness' (Reay and Lucey, forthcoming). Our research suggests that some working-class boys in Year 6 may find the resolution to this potentially disastrous situation in the position of the 'bright but naughty' boy, distancing themselves as a defensive strategy from working hard at school (Mac an Ghaill, op cit; Sewell, 1995, 1997). These are boys who are clearly very able and who also enjoy school work on one level, but who on another, have to hide their ability and enthusiasm for fear of being viewed unfavourably by their peers. Displaying an exaggerated masculine identity may get them into trouble with the teacher, but it reasserts their 'sameness' with the other boys (Connell, 1989, 1995; Jackson, 1997). We do not go along with the idea that this constitutes 'resistance' in the way that it has traditionally been understood, but as one of the ways in which some working-class boys desperately try to maintain the status quo in the face of enormous change.

Working With Parents

Parents are viewed as crucial in the process of children learning to read and certainly in our study, teachers made strong connections between parental practice and children's performance in literacy. All parents had some kind of practice around literacy which would be recognized as 'good' practice, but there were no unambiguous connections between the amount or kind of reading parents did with their children and how much the children read of their own volition (Webster et al., 1996). Within the 'crisis of masculinity' discourse it is fathers who have emerged as the most influential agents in the promotion of reading and are advised to spend more time reading with their sons (Wragg, 1997a). Literacy practices within the families of the low achieving working-class children served an important function of maintaining close, loving relationships between one or both parents, and sometimes for the whole family, but would be viewed as unhelpful or irrelevant in pedagogical terms. (See Chapter 7 for a fuller discussion of this issue.) Particularly important is the telling of stories. For Kalvinder's family, the telling and reading of Hindu parables and other Indian folk stories are a source of immense pleasure and cultural knowledge for her and her parents. David's father tells him stories about World War Two and the 'Wild West'. His father's knowledge is gained from the documentaries and general knowledge programmes he watches. David is enthusiastic about these subjects but finds the written material just too difficult to deal with. However, when first given the story in spoken form (such as on the television news) he is able to make far greater headway with the same story in written form (in the newspaper). This is, in fact, one of the extremely effective strategies used in 'reading recovery' schemes.

All of the working-class parents who took part in the study understood the necessity for their children to do well at school and tried to give the message that it is important for them to work hard, particularly with reference to securing a 'good job' in the future. However, 'success' becomes a very relative concept here because for most of these parents, their children are achieving more and are happier than they were at school.

> I know I think he is quite a good reader, I don't know about for his age, but at his age I couldn't read like him so as far as I'm concerned he's better than what I was and that's good enough for me, so that's fine.
>
> (White, working-class mother)

Race and social class intersect powerfully for Kalvinder's parents, who themselves had very different experiences of primary education in rural India and for whom English is their second language. Although Kalvinder is achieving poorly at school, her mastery of the English language compared to their own makes it difficult for them to see her as 'failing'.

> At the moment she is always all right – she is happy doing – always busy at home, doing something, painting whatever, drawing, she's all right at school I think.
>
> (British Pakistani father)

The working-class parents' experiences of education were coloured by indifference, lack of motivation, unhappiness and failure. Not surprisingly then, there are a number of unconscious fears and anxieties around their children's education which tend to act as 'blocks' to working with the school in the way that middle-class parents are able to do. This surfaces as their desire for their children above all to be happy, a desire which is at times understood by the teachers as parents not being interested in their child's progress, although our case studies show that nothing could be further from the truth. However, one of the things which clearly differentiates the middle-class and working-class parents is the *level* to which middle-class parents are prepared to push their children in order to achieve and maintain high academic performance (Allatt, 1993). While David's mother (who left school at 15) is sure 'he will do the best he can, without being pushed', Hassan's professional, educated mother stresses that 'he is one of those children that needs a push, all the time, he needs that added bit of pressure'.

This highlights class-differentiated conceptions of children's happiness (David et al., 1994; Reay, 1998b). While working-class parents' concerns for their child's happiness tended to be located in the here and now, middle-class parents' conceptions of happiness were also projected into the adult future where it was inextricably connected to educational success (Reay and Ball, 1998). We suggest that for some of the parents of failing children, who themselves have experienced educational failure, it is very difficult to push their child and distressing to hear that the child may be finding school work very 'hard'. Instead, the parents want to protect their child from these difficult feelings and preserve their childhood as a time of happiness and freedom from worry and expectation.

> Just for him to be happy and do well and get on with life and whatever he wants to do I'm behind him, as long as he's happy I'm happy.
>
> (White working-class mother)

(…) as long as they're happy and they're getting on and they're trying hard, that's fine.

(Mixed-race Afro-Caribbean/white British father)

Perhaps this sheds light on some working-class parents' ambivalence around their children's education. They may encourage the child to do well in order that they 'get on in life' whilst at the same time being seriously doubtful about the benefits of academic knowledge or qualifications (Mac an Ghaill, op cit.). Sally is a high-achieving working-class girl. While her mother is supportive of the idea of Sally one day sitting A-levels, she balks at the notion of her going to university; unlike the middle-class parents, she is not sure what university is *for* or how it can enhance one's credentials – not surprising since no one in her or her partner's family had ever been to university.

I don't think actually going to university and doing all these qualifications actually is the be all and end all of everything 'cos I think at the end of the day it's what makes you happy.

(White working-class mother)

For working-class children, doing well at school is no longer a guarantee of getting a 'good job'. Our research indicates clearly that for middle-class boys and girls, outstanding performance at school and in examinations is often viewed as ordinary by teachers and parents and to get anything less is tantamount to failure (Lucey et al., op cit.). What chance do ordinary working-class children have, even those who achieve 5 GCSEs grades A–C?

I mean if teachers are honest, which hopefully most teachers are, they can't say to kids 'if you do this you're going to get a job', because even if you do get better at reading, you may still not get a job. You've got to be very good at it, haven't you now?

(Teacher in working-class school)

This strengthens our argument that both policy and practice around home–school relations cannot assume that working-class parents can simply be inculcated into what is essentially a bourgeois school culture in the relatively easy way in which middle-class parents are able to (Reay and Ball, op cit.; Mac an Ghaill, op cit.). In July 1997 the Minister for Education announced government proposals for improving literacy which included asking parents to sign a pledge to read with their children for at least 20 minutes a day (*Guardian*, 1997a). Parents whose literacy skills were so poor that they could not fulfil this promise would be identified by the school and offered basic literacy classes themselves. Parents (and by now we are clear that it is working-class parents who are being talked about) who failed to discharge their responsibilities to their children would have to be tackled in other ways. In no way do we wish to dismiss these proposals altogether as we are sure that some parents will be able to take up and experience them as helpful. Clearly, any serious attempt to effectively manage the literacy curriculum must involve parents in the process. But we do argue that some such proposals are unable to grasp the deeply affective links between learning and emotional processes and, in this light, seem wilfully punishing of working-class parents who may feel that, as children themselves, they have already been let down by the education system.

The government's proposal to pilot up to 25 Education Action Zones in areas with a mix of underperforming schools and high indicators of social disadvantage promises to bring together parents, local businesses and other representatives from the community in which to plan, implement and monitor pragmatic approaches to raising educational standards (DfEE, 1997b). For some, the EAZ initiative is viewed as a 'Trojan horse' which will promote the privatisation of schooling and erode pay and conditions for teachers (Socialist Teachers Alliance, 1998). Other commentators note that while there are positive 'redistributional' and 'welfare-integrational' possibilities contained in EAZ policy stemming from an implicit recognition of the links between educational underperformance and structural processes, these aims may be seriously at odds with 'the perpetuation of markets, managerialism and privatisation', which 'will almost inevitably foster redistributions in favour of the most advantaged and are likely to produce exclusions and circumscribe institutional and individual autonomy over many of the things that matter' (Gewirtz, 1998, p. 24).

A Crisis of Work and of Working-Class Masculinity

Central to many of the discourses through which the failure of boys, particularly working-class (black and white) boys in the education system is understood, is the notion that there is a contemporary crisis in masculinity itself. This crisis and the eruption of such panic over boys' educational achievement, is closely tied to changes in the structural and social organization of work in the last 20 years (Wragg, 1997a). Once again the theme of feminization appears, with the massive decline of the manufacturing base and the subsequent loss of traditional, male, manual jobs alongside the immense growth in women's participation in waged labour. Some argue that there has been a feminization of men's jobs (Jensen et al., 1988; Callender, 1996; Hakim, 1996; Wilkinson, 1994) as today's working practices no longer require physical strength, rather a smart appearance, a good manner and keyboard skills – that is, unless they are badly paid and unregulated jobs in service industries such as security or fast food (Leidner, 1993). It is in this socio-economic setting that female success appears (though quite unfairly) to be taking jobs away from boys. Within this scenario it is working-class

47

masculinity which is faced with huge challenges. As we have discussed above, middle-class boys have traditionally done well at school and gone on to higher education and then into a profession: their sense of being masculine is not challenged by these changes in the same way. It is working-class boys who are called upon to adapt to profound shifts in the economic and social organization of society, which strike at the very essence of what it means for them to be boys and become men.

Conclusion

In this chapter we have tried to explore some of the ways in which questions of identity or self are at the very heart of schooling. We have also attempted to show how the development of that self takes place not only at the level of individual psychological processes, but is also grounded in immensely complex historical, cultural, social and economic relations. Gender, race and class highlight the level of complexity when educational disadvantage generally and the underachievement of boys in particular are considered in this way.

Contemporary educational policy and practice cannot stand alone, to be regarded as somehow outside of the national and global economic context in which it is formed and takes place. There are no simple pedagogic solutions to the complex effects of, for instance, the absence of a youth labour market, the restructuring of the adult labour market and the effects of globalization. The current Labour government is committed to finding appropriate ways to enhance the academic motivation of working-class boys and help working-class parents to reorientate their educational values and aspirations for their children. But we have tried to show how for the working-class children, having aspirational parents who 'do all the right things' is no guarantee of the kind of educational success routinely achieved by the middle-class children. More importantly, we suggest that these kinds of solutions are based on a meritocratic fiction that *everybody*, if only they do well at school, can somehow bypass the chronic ailments of late industrial capitalism.

New Labour are keen to promote an ethos of excellence in relation to educational policy and practice, an aim which is of course, to be applauded. However, the pursuit of such excellence too often relies on an increasing credentialism which targets and then finds consistently wanting, the very groups it sets out to incorporate. In this 'performance culture' it is the children of the middle classes who are expected to, and do, achieve the kinds of outstanding examination results which are becoming increasingly necessary as entry requirements into fiercely competitive professional job markets. A more realistic picture is that this emphasis on qualifications will lead to a deepening polarization in the economy between the securely over-employed and the insecurely under-employed.

It is in this context that the crisis of masculinity, jobs and the future reaches its peak. The working-class boys' anti-reading and anti-school position is not resistance, as the followers of Willis (1977) argued, but a defence against fear. They act against study for fear of the loss of masculinity, a masculinity which is already seriously under threat in terms of the disappearance of the jobs which required it. Paradoxically however, the willingness and ability to study is the very thing they need for jobs requiring a different kind of masculinity. Today's definition of literacy fits a post-industrial economy which is based not on production but on information and services. These changes have produced a troubling of masculinity, but while this is projected onto women and girls, and assumed to affect *all* boys, the tendency of public and educational policy to look for 'quick fix' solutions to easily identifiable problems means that the processes, through which a sustained improvement in the educational and life chances of working-class children and young people may be achieved, remain relatively unexamined.

Notes

1   See *Guardian*, 1997a, 1997b, 1998; TES, 1997; *Observer*, 1998; Wragg, 1997b.
2   In January 1998 Stephen Byers, then Minister for School Standards released to the press details of a 'co-ordinated' plan of action to tackle the underachievement of boys (Department for Education and Employment, 5 January 1998).
3   As opposed to the 'first wave' of feminists who campaigned for women's legal and political rights around the turn of this century.
4   'Gender Differences in Literacy at Key Stage 2' is a small, qualitative research project commissioned by the London Borough of Greenwich (Walkerdine and Lucey, 1997). This research was carried out in two contrasting primary schools. School A was located on the edge of a large council estate in an area which had witnessed enormous social and economic upheaval in the last 20 years. The pupils in this school were from mainly working-class families and the intake reflected the racial and ethnic diversity of the area. School B was a long-established Church of England school with a far higher intake of children from professional middle-class families. This school had maintained its place as amongst the highest achieving in the borough for some years.
5   Proposed government initiatives to increase the number of male teachers in primary schools is a direct response to the view that boys' development as learners is hampered by the over-predominance of women teachers.
6   In Project 4:21 Transition to Womanhood, we found that middle-class girls whose parents were the first in their families to go on to higher education and enter a professional career, had far more trouble sustaining a straightforward educational route (Lucey et al. forthcoming). We would suggest that ambivalence around the two contrasting identity positions is far more likely to emerge amongst the sons of such parents, whose familial, social and peer milieu is more likely to include a much higher proportion of working-class people.
7   See Sally Tomlinson's chapter in this volume for a fuller discussion of the formation and impact of disadvantage on ethnic minorities in Britain.
8   'Project 4: 21 Transition to Womanhood' is a longitudinal study of young women who have grown up in Britain in the 1980s and 1990s. See Lucey et al. (forthcoming).

References

Allatt, P. (1993) 'Becoming privileged: the role of family processes', in Bates, I. and Riseborough, G. (eds), *Youth and Inequality*, Buckingham, Oxford University Press.

Alloway, N. and Gilbert, P. (1997) 'Boys and literacy: lessons from Australia', *Gender and Education* 9, 1, pp. 49–58.

Bleach (1996) 'What difference does it make? An investigation of factors influencing the motivation and performance of Year 8 boys in a West Midlands comprehensive school', *Educational Research Unit*, University of Wolverhampton.

Child Poverty Action Group (1997) *Britain Divided*, London, CPAG.

Callender, C. (1996) 'Women and employment' in *Women and Social Policy: An introduction*, Hallett, C. (ed.) London, Harvester Wheatsheaf.

Clancy, K. (1997) 'Academic as anarchist: working-class lives into middle-class culture', in Mahony, P. and Zmroczek, C. (eds) *Class Matters: Working class women's perspectives on social class*, London, Taylor & Francis.

Cohen, M. (1996) ' "A habit of healthy idleness": boys' underachievement in historical perspective', ESRC seminar series, *Gender and School: Are boys now underachieving?*, London University, Institute of Education.

Connell, R.W. (1989) 'Cool guys, swots and wimps: the interplay of masculinity and education', in *Oxford Review of Education* 15, 3, pp. 291–303.

Connell, R.W. (1995) *Masculinities*, Cambridge, Polity Press.

David, M., West, A. and Ribbens, J. (1994) *Mother's Intuition: Choosing secondary schools*, London, Falmer Press.

Davies, B. (1993) *Shards of Glass: Children reading and writing beyond gendered identities*, Sydney, Allen & Unwin.

Department for Education and Employment, (1997a) Secondary School League Table Results, London, DfEE.

Department for Education and Employment (1997b) 'Education action zones: an introduction', London, DfEE.

Department for Education and Employment (1998) 'Byers outlines co-ordinated action to tackle boys' underachievement', press release, 5 January 1998, London, DfEE.

Douglas, J.W.B., Ross, J.M. and Simpson, H.R. (1968) *All Our Future: A longitudinal study of secondary attainment*, London, Peter Davies.

Eldridge, J. (1997) 'Future imperfect: gender, literacy and schooling in 1990s Britain', unpublished Ph.D Thesis, University of London, Goldsmiths' College.

Equal Opportunities Commission and Office for Standards in Education (EOC) (1996) *The Gender Divide: Performance differences between boys and girls at school*, London, HMSO.

Gewirtz, S. (1998) 'Education policy in urban places: making sense of action zones', paper presented to Social Policy Association Annual Conference: 'Social policy in time and place', University of Lincolnshire and Humberside.

Gilborn, D. and Gipps, C. (1996) 'Recent research on the achievements of ethnic minority pupils', OFSTED Reviews of Research, London, HMSO.

Guardian (1997a) 'Parents told to sign reading pledge', 29 July, p. 1.

Guardian (1997b) 'Up, up and away', 29 July, p. 18.

Guardian (1998) 'Girls on top form', 6 January, p. 6.

Hakim, C. (1996) *Key Issues in Women's Work*, London, Athlone.

Hall, C. and Coles, M. (1997) 'Gendered readings: helping boys develop as critical readers', in *Gender and Education* 9, 1, pp. 61–68.

Jackson, D. (1997) 'Breaking out of the binary trap: boys' under-achievement, schooling and gender relations', ESRC Seminar Series, *Gender and Education: Are boys now underachieving?*, London, Institute of Education.

Jensen, J., Hagen, E. and Reddy, C. (eds) (1988) *Feminization of the Labour Force*, Cambridge, Polity Press.

Leidner, R. (1993) *Fast Food, Fast Talk*, Los Angeles, CA, University of California Press.

Lucey, H., Melody, J. and Walkerdine, V. (forthcoming) *Millennial Girls: Class and gender in the 21st century*, London, Macmillan.

Mac an Ghaill, M. (1994) *The Making of Men: Masculinities, sexualities and schooling*, Milton Keynes, Open University Press.

Mahony, P. (1997) 'The underachievement of boys: old tunes for new fiddles?', ESRC seminar series, *Gender and School: Are boys now underachieving?*, London University, Institute of Education.

Mahony, P. and Zmroczek, C. (1997) *Women and Social Class*, London, Taylor & Francis.

Millard, E. (1997) *Differently Literate: Boys, girls and the schooling of literacy*, London, Falmer Press.

Murphy, P. and Elwood, J. (1998) 'Gendered experiences, choices and achievement – exploring the links', *International Journal of Inclusive Education* 2, 2, pp. 95–118.

Observer (1998) 'Boys performing badly', 4 January.

Office for Standards in Education (OFSTED) (1993) *Boys and English: A report from the Office of Her Majesty's Chief Inspector of Schools*, London, Department of Education, ref: 2/93 NS.

Plummer, G. (1998) 'Forget gender, class is still the real divide', *Times Educational Supplement*, 23 January, p. 21.

Raphael, R.L. (1995) 'Reconceptualizing equal opportunities in the 1990s: a study of radical teacher culture in transition' in Griffiths, M. and Troyna, B. (eds) *Anti-Racism, Culture and Social Justice in Education*, Stoke-on-Trent, Trentham.

Reay, D. (1997) 'The double bind of the working class feminist academic: the success of failure or the failure of success?' in Mahony, P. and Zmroczek, C. (eds) *Class Matters: Working class women's perspectives on social class*, London, Taylor & Francis.

Reay, D. (1998a) 'Cultural reproduction: mothers and their children's primary schooling' in Grenfell, M. and James, D. (eds) *Bourdieu and Education: Acts of practical theory*, London, Taylor & Francis.

Reay, D. (1998b) 'Classifying feminist research: exploring the psychological impact of social class on mothers' involvement in children's schooling', *Feminism and Psychology* 8, 2, pp. 155–71.

Reay, D. and Ball, S.J. (1998) 'Making their minds up: family dynamics of school choice', *British Educational Research Journal* 24, 4, pp. 431–448.

Reay, D. and Lucey, H. (forthcoming) 'Children's perspectives on secondary school choice'.

Reid, I. (1994) *Inequality, Society and Education*, Loughborough, Loughborough University of Technology.

Reynolds, T. (1998) 'Class matters, "race" matters, gender matters' in Mahony and Zmroczek (eds) *Women and Social Class*, London, Taylor & Francis.

Sammons, P. (1995) 'Gender, ethnic and socio-economic differences in attainment and progress: a longitudinal analysis of student achievement over nine years', *British Educational Research Journal* 21, 4, pp. 465–485.

Sewell, T. (1995) 'A phallic response to schools: black masculinity and race in an inner-city comprehensive', in Griffiths, M. and Tryna, B. (eds) *Anti-Racism, Culture and Social Justice in Education*, Stoke-on-Trent, Trentham Books.

Sewell, T. (1997) *Black Masculinities and Schooling: How black boys survive modern schooling*, Stoke-on-Trent, Trentham Books.

Shaw, J. (1995) *Gender, Education and Anxiety*, London, Taylor & Francis.

Smith, T. and Noble, M. (eds) (1995) *Education Divides*, London, CPAG.

Socialist Teachers Alliance Pamphlet (1998) *Trojan Horses: Education action zones*, London, Socialist Teachers Alliance Pamphlet.

Steedman, C. (1986) *Landscape for a Good Woman, a Story of Two Lives*, London, Virago.

Sutherland, M. (1983) 'Anxiety, aspirations and the curriculum', in Marland, M. (ed.) *Sex Differentiation and Schooling*, London, Heinemann Educational Books.

Swann, J. (1992) *Girls, Boys and Language*, Oxford, Blackwell.

Tattum, D. and Herbert, G. (1997) *Bullying: Home, school and community*, London, David Fulton.

Times Educational Supplement (TES) (1997) 'Two nations', 25 April, p. 1.

Walkerdine, V. (1988) *The Mastery of Reason*, London, Routledge.

Walkerdine, V. (Ed) (1989) *Counting Girls Out*, London, Virago.

Walkerdine, V. (1990) *Schoolgirl Fictions*, London, Verso.

Walkerdine, V. and Lucey, H. (1997) 'Gender differences in literacy at KS2 in Greenwich primary schools', *Final Report to Greenwich Education Authority*.

Webster, A., Beveridge, M. and Reed, M. (1996) *Managing the Literacy Curriculum*, London, Routledge.

Whyte, J. (1986) *Girls into Science and Technology: The story of a project*, London, Routledge & Kegan Paul.

Wilkinson, H. (1994) *No Turning Back: Generations and the genderquake*, London, Demos.

Willis, P. (1977) *Learning to Labour: How working class kids get working class jobs*, Farnborough, Saxon House.

Wragg, T. (1997a) *The Cubic Curriculum*, London, Routledge.

Wragg, T. (1997b) 'Oh Boy', *Times Educational Supplement*, 16 May, p. 4.

4 Pupil Absenteeism in the Primary School

Tim Carroll

In this chapter, an explanation of the term pupil absenteeism is offered and consideration is given to the use of data from the school attendance register as a basis for quantifying pupil absenteeism. Reasons are presented for researching pupil absenteeism at the primary rather than secondary school level. Two studies of pupil absenteeism in the primary school are described. The accounts deal with the selection of the Poor Attenders and the Better Attenders, with whom they are compared, and demonstrate that the Poor Attenders do indeed have real attendance problems, and reveal that the Poor Attenders have home environments which may contribute to their attendance problems. Suggestions are made for dealing with pupil absenteeism in the primary school, particularly at the infant school level.

Introduction: The Meaning of the Term 'Pupil Absenteeism'

The term pupil absenteeism is used in preference to alternatives such as parental condoned absence, truancy or school phobia/school refusal because it does not carry with it specific connotations, namely that the problem lies with the parents, as implied by the term parental condoned absence, or with the child, as suggested by the labels truancy and school phobia/refusal. The term truancy is used to describe the behaviour of a child who absents him/herself from school without parental knowledge, whereas the diagnosis school phobia/refusal is employed by psychiatrists and psychologists when a child refuses to go to school because of fear of school or fear of leaving home (Kahn et al., 1981).

Pupil absenteeism can be quantified by use of data from the school attendance register, something which schools in Britain are required by law to take twice a day. In completing the register a teacher has to indicate for each absent child whether the absence is for an authorized or unauthorized reason. The former includes officially granted leave, sickness and religious reasons (Kahn, 1995). Unauthorized absence is defined as 'Absence without permission from a teacher or other authorized representative of the school. This includes all unexplained or unjustified absence'. (Department for Education and Employment (DfEE), 1995, p. 8). Unfortunately, the registers are open to abuse, particularly as a consequence of the passing of the 1992 Education (Schools) Act which requires schools to publish their rates of unauthorized absence. This problem is acknowledged in paragraph 6 of a 1994 DfE document: 'Representations have however been made to the Department alleging unacceptable variations in practice between schools in authorizing absence'. The fact that such representation has been made casts doubt on the reliability of attendance data gathered since 1992 on individual children and schools.

Fortunately, many of the important research studies on pupil absenteeism which have utilized data from the school register, including the two which are reported on in the next sections of this chapter, were carried out before 1992 and have not therefore been affected by the aforesaid problem. Most of these studies have used attendance data as a basis for identifying poor attenders. However, different percentage cut-off points based on different periods have been employed, e.g. 87.6 per cent for two years (May, 1975), 50 per cent for one term (Galloway, 1982) and 85 per cent for two terms (Southworth, 1992). The problem with all these studies is the use of a single period of time. The problem stems from the fact that, as revealed by Upton (1978), for most children who have a behaviour problem, it is transitory, whereas for those whose behaviour problem is present over two non-contiguous periods, for example during both Years Two and Six, as in Upton's study, theirs may be deemed a severe problem. That being so, what is required, if one can equate a behaviour problem with an attendance problem, is a definition of a poor attender which is based on two, non-consecutive school years, e.g. top infants and top juniors. Such a definition was, in fact, employed in the studies to be described in the next sections though the attendance rate cut-off to define the poor attenders, namely 80 per cent or less in both Years Two and Six, was more severe than that taken by Southworth (1992) but less extreme than that employed by Galloway (1982).

Two Linked Studies of Poor Attenders

An account of two studies of primary school poor attenders now follows. Both were completed during the early 1980s when the author was at the Department of Education in the University of Wales Swansea. However, whereas the first study made use of data resulting from research designed by others, namely the National Child Development Study Team, the second was based on the first but was designed and directed by the present writer.

The Selection of the Poor Attenders (PAs)

Even though school attendance problems are much more severe at the secondary than at the primary school level, as demonstrated in the USA by

Easton and Engelhard (1982) in their longitudinal research and by the DfEE in their published rates of unauthorized absence for primary and secondary schools in England for the years 1992 to 1995 (Isham, 1997), this study is based on primary school pupils and for two reasons. In the first place, as has been correctly pointed out by O'Keeffe and Stoll (1995), not much is known about primary school pupils with attendance problems. However, it is known from longitudinal studies carried out by Douglas and Ross (1965), Fogelman and Richardson (1974), and Easton and Engelhard (1982) that absence from primary school has the greatest effect on the attainments of children from the lowest social classes, but slight, or even negligible effects on children whose fathers have non-manual occupations.

Second, given the importance of the primary school years during which time most children become literate, numerate and socialized, it is important to know whether some primary school children do have a persisting school attendance problem and, if so, what might account for it.

Two groups of pupils were investigated. The first was taken from the National Child Development Study (NCDS) cohort of children – for the most part, all those born in England, Scotland and Wales during one week in March 1958 – who were followed up at the ages of 7, 11 and 15 years, and also during adulthood. The data gathered by health visitors and teachers when the children were of primary school age form part of the basis of what follows. The former interviewed the parents (usually the mother) and the latter, amongst other things, completed a questionnaire which included questions relating to the children's families. With the agreement and support of the National Children's Bureau and the SSRC Survey Archive the author gained access as a secondary researcher to this very large body of data, part of which was used for generating a group of Poor Attenders (PAs) and one of Better Attenders (BAs) together with information about them and their families. The Poor Attenders (subsequently to be referred to as the NPAs) numbered 140 and had percentage attendance records of 80 or less for the first half of both Years Two and Six. The Better Attenders (subsequently to be referred to as the NBAs) numbered 7,373 and all had attendance records better than the NPAs. The NBAs constituted the remainder of the cohort having attendance data for both Years Two and Six and were representative of the original, total cohort.

The second group of pupils contained all the Year Six pupils in a single LEA in South Wales who had percentage attendance records of 80 or less for the whole of Year Two and the first half of Year Six (subsequently to be referred to as the WPAs) and a further group of pupils, all of whom had attendance records better than the WPAs and who subsequently will be termed the WBAs. The WBAs were identified by selecting for each WPA, where possible, a pupil of the same gender, in the same school class and born within the same season of the year. In total the WBAs numbered 133, seven fewer than the number of WPAs which coincidentally, was identical to the number of NPAs. Aside from data gathered from the attendance registers, the Education Welfare Service (EWS), the Educational Psychology Service (EPS) and Child Guidance Service (CGS), all the information about the children in the Welsh Study (WS) which is presented here was obtained from the pupils' respective class teachers.

The data from both the WS and the NCDS provided the basis for learning more about the attendance problems of the PAs and for comparing the PAs and BAs in terms of certain home background factors when they were in Year Six. The findings will be presented in the next sections.

An Investigation of the Attendance Problems of the Poor Attenders (PAs)

If it can be shown that proportionally more PAs than BAs: (a) were considered by their respective parents and teachers to have difficulties relating to school attendance; and (b) were known to outside agencies because of attendance problems; and, furthermore, if it can be demonstrated that, between Years Two and Six, the Poor Attenders had a worse attendance record, then the arbitrary choice of the 80 per cent cut-off point will be vindicated.

In the NCDS when the children were eleven the parent was asked by the health visitor to indicate how much time altogether the child had missed from school during the previous school year because of ill-health or emotional disturbance. For 63.1 per cent of the NBAs but only 11.5 per cent of the NPAs these reasons accounted for missing school for less than a week whereas, for 52.2 per cent of the NPAs but only 5.1 per cent of the NBAs, these reasons accounted for missing school for more than one month. Like all the differences to be reported on in this and the next section, the differences when examined using the Likelihood Ratio Chi-square Test (Gabriel, 1966) were found to be highly significant statistically.[1]

In the NCDS each Year Six teacher completed a behaviour rating scale on the study child which required him or her to indicate whether the phrase 'has truanted – once or twice, often suspected of truancy' described 'the child's behaviour … over the past term or so'. Analysis of the resulting data revealed that 8 per cent of the NPAs but only 1 per cent of the NBAs were so rated.

Concerning attendance in Years Three, Four and Five, such data were obtained in the WS only. The median percentage attendance rates were found to range between 91.8 and 95.7, and 71.8 and 77.2 for the WBAs and WPAs respectively and, for all five years taken together, the respective medians were 92.3 and 73.7. As revealed by the Mann–Whitney U Test (Siegel, 1956) all the differences between the WBAs and WPAs were highly significant.

The final source of evidence for an attendance problem came from knowing whether a child had been referred to an outside agency because of such a difficulty. In the Welsh Study the Education Welfare Service (EWS), the Educational Psychology Service (EPS) and the Child Guidance Service

(CGS) in the county were each asked whether any of the study children were or had been known to them because of attendance problems. Although no differences were found between the attendance groups for the EPS and CGS, in the case of the EWS 52.6 per cent of the WPAs but only 8.5 per cent of the WBAs were or had been known to the Service.

Taken together the NCDS and WS findings certainly vindicate the semi-arbitrary choice of the 80 per cent cut-off point for attendance during the first half of both Years Two and Six for defining the PAs. That being so, it is possible to claim that, as a group, the PAs who are the subject of this study did indeed have a real attendance problem and that they did warrant further investigation in terms of their home environment.

The Home Environment of the Poor Attenders (PAs)

In considering the children's home environment two key elements will be examined, namely the physical and the social environments. From the outset it is important to note that, as possible causes, direct or, more likely, indirect, of absence from school, it is probable that the various home factors to be presented here would not have acted in isolation but interactively.

Concerning the physical environment of the home, housing and financial status will provide the focus of this study. Housing itself may be considered in terms of the house/home as a totality and roominess. Data on these variables were obtained in the NCDS only and were collected by the health visitors who went to the homes of the Study children. Because the findings to be presented significantly differentiated between the NPAs and the NBAs when they were 7 and 11 years of age, only the results relating to the children's homes when they were 11 will be given in order to illustrate the differences. All the figures to be presented are percentages.

It was found that more of the NPAs (72.4) than the NBAs (42.6) lived in council-rented homes, whereas more of the NBAs (45.4) than the NPAs (16.4) dwelt in homes which were owned or being bought by their parents. In addition, more of the NPAs (27.6) than the NBAs (10.8) lived in homes which were overcrowded (more than 1.5 persons per room). Not surprisingly, therefore, more of the NPAs (32.5) than the NBAs (15.9) shared a bedroom with more than one other person, a difference which was even more marked with respect to sharing a bed with someone else (38.3 and 17.2 per cent of the NPAs and NBAs respectively). If the corollaries of bedroom and/or bed sharing are more disturbance and less sleep, and more opportunities for contracting contagious illnesses, then it may be concluded that a disproportionate number of the NPAs would be physically more tired and more susceptible to illness and, as a consequence, more likely to be irritable, and lacking in concentration at school. One effect of illness would be to reduce school attendance; that of irritableness, to lead to social problems at home and at school; and that of poor concentration, to doing less well at school.

The data on the financial circumstances of the homes fall into three areas, namely the social class of the father, whether the mother was in paid employment and the presence of financial problems. In both the NCDS and WS more of the BAs (31.1 and 11.3 per cent respectively) than the PAs (12.3 and 4.8 respectively) had fathers in non-manual occupations. However, even more marked was the situation relating to there being no father in the home or the father being unemployed. For the NBAs and WBAs the percentages were 7.8 and 14.5 respectively whereas for the NPAs and the WPAs they were 16.9 and 43.6. To some extent the picture as it related to the mothers working reflected that for the fathers, namely in the NCDS and WS 37.9 and 55.4 per cent respectively of the BAs' mothers were not in paid employment whereas 54.3 and 72.4 per cent respectively of the PAs' mothers were unemployed.

A reliable indicator of financial problems is being eligible to receive free school meals. On the basis of information provided by the schools it was found that in both the NCDS and WS more PAs (30.4 and 41.3 per cent respectively) than BAs (9.9 and 18.8) were receiving or were eligible to receive free school meals when they were in Year Six.

Concerning the social environment of the home, this may be said to be determined by the parental situation, namely the number of parents, and by sibling influences, e.g. the actual number of siblings and their age relative to the children being studied. With respect to the parental situation, examination of the NCDS and WS data showed that more of the PAs (9.3 and 15.9 per cent respectively) than the BAs (4.6 and 6.5) came from a one-parent family. As for sibling influences, when the children were in Year Six comparable results emerged in that proportionally more of the BAs than the PAs came from families with fewer than three children in them (44.2 and 31.3 per cent of the NBAs and NPAs respectively, and 38.3 and 28.3 per cent of the WBAs and WPAs respectively) and proportionally more of the PAs than the BAs came from families with more than three children in them (52.2 and 31.1 per cent of the NPAs and NBAs respectively, and 47.1 and 23.3 per cent of the WPAs and WBAs respectively).

Further insight into the kind of social pressures influencing the child is gained by looking at the number of children living in the Study child's household who were younger or older than the Study child. In order to simplify the analysis and draw attention to the proportions falling into the more extreme categories, the variables were reduced to being dichotomous, the extreme category for both the number of younger and older children for the NCDS and WS variables being three or more. Analysis of the data revealed that, in the NCDS when the children were aged seven, 27.2 per cent of the NPAs but only 13 per cent of the NBAs had three or more older siblings, and 20 per cent of the NPAs but only 7.9 per cent of the NBAs had three or more younger siblings, i.e. there were proportionally more PAs in both extreme categories. However, at eleven years of age the results were less clear cut. Although the WS data confirmed the NCDS findings with respect to there being a greater proportion of PAs in the '3 or more older children in the family' category (NBAs and NPAs: 8.4 and 21.7 per cent respectively; WBAs and WPAs: 18.1 and 34.8 per cent respectively), they did not do so in the case of the younger children, the WBAs and WPAs being virtually the same in terms of the proportions in the two categories, namely 3.7 and 3.6 per cent respectively.

Considering the results overall, it may be concluded that more PAs did indeed come from larger families, and that, for between one fifth and one third of those families, they tended to be the younger ones. Had the findings been unambiguous in the NCDS and Welsh Study, it would have been possible to have argued that one of the possible explanations of poor attendance in the children studied was the additional pressure on the family, in particular on the mother, of having to cope with children younger than the Study child. In the case of the NCDS findings, this argument could well have applied at both ages. As for the Welsh Study, such an argument could not really be used, simply because there were so few Study children with younger siblings (3.7 and 3.6 per cent WBAs and WPAs respectively). Several explanations to account for the consistent finding that more of the PAs were the younger members of the family could be offered, e.g. that as a consequence of being amongst the youngest in the family, they were overdependent on their mother and consequently found it more difficult to leave her and go to school on certain occasions, particularly those when other home and/or school problems had to be faced; that they were more vulnerable to contracting illnesses brought home by the older children; or that the attitude towards school of the older siblings was such as to make it more likely that the youngest missed school for slight or trivial reasons. However, without further evidence, it is difficult to say which explanation comes nearest to the truth.

In order to provide an overall picture of the material and social circumstances of the home, use was made of Wedge and Prosser's (1973) definition of disadvantage. It commended itself because, as well as seeming reasonable for the reasons given by Wedge and Prosser, it was also one which could be quantified in exactly the same manner that they had quantified it. This was so because the study for which they had employed the definition also involved the NCDS cohort of children. In Wedge and Prosser's terms, a child was said to be disadvantaged if all three of the following conditions covering family composition, income and housing applied:

1   that at either 7 or 11 years of age or both, the child came from a large family or a family with but a single parent;
2   that at eleven, either:

    (a) at least one of the children in the family was receiving free school meals; or

(b) during the previous year the family had received supplementary benefit; and

3   that at 7, 11 or both ages, the child came from either an overcrowded home (as defined previously) or a home lacking sole use of a hot water supply.

On the basis of applying these criteria it was found that 18.5 per cent of the NPAs but only 5.9 per cent of the NBAs proved to be disadvantaged. Concerning the proportion for the NBAs, this is identical to that obtained by Wedge and Prosser in their analysis of the same data, though with a larger sample (10,504 children) of the same cohort. The fact that the figures are the same and that Wedge and Prosser's sample was said by them to be representative of the original, total NCDS cohort in terms of the variables they examined underlines the extent to which the sample used in this research is representative of the total cohort.

Wedge and Prosser painted a detailed and rather dismal picture of the background and characteristics of 'their' disadvantaged children. That same picture applies to nearly one-in-five of the NPAs in this study. That being so, it seems reasonable to conclude that being disadvantaged could well have played a part in bringing about the poor school attendance of the NPAs. However, the fact that just over 80 per cent of the group was not disadvantaged according to the chosen criteria, indicates that other factors played an important part in the difference in attendance of the two groups, namely some of the specific aspects of the physical and social environment of the home considered here. Clearly, the relationship between the home factors and absence from school is not a simple one. In particular, each home factor would not have acted in isolation but interactively. However, for analysis and presentation purposes it was necessary to consider most of the variables separately, though some combinations of variables were examined. Underlying the approach taken here is the view that the various home factors, in combinations which vary from one child to another, make certain children more vulnerable to the stresses of their lives, absenting themselves from school being but one of the ways in which they respond to such stress in certain situations. Before moving on to consider how help may be given to poor school attenders, their families and their schools, it is important to note that it is highly unlikely that the same PAs were rated at the 'detrimental' level on all of the significant factors. Thus, if each of the significant home factors was a part-cause or concomitant of poor school attendance, it is probable that each would have had a slightly different effect, the difference being determined by the unique characteristics of each child and his or her environment. That being so, the temptation to offer 'blanket' solutions to dealing with pupil absenteeism should be avoided in favour of approaches which take account of the characteristics and needs of the individual case, whether it be a child, family, school class or whole school.

Dealing with Pupil Absenteeism in the Primary School

The fact that the NPAs and WPAs had poor attendance records in Year Two as well as subsequently implies that efforts to deal with pupil absenteeism in the primary school should begin in the first two years of compulsory education. However, in view of the findings relating to home factors reported earlier in this chapter, it would seem more appropriate to concentrate, not on the poor attendee *per se* – unless of course (s)he has other problems – but on his or her family. If a Year One or Two pupil has a poor attendance record *and* there are well-founded concerns about the child's academic and/or social development it would be appropriate to call in the school psychologist (Carroll, 1995) or educational psychologist (Carroll, 1996) (see also Chapter 12). The two papers by Carroll differ in that the latter is about the role of the educational psychologist in dealing with pupil absenteeism in Britain whereas the earlier one has a wider perspective in that it looks at the problem in Germany and Sweden as well as in Britain. This broader perspective is salutory because it shows that the problem is dealt with differently in the three countries. If there is a common denominator, it is the fact that in all three countries the school would involve the family from the outset, particularly in Sweden and Germany where there is no equivalent to the education welfare officer (Carroll, 1995).

In Britain, if a child of infant school age is thought to have an attendance problem but no other obvious difficulties, the school has the possibility of involving the education welfare officer (EWO). Unfortunately for primary schools EWOs spend the majority of their time dealing with secondary school absentees and therefore have insufficient time for those of primary school age (Mosley, 1968; Baylis, 1985). Furthermore, as shown by Galloway et al. (1981a), the families who are subject to legal proceedings as a consequence of the direct action taken by EWOs tend to live in socially deprived areas. Given the association reported earlier in this chapter between deprivation and pupil absenteeism, the possibility that legal action could be taken inappropriately is a worrying one indeed, particularly when it is realized that Galloway et al. (1981a) considered that the decision-making of EWOs is open to criticism, and that Galloway et al. (1981b) pointed out that it has not been possible to demonstrate that legal action is followed by better attendance.

However, it is not always necessary to involve EWOs. Improvements in attendance can be achieved when the school phones the parents as soon as there is concern about attendance (Sheats and Dunkleberger, 1979). If primary schools in Britain were to encourage teachers to visit homes when an attendance problem was suspected, something which is common in Sweden, and also in Germany where there appears to be a negligible school attendance problem (Carroll, 1995), it is possible that the problem could be reduced and, in the case of infant school pupils such as the PAs in the two studies reported in the previous sections, the problem could be 'nipped in the bud', thus preventing it from continuing.

Attractive though these alternatives are, it should not be forgotten that, as reported earlier, home problems appeared to be related to poor attendance. In Britain it is the case that EWOs are trained to deal with home problems, particularly of a financial or material kind (Macmillan, 1977; Isham, 1997). That being so, what appears to be needed is an approach involving joint home visiting by both the EWO and the child's primary school class teacher. Such an approach would be safer for the teacher and would be enlightening for the parents, EWO and teacher. In its plans for tackling truancy in Scotland the Scottish Office (1995) also offers cautious support for such an approach. Given that EWOs themselves and the DfEE strongly advocate the principle that EWOs and schools should work closely together (Isham, 1997), it is possible that EWOs would welcome the idea of joint EWO/teacher visits to homes.

With respect to dealing with pupil absenteeism at a school and LEA level, both previous and current Governments in Britain have attempted and are attempting to reduce pupil absenteeism. In the case of the previous Government, it introduced the publication of unauthorized absence rates on a school basis so that parents can make better informed school choices for their children. However, as revealed by Carroll (1992), such an approach is open to criticism and will continue to be until such time that, in publishing the school results, account is taken of certain home environment factors, e.g. financial problems and family size. As for the present Government, in the report of its Social Exclusion Unit (1998) it is indicated that Ministers will be given the power to set attendance targets for the schools with the poorest records and to take further action if the targets are not achieved. Even more recently the Government's new schools standards Minister, Estelle Morris, has declared that 'All of us must work together to tackle this problem' (the reduction of truancy). 'The Government is introducing new measures through the Crime and Disorder Bill to reinforce parental responsibility' (Lepkowska, 1998, p. 5). According to Lepkowska, Morris went on to say that LEA targets would be announced in the future and that their publication would make some LEAs 'feel quite ashamed' and keen to take action. If such targets take no account of the effect of social deprivation on school attendance and if LEAs with signifi-cant pockets of deprivation are not given additional support, it will be unjust for the current Government to take punitive action against LEAs and schools which fail to meet the targets. What such LEAs need are more resources for:

1   combating deprivation;
2   training and employing more education welfare officers and educational psychologists;
3   training primary school teachers to work with parents; and
4   establishing more Standards Fund projects aimed at tackling pupil absen-teeism, particularly in primary rather than secondary schools which in the past have received far greater attention, e.g. via the Compact programmes which have been aimed in part at improving the school attendance of Year Eleven pupils (Saunders et al., 1995).

In so far as the current Government has, as part of its drive to raise standards, introduced legislation (The Schools Standards and Framework Act, 1998) which sets a limit of thirty on infant school class sizes, it is clear that the Government recognizes the importance of the infant school years. It remains to be seen whether better staffed infant schools will be able to tackle the problem of pupil absenteeism from the outset, i.e. from Year One onwards. Given the conclusion of the excellent annotation on class size by Bennett (1998), it would appear that the Government will have to reduce infant class sizes yet further and will need to introduce training for teachers aimed at giving them the skills and competencies for working effectively with smaller classes. Only then is it likely that reduced class sizes will have a beneficial effect on pupil attendance and educational performance.

Acknowledgements

The author would like to acknowledge the much valued help which he was given by the National Children's Bureau and the SSRC Survey Archive at the University of Essex, and headteachers and teachers in the LEA in which he conducted the second study.

Notes

1   Should any reader wish to view the original data the author will be very happy to provide them.

References

Baylis, S. (1985) 'A review of research before the Commons Education Committee', *Times Educational Supplement*, 10 May, p. 6.

Bennett, S. N. (1998) 'Annotation: class size and the quality of educational outcomes', *The Journal of Child Psychology and Psychiatry* 39, 6, pp. 797–804.

Carroll, H.C.M. (1992) 'School effectiveness and school attendance', *School Effectiveness and School Improvement* 3, 4, pp. 258–271.

Carroll, H.C.M. (1995) 'Pupil absenteeism: a Northern European perspective', *School Psychology International* 16, pp. 227–247.

Carroll, H.C.M. (1996) 'The role of the educational psychologist in dealing with pupil absenteeism', in Berg, I. and Nursten, J.P. (eds) *Unwillingly to School*, London, Gaskell.

Department for Education (DfE) (1994) *1994 Performance Tables: Information on pupil absence*, London, DfE.

Department for Education and Employment (DfEE) (1995) *National Pupil Absence Tables 1995*, London, DfEE.

Douglas, J.W.B. and Ross, J.M. (1965) 'The effects of absence on primary school performance', *British Journal of Educational Psychology* 35, pp. 28–40.

Easton, J.Q. and Engelhard, G. (1982) 'A longitudinal record of elementary school absence and its relationship to reading achievement', *Journal of Educational Research* 75, 5, pp. 269–274.

Fogelman, K. and Richardson, K. (1974) 'School attendance: some results from the National Child Development Study', in Hersov, L. and Berg, I. (eds) *Out of School*, Chichester, Wiley.

Gabriel, K.R. (1966) 'Simultaneous test procedures for multiple comparisons on categorical data', *Journal of the American Statistical Association* 61, pp. 1,081–1,096.

Galloway, D. (1982) 'Persistent absence from school', *Educational Research* 24, pp. 188–196.

Galloway, D., Ball, T. and Seyd, R. (1981a) 'The selection of parents and children for legal action in connection with unauthorised absence from school', *British Journal of Social Work* 11, pp. 445–461.

Galloway, D., Ball, T. and Seyd, R. (1981b) 'School attendance following legal or administrative action for unauthorised absence', *Educational Review* 33, 1, pp. 53–65.

Isham, B. (1997) 'The education welfare service: working in partnership', in Martin, C. and Hayman, S. (eds) *Absent from School: Truancy and exclusion*, London, The Institute for the Study and Treatment of Delinquency.

Kahn, A.N. (1995) 'Compulsory school attendance in Britain', *Journal of Law and Education* 24, 1, pp. 91–102.

Kahn, J.H., Nursten, J.P. and Carroll, H.C.M. (1981) *Unwillingly to School: School phobia or school refusal*, Oxford, Pergamon Press.

Lepkowska, D. (1998) 'Morris plans crackdown on truancy', *The Times Educational Supplement* 31 July, p. 5.

Macmillan, K. (1977) *Education Welfare: Strategy and structure*, London, Longman.

May, D. (1975) 'Truancy, school absenteeism and delinquency', *Scottish Educational Studies* 7, 2, pp. 97–107.

Mosley, L.G. (1968) 'The primary school and preventive social work', *Social Work* 25, 2, pp. 7–10.

O'Keeffe, D. and Stoll, P. (1995) 'Truancy and the primary school', in O'Keeffe, D. and Stoll, P. (eds) *Issues in School Attendance and Truancy*, London, Pitman Publishing.

Saunders, L., Morris, M. and Storey, S. (1995) *National Evaluation of Urban Compacts*, London, DfEE.

Scottish Office (1995) *The Truancy File*, Glasgow, the Quality in Education Centre for Research and Consultancy.

Sheats, D. and Dunkleberger, G.E. (1979) 'A determination of a principal's effect in school – initiated home contacts concerning attendance of elementary school students', *Journal of Educational Research* 72, 6, pp. 310–312.

Siegel, S. (1956) *Nonparametric Statistics*, New York, McGraw-Hill.

Social Exclusion Unit (1998) *Truancy and School Exclusion*, London, HMSO.

Southworth, P. (1992) 'Psychological and social characteristics associated with persistent absence among secondary aged school children with special reference to different categories of persistent absence', *Personality and Individual Differences* 13, 3, pp. 367–376.

Upton, G. (1978) *A Developmental Study of Children's Behaviour and Adjustment at Home and School from 7 to 11 Years*, unpublished Ph.D. thesis, Cardiff, University of Wales.

Wedge, P. and Prosser, H. (1973) *Born to Fail*, London, Arrow Books in Association with the National Children's Bureau.

5 Promoting the Educational Achievement of Looked-After Children

Sonia Jackson

Children who are looked after by local authorities for more than a short time usually perform poorly at school and are at high risk of dropping out or leaving with few or no qualifications. In addition to the problems they share with other children from severely disadvantaged homes, they also suffer from discrimination within the education system at both institutional and individual levels because of their care status. Frequent changes of placement mean that their schooling is usually disrupted and social workers consistently give low priority to children's educational needs despite their great importance both in the short and long term. Market-oriented changes in education policy and organization have caused a further sharp deterioration, with looked-after children being much more likely than others to be excluded or denied school places.

This chapter presents evidence from research by the author that educational success can have a critical impact on the life chances of looked-after children. It suggests that their present low level of attainment is due to weaknesses in the care and education systems rather than to the characteristics of individuals. Schools and teachers, working closely with social workers and carers, need to understand the difficulties faced by children living away from home and make special efforts to build their self-esteem and promote their attainment.

Introduction

Children in public care are an overlooked group within the education system, both because of their small numbers and because they are seen to be the concern of social workers rather than teachers (Jackson, 1987). In most areas looked-after children make up fewer than one in a thousand of the age group, and they are not evenly distributed, so that a school may go many years without encountering a looked-after child and have no awareness of their particular difficulties. Research going back to the 1960s shows that even after controlling for other adverse factors children in substitute care fall far behind their peers at school and are in constant danger of dropping out of mainstream education (Jackson, 1994), but it is only in the last few years that the issue has attracted serious attention. There is still a strong tendency to attribute low attainment to the characteristics of the children themselves instead of locating the problem where it belongs, with the care and education systems and their failure to work effectively together. It is nevertheless possible for individuals to achieve educational success despite the enormous odds against them, and their experiences have much to tell us about how looked-after children might be enabled to do better at school.

The care of children and young people who cannot live with their own families is governed by the Children Act 1989. The Act introduced the term 'looked-after' to emphasize that accommodation by a local authority should be offered as a service to a family in difficulties rather than being a punishment for failure – 'in care' now legally applies only when children are subject to a court order. The intention was to normalize the child's experience as far as possible, a principle already endorsed by the historic Children Act of 1948.

With regard to education this is unequivocally stated in the Guidance and Regulations to the 1989 Act: 'Children who are looked-after or accommodated have the same rights as all children to education, including further and higher education, and to other opportunities for development' (Department of Health, 1991a, pp. 9–10). Guidance on both family placements (foster care) and residential care recognizes the educational disadvantage suffered by most looked-after children and provides excellent advice on how it might be overcome. It is clearly the intention of the Act that local authorities in their capacity as corporate parent should give the same attention to the education of the children they look after as a concerned parent would, including supporting them through further and higher education (Department of Health, 1991b). This has not happened, and in the ten years since the Act was passed the gap between the educational attainment of children in the community and those looked after away from home has grown ever wider (Broad, 1998; Blyth and Milner, 1998).

Characteristics of Looked-After Children and Their Families

The latest available figures show 51,600 children looked after by local authorities in England and about 2,800 in Wales.[1] Numbers have been gradually rising after a low point in 1994, and although as a proportion of the population far more older children are looked after than younger ones, the average age of the care population has been falling throughout the 1990s. Four out of ten looked-after children are nine years or under, but there is a heavy concentration in the literature on the older age group, probably because they are seen as more problematic. Their problems are not usually of their own making: contrary to popular perception, only 6 per cent of children enter the care system because they have been convicted or even accused of an offence (Department of Health, 1998).

The majority of children who come into local authority care are swiftly reclaimed by their families – nearly half are looked after for less than eight weeks and two out of three return home in less than six months. But those who remain for more than six months are likely to stay for long periods, and may spend the rest of their childhood in public care.

Bebbington and Miles, in a much quoted paper, showed that these children are drawn overwhelmingly from the poorest and most disadvantaged families. They are much more likely than most children to have a single parent trying to manage on a low income, to come from a minority ethnic background, to live in substandard accommodation and have many siblings. But even when all these material disadvantages are combined the chances are only one in ten that a child will enter the care system (Bebbington and Miles, 1989). For this to happen there have to be other factors, most commonly the mental illness of a parent, domestic violence or physical and/or sexual abuse (Osborn and St Claire, 1987). Only severe, substantiated maltreatment is likely to result in a child's removal from home (Gibbons et al., 1995) and every attempt is made to keep families together whenever possible. Thus children who remain long in care are even more likely than in the past to come from divided and troubled families with multiple problems. Not surprisingly many of them display behavioural and emotional problems arising from abuse and neglect, the trauma of coming into care and the effect of multiple placement moves – see also Chapter 6. However, just as there is a misperception that children mainly enter local authority care as a result of bad behaviour, there is a similar mistaken impression that most of them have learning disabilities, whereas, apart from those with congenital abnormalities or brain-damage as a result of abuse, the great majority have intelligence within the normal range.

Instability of Care

In the past children in long-term care might have expected to stay in one placement for many years, but the care system has now collapsed into a state of chronic instability (Jackson and Thomas, 1999). Most residential units have become temporary stopping places and foster care has been described by its own organization, the National Foster Care Association, as 'in crisis' (National Foster Care Association, 1997).

Government statistics give figures for the number of children who have moved placement more than three times during the year, implying that this is an acceptable level of instability, or at least only to be expected. A survey of four thousand children carried out by the Who Cares? Trust (Shaw, 1998) found that 28 per cent had moved more than six times and 9 per cent of children under eleven had moved more than ten times.

The experience of many looked-after children today is analogous to that of refugees or displaced persons, especially if they are taken from home under an Emergency Protection Order or, as frequently happens, they are moved without warning to a new placement. Like displaced children in war, they have to leave their known surroundings, precious possessions, pets, friends and familiar routines. And they may have to do this not just once but over and over again.

It is instructive to look at what happened to children caught up in the conflict in Yugoslavia. In one month in 1992 70,000 children arrived in Slovenia, forced to abandon their homes by the war in Bosnia. Some had no relatives or their parents were too disorientated to care for them. The leading Slovenian psychiatrist, Dr Anica Kos, quickly set up schools in the refugee camps, insisted that children attended regularly and that high academic standards were maintained. She argued that normalization is the best treatment for trauma. School provided a structure to the day and targets to aim for. It started to give back a certain logic and predictability to life for these children whose entire world had been turned upside down. A five year follow up found that the children had recovered personally and educationally and were doing as well in tests and examinations as their Slovenian peers (Kos, 1998).

School could be equally important as a source of continuity in the lives of looked-after children, yet it is often assumed that a change of care placement must mean a change of school, and for reasons I discuss later, weeks or months may pass before the child is found a new school place.

Education and Future Life Chances

When the first local authority Children's Departments were established in 1948 almost all working-class children still left school at age 14 or 15 with minimal education. There were large numbers of unskilled jobs available for careleavers, so educationally and occupationally they were not significantly more disadvantaged than other children. If a child showed special talent the newly appointed Children's Officers would make great efforts to nurture it and enable the child to continue in education (Holman, 1998), but generally it was assumed that children in care would finish school as soon as they reached statutory leaving age. That has continued to be the case in the utterly changed climate of the 1990s, and is one of the reasons why the average level of attainment of looked-after children is so poor. Despite the emphatic statement in the Guidance to the Children Act 1989 that 'young people who have the ability should be encouraged most strongly to continue their education beyond compulsory school age' and that 'every encouragement should be given to young people to undertake higher education' (Department of Health, 1991a), the vast majority of looked-after children still leave school at sixteen or earlier, and fewer than one in a hundred goes to university. It is estimated that only 3 per cent of young people leaving care between the ages of 16 and 18 have five GCSE passes at Grade C or above, compared with over 60 per cent in the general population. However, none of these figures is reliable since most local authorities still keep no central records of examinations taken or passed by the children they look after.

It is not in doubt, however, that local authorities have lamentably failed to look after 'their' children's educational needs, as was acknowledged by the highly critical joint report by the Social Services Inspectorate and OFSTED (SSI/OFSTED, 1995). This concluded:

> The care and education services in general are failing to promote the educational achievement of children who are looked-after. The standards which children achieve are too low and often the modest progress they make in primary schools is lost as they proceed through the system. Despite the clear identification of this problem in several research studies and by committees of enquiry little has been done in practice to boost achievement.

Studies of careleavers show that the consequences of failing to obtain educational qualifications are very serious, often condemning young people to life on the margins of society (Biehal et al., 1995; Broad, 1998). For example careleavers make up 30 per cent of homeless young people although less than 1 per cent of the age group (Hutson, 1997). An inquiry by the Howard League into the use of prison custody for teenage girls found that 40 per cent of 15 to 17-year-olds had been in care (Russell, 1998). These effects are not short-term; with fewer and fewer jobs available for poorly educated people the employment prospects of those formerly in care get progressively worse as they grow older (Cheung and Heath, 1994) and their opportunities for participation in mainstream society less.

Very little is known about the small minority of looked-after children whose school attainment reaches average or better levels. However, a study which I undertook with support from the Leverhulme Trust throws some light on their experiences and shows that educational attainment can be a powerful protective factor against the social exclusion suffered by so many children who pass through the care system.[2]

High Achievers Who Have Been in Care

Subjects were contacted by means of letters and articles in newspapers and by an insert in the magazine *Who Cares?* which is distributed through social service departments to about half of young people over age 10 in the care system.

The leaflet asked for people who had spent more than a year in care and obtained five or more O-levels or GCSEs at Grades C or above, or were in further or higher education, to contact the researcher if they would like to take part in the study. In all 154 out of 256 initial responses met the criteria and the respondents received a 90 item questionnaire which was designed to elicit as full a picture as possible of the their care and educational experiences and their family background. One hundred and five questionnaires were returned fully completed (68 per cent). Thirty-eight of the most successful subjects were interviewed in depth (Jackson, forthcoming; Jackson and Martin, 1998).

Following the interview, which usually took between two and three hours, the participant was asked to complete the General Health Questionnaire and self-administered tests of self-esteem and self-efficacy. Those who took part in the second phase are referred to in this chapter as 'high achievers'. The background of those interviewed was found to conform quite well to what we know of the care population generally. Sixty three per cent categorized themselves as white British, 12.4 per cent black (African/Caribbean), and 20 per cent were of Asian, Chinese or mixed parentage. More of the respondents were female, which is typical of self-recruited research populations.

At a later stage we re-contacted other people who had responded to the initial appeal and asked them to complete the original questionnaire together with the self-administered tests. Most of them had not achieved any educational qualifications – the best was three GCSEs – so we were able to use them as a comparison group, matched with a successful young person of the same age, sex, geographical area and similar care experience to consider the effects of educational achievement on adult lifestyle. Of the 49 people in this group who were sent the postal questionnaire and the four self-administered scales of psychological well-being, 22 people (10 males and 12 females with a mean age of 25 years) returned fully completed questionnaires.

The results were striking. The post-care experience of the people in the comparison group was very different from that of our study group, conforming much more closely in terms of outcomes to what we know of careleavers in general (SSI, 1997). All were unemployed, all had experienced homelessness (compared with only one of the study group), many had drug or alcohol problems, most of the women were single mothers and all of the men had been in trouble with the law. Three young men were currently serving prison sentences. By contrast, the higher achievers were either on satisfying career paths or studying, many owned their own houses, were in stable relationships and were generally happy with their current life style. The in-care experience of the two groups was, however, remarkably similar and there was no evidence that the high achievers had faced fewer adverse factors in their lives. It seems that they had overcome the many obstacles they faced by extraordinary determination and persistence. In other words they were exceptionally resilient individuals.

Resilience, which is defined by Garmezy (1993) as normal development despite adversity, is the product of the interaction between negative or risk factors and protective factors in children's lives. Taking an ecological perspective, as expounded by Fraser (1997) personal qualities and environmental conditions are part of the equation which determines whether the child will sink or swim. Rutter (1987) has further developed the theory to suggest that there are turning points in the lives of individuals which may initiate downward or upward spirals – risk and protective processes. Elsewhere he has described these as links in a chain, with each event or process depending on the one before (Rutter, 1988). A longitudinal study of adolescents in New Zealand found that risk factors have a cumulative effect on outcomes, so that one or two adverse elements in a child's life may be insignificant, but each additional factor greatly increases the likelihood of serious problems in adolescence (Fergusson and Lynskey, 1996). It is instructive to look at the lives of looked-after children in the light of this theoretical framework.

Risk Factors for Educational Failure

Risk factors for educational failure among the high achievers were very clear. They can be grouped into four categories: damaging pre-care experiences, inadequate support for school progress in the care environment, low expectations of social workers and schools, and the failure of social and education services to work together.

The severely disadvantaged background of most looked-after children has already been mentioned. Nearly a third of the high achievers (32.4 per cent) had suffered physical, sexual or emotional abuse and/or neglect before coming into care, which a study of foster children in Oxford found was particularly associated with continuing low educational attainment despite much improved living conditions (Heath et al., 1994).

Other risk factors were also prominent in the pre-care lives of almost all subjects, for instance conflict between parents, disability and ill-health (especially mental health problems), poverty, inadequate housing, living in a poor neighbourhood, isolation and racism. Once in care, an almost complete absence of educational support was a common experience. This was particularly true of residential care. Many subjects reported that no one took any interest in what went on at school, other than making sure you were properly dressed in the morning. 'No one ever asked what you'd done in the day or said well done if you got a good mark. It was "get your uniform off and it's time for tea."' No facilities were provided for doing homework, there were seldom any books, and few respondents could remember ever being read to by a member of staff. It was difficult to find a quiet space to read or work. 'The bedrooms were locked in the day and you weren't allowed upstairs. You could work in the dining room after tea but it smelt of food and made me feel ill.' Sarah remembered putting a board on her bed and trying to do homework in the dim light of a 40 watt bulb. Tracey found a plank to stretch between lockers in the cloakroom. It takes strong motivation to overcome practical obstacles like these. A further difficulty was that because most residential staff had very limited education themselves they had no conception of what was involved in studying for examinations and were inclined to complain about young people who shut themselves up in their rooms to work and refused to participate in the social life of the home.

Placement moves carried a great risk of disrupting school progress, especially when they occurred at critical times, such as during Year 10 when GCSE choices had been made, and the new boy or girl would be slotted into classes in less popular subjects where there was a space. Many authorities pursue a policy of moving young people at age 16 to 'semi-independent' living, which could hardly be more disruptive at the time when they are sitting vitally important public examinations and need maximum support to continue their education, either at school or in college (Action on After-care Consortium, 1996). Moves were often made within a week or two of the end of term, or involving a change of school three or four weeks into the start of a new term, when they could equally well have occurred in the holidays – a point noted by Fletcher-Campbell (1990) and Bullock et al. (1993). These seemingly small matters could make all the difference between a child's continuing to do well and initiating a rapid deterioration (an example of a risk factor becoming a risk process). In short, the accounts of these subjects fully confirmed the risk factors for school failure identified in earlier research (Heath et al., 1989, 1994). The only factor which by definition could not apply in the case of the high achieving subjects was low ability or lack of intelligence. Some said that they had always had a clear sense of their own ability, but others had accepted the negative attributions of caregivers, teachers or peers and had carried the low self-esteem which this induced into adulthood, despite their achievements.

Bella came into care at age 14 after many years of sexual abuse by her father:

> I was useless, absolutely useless. I had no confidence at all. I couldn't do anything right. I was always messing about – attention-seeking and misbehaving. I just believed I was stupid. Kids do, don't they, when they are told they are.

Teachers are sometimes unaware of the wounds their casual words can inflict on the fragile self-concept of a looked-after child. They would probably be amazed to know that that child could remember and repeat them to an interviewer ten years later

Protective Factors

Conversely sympathetic teachers can have an equally strong positive impact, both by expressing interest and confidence in a child and as a role model. Teachers were much more often mentioned as encouragers and motivators than social workers, making time to talk and listen and providing extra support, often out of school hours. Teachers tended to have a wider view of career possibilities than care workers and could give better informed advice. They might inspire the child with the ambition to go to college and provide them with a goal and a stimulus to 'planful behaviour' – another characteristic of resilient people (Rutter et al., 1990).

Further and Higher Education

Several of the high achievers had experienced multiple problems at school but struggled back via further education. Most notable was a young woman who spent only one term in mainstream school and was moved over thirty times before leaving care at 15, but eventually obtained a good honours degree from a leading university. Apart from the lack of encouragement to continue their education, some of our respondents found that achieving a university or college place was only the start of their problems. Unless schools liaise closely with social workers to organize essential financial support, aspirations are likely to be disappointed. Many local authorities still do not recognize their responsibility to provide at least as much support for young people in further or higher education as a concerned parent would do, and some of our subjects had to fight for every penny. Some authorities made no allowance at all for vacations, when most students can return to their family homes, and one young woman was reduced to sleeping in a railway station over the Christmas holiday. The experience of the people in our study appears to be typical. A comparison of provision by local authorities for financial support of careleavers in further and higher education actually showed a decline between 1994 and 1996 (Broad, 1998).

Locked Out of School: The Effects of Education Reform Acts on Looked-After Children

The shift in power from Local Education Authorities to individual schools and their heads has left looked-after children in a very vulnerable position. The Children Act 1989 makes it clear that children are to be looked after by the local authority as a whole, not simply by the social services department. This responsibility has never been taken seriously, and if it was hard previously for LEAs to accept the idea that they had special obligations towards children in public care, it is still more difficult now that headteachers make their own decisions about allocation of school places. They argue that their first duty is towards pupils already in the school. They fear not only that looked-after children will depress SATS scores and GCSE results but that they will be a disruptive influence in the classroom and interfere with the work of better motivated students. These ideas are often quite unrelated to objective facts about the child in question, but may lead to their being kept out of school for months at a time (Fletcher-Campbell, 1997). The difficulty in obtaining school places means that there is rarely any question of making a positive choice of a particular school; it is simply a question of which is prepared to offer a place. Fletcher-Campbell comments that, unlike parents, social workers are rarely concerned about the academic reputation of the school even when looking for a place for a potentially high-achieving child.

The negative impact of the Education Reform Act 1988 and the Education Act 1993 on vulnerable children generally, but particularly on children in the care system has been well documented. The effect of this legislation has been to make it almost impossible for local authorities to fulfil their duty under the Children Act 'to safeguard and promote the welfare of children within their area who are in need', at least as far as their education is concerned (Sinclair et al., 1994; Blyth and Milner, 1998). So many looked-after children are excluded, officially or unofficially, that in some residential units it seems to be accepted as the norm. An anti-school culture develops and children who enter the system having attended school in the normal way quickly become infected by it (Berridge and Brodie, 1998). However schools cannot escape their share of responsibility; it has been estimated that a child in residential care is eighty times more likely to be excluded than one living in his or her own home (Searle, 1996).

For a proportion of young people who come into the care system as adolescents, usually as a result of conflict with their families, school troubles go back many years. They may have dropped out of school semi-voluntarily, or been pushed out, and are now so far behind that there is no realistic prospect of their returning to mainstream education. This does not of course mean that their education should be abandoned. But as noted above, the acute problems of the minority are generalized to apply to all looked-after children, with the result that many who want to attend school and who could do perfectly well given adequate help and support, are written off in the same way.

Aiming for Success

At present there is overwhelming evidence that entering the care system is an additional risk factor for educational failure, compounding all the other adverse elements in children's lives. This is not inevitable. Coming into care could be seen as a potential turning point for many children previously living in conditions which failed to meet their most basic needs. Care can and should be a protective factor, or the start of a protective process for educational resilience.

Among the High Achievers there were some who had no doubt at all that coming into care had been a positive turning point for them and that they would have had no chance of educational success had they remained with their families. Helen was sexually and physically abused by her father over a period of five years after coming from Hong Kong to join her family in Wales. Care provided her with a means of escape from a grim future:

> If I hadn't gone into care I'd still be in my parents' take away, working for about £30 a week, having no life at all, no friends, staying in cleaning, doing the dishes…Care meant I got my freedom, and time to study, and people to talk to as well. It was more of a family than I ever had with my parents. If I was at home I know for a fact that I wouldn't have made it to college.

Helen was helped by the stability of her placement – three and a half years in one residential home, and by her close relationship with one of the care workers, who offered her a home after she completed her law degree. Most of our respondents reported a special relationship with at least one person who made time to talk with and listen to them. The presence of a positive adult role model in the child's life setting as well as the amount of time spent with that person has been found in other studies to be important in fostering resilience (Werner, 1994; Maluccio et al., 1996).

For the people in our study the key adult was much more likely to be a teacher than a social worker. But teachers had quite a difficult path to tread, since, what all children in care agree, is that they do not want to be picked out or treated differently in any way. They want teachers to recognize the particular difficulties they face, but they do not want allowances made for them, which they recognize will disadvantage them in the longer term. It is important for teachers to know when a child in their class is living away from home, but they need to keep that knowledge to themselves and never say anything which will reveal the looked-after child's care status to their fellow pupils.

New Initiatives

It is now well over ten years since attention was first drawn to the blighted educational chances of children in care (Jackson, 1987) and although progress has been disappointingly slow there have been some improvements at policy level and several innovative schemes and demonstration projects. The Department of Health commissioned and threw all its support behind the Looking After Children System (LAC), in which age-related Assessment and Action Records set targets for looked-after children's development and ask questions about the actions needed to lead to their fulfilment. The LAC system has now been adopted by 92 per cent of local authorities and should lead to a much clearer focus on children's educational needs, from babyhood onwards (Ward, 1995; Jackson, 1998).

Some local authorities have developed specialist support services for children in need and looked-after children which aim to keep them in mainstream education and promote their achievement. The first of these, the Manchester Teaching Service for the Social Services, was created by closing all the on-site education units in community homes and using the resources to pay support teachers (Walker, 1990,1994). A number of other local authorities have now established similar services, spanning the divide between education and social services departments. A study by the National Foundation for Educational Research of the work of these services found that they were greatly valued and did an excellent job of advocating for looked-after children and supporting them and their carers (Fletcher-Campbell, 1997). Unfortunately, not being part of core services, they are chronically underfunded, often confined to particular areas, and always vulnerable to cuts. It could be argued that what they do is basically the task of social workers, but it is unrealistic to expect social workers to have sufficient knowledge or confidence in dealing with the education system to be effective in the way that a specialist service can be.

The Who Cares? Trust has always given high priority to education among its activities. Following a guide for young people to help them assert their educational rights (Who Cares? Trust, 1994) it has published guides for school governors and elected members (Fletcher, 1996, 1998), suggesting ways in which they can play a key role in improving the education of looked-after children. It also sponsored an innovative book-buying scheme, designed to give looked-after children the opportunity to own their own books and encourage carers to spend more time reading with them (Bald et al., 1995). At the strategic level, with support from the Gulbenkian Foundation, the Trust has launched the Equal Chances project, working with two local authorities to create a truly integrated care and education service for looked-after children with the aim of raising their attainment to at least the level of home-based children living in the same area. An important and innovative feature of this scheme is that it includes children and young people in the planning and implementation, helping them to communicate their views to managers and policy-makers and to support each other.

Government initiatives have in the past been confined to exhortations, not backed with money, and those emanating from the DfEE usually make no specific mention of looked-after children except in connection with problematic behaviour or special educational needs. Successful bids for Educational Action Zones, announced in June 1998, all included in their targets increasing the proportion of children reaching expected levels in key subjects, raising attendance levels and substantial improvements in GCSE results but none appear to make any specific reference to looked-after children, and there is a strong probability that whatever benefits result for other children this most vulnerable group will be left out once again.

More hopefully, following a highly critical report from the House of Commons Select Committee on Health (July 1998) the Government has finally recognized the many inadequacies of local authority care and pledged itself to take effective action, explicitly including better educational attainment as one of its objectives. The *Quality Protects Framework for Action*, launched by the Secretary of State for Health, Frank Dobson, on 21 September 1998, states that the quality of the public care system has been unacceptably low and that the Government is committed to taking action 'to strengthen local authorities' management of these vital services'. Detailed objectives, performance indicators and targets are set out in the documentation and local authorities are required to submit action plans and achieve Key Tasks by 2002. Education is given more prominence than ever before in government guidance on children in public care, and Sub-objective 4.1 is worth quoting in full:

> To bring the overall performance of children looked after, for a year or more, at key stage SATs and GCSE closer into line with local children generally. This is perhaps the single most significant measure of the effectiveness of local authority parenting. The very reasons why children will

need to be looked after will bring some degree of disadvantage, but this must never be used as an excuse to lower aspirations.

(Department of Health Social Care Group, 1998)

Conclusion

The educational disadvantage suffered by looked-after children is so extreme that, at present, only the most resilient have any chance of success. Yet despite growing evidence of the widening gap between the attainment of children living away from home and those with their own families there has been little serious effort in the past to tackle the problem. The ambitious objectives of the new initiative cannot be achieved without a fundamental shift in the attitudes and assumptions of local authority officers and councillors. The importance of elected members has previously been overlooked, and it is significant that Frank Dobson chose to write a long letter to every local councillor in support of *Quality Protects*, correctly recognizing their key role in bridging public and professional viewpoints if the old class-based assumptions about the educational needs and potential of children in care are to be overturned. It is astonishing, for example, that some local authorities are still prepared to approve people who are illiterate as foster carers, whereas it should be recognized that, in order to provide the high level of skilled support and encouragement that the majority of looked-after children require to function well at school, carers need themselves to be very well educated, preferably to degree standard. Currently no educational qualifications at all are required to become a residential worker or foster carer.

Second, local authorities need to make a corporate commitment to all children in their care, whatever their legal status, and recognize their primary duty to support them in mainstream education, providing whatever additional resources are required. No looked-after children should be excluded from school unless they are genuinely uncontainable in the classroom, and then only after every effort has been made to understand and help with their problems. Looked-after children should have the *first* claim on places in the most effective schools, because that is what we would want for our own children, and while they are in the care of the local authority they *are* our children. Targets should be set for the school attainment of the looked-after population in each local authority area in collaboration with schools and the children themselves, and these should be an integral part of the children's services plans that all authorities are required to produce.

The policy of routinely abandoning young people to 'independent living' at age 16 should be ended at once and replaced by the expectation that the majority will continue in education at least until they leave formal care at age 18, and if they go to college or university, they should be able to rely on a warm supportive home environment to return to in vacations. The fact that in many areas this would be seen as a radical suggestion shows how far we

77

have to go. But not until looked-after children have the same chances to succeed in education as children who grow up in their own homes will we finally have left behind the legacy of the Poor Law.

Postscript: Just as this book was going to press the Department for Education and Employment and the Department of Health jointly issued draft guidance on the education of children looked after by local authorities (1999). In contrast to the previous 1994 guidance, which was only advisory, it is proposed to give statutory force to key recommendations. In future every looked-after child must have a Personal Education Plan; every school must appoint a designated teacher; local authorities must set up systems for sharing information between LEAs, social services departments and schools; and no child should be without a school placement for more than 30 days. Local authorities that do not fulfil these requirements would be in breach of the law. The guidance was launched by the Secretary of State, David Blunkett, at the 1999 annual conference of LEAs. Whatever its final form its real significance is that, for the first time, the government has acknowledged past failures and thrown its full weight behind a national initiative to raise the educational achievement of children looked after by local authorities.

Acknowledgements

The author would like to thank the Leverhulme Trust for funding the research on 'high achievers' referred to in this chapter. Thanks also to Rosemary Knight, Jaqueline Lile and Pearl Martin who provided substantial help with different stages of this research.

Notes

1   Information from Department of Health Personal Social Services Local Authority Statistics refers to children looked after on 31 March 1997 (Department of Health, 1998). Provisional figures for Wales supplied by the Welsh Office refer to 31 March 1996.
2   The findings from this research, which was funded by the Leverhulme Trust, are reported in more detail in Jackson and Martin (1998) and in Jackson (forthcoming).

References

Action on After-care Consortium (1996) *Too Much Too Young: The failure of social policy in meeting the needs of care leavers*, Ilford, Barnardos.
Bald, J., Bean, J. and Meegan, F. (1995) *A Book of My Own*, London, Who Cares? Trust.
Bebbington, A. and Miles, J. (1989) 'The background of children who enter local authority care', *British Journal of Social Work* 19, 5, pp. 349–368.
Berridge, D. and Brodie, I. (1998) *Children's Homes Revisited*, London, Jessica Kingsley.
Biehal, N., Clayden, J., Stein, M. and Wade, J. (1995) *Moving On: Young people and leaving care schemes*, London, HMSO.
Blyth, E. and Milner, J. (1998) *Social Work with Children: the educational perspective*, London, Longman.

Broad, B. (1998) *Young People Leaving Care: Life after the Children Act 1989*, London, Jessica Kingsley.

Bullock, R., Little, M. and Millham, S. (1993) *Going Home: The return of children separated from their families*, Aldershot, Dartmouth.

Cheung, S. and Heath, A. (1994) 'After Care: the education and occupation of adults who have been in care', *Oxford Review of Education* 20, 3, pp. 361–375.

Department for Education and and Employment/Department of Health (1999) *Draft Guidance on the Education of Children Looked After by Local Authorities*, issued June 17, London, DfEE/DoH.

Department of Health (1991a) *The Children Act 1989 Guidance and Regulations*, vol. 3 *Family Placements*, London, HMSO.

Department of Health (1991b) *The Children Act 1989 Guidance and Regulations*, vol. 4, *Residential Care*, London, HMSO.

Department of Health (1998) *Children Looked After by Local Authorities, Year Ending 31 March 1997 England* (Personal Social Services Local Authority Statistics A/F/97/12), London, Department of Health.

Department of Health Social Care Group (1998) *Quality Protects: Objectives for Social Services children*, London, Department of Health.

Fergusson, D.M. and Lynskey, M.T. (1996) 'Adolescent resiliency to family adversity', *Journal of Child Psychology and Psychiatry* 37, 3, pp. 281–292.

Fletcher, B. (1996) 'Who Cares? about education: the education of children who are looked after by local authorities', *A Guide for School Governors*, London, Who Cares? Trust.

Fletcher, B. (1998) 'Who Cares? about education: the education of children who are looked after by local authorities', *A Guide for Elected Members*, p. 24, London, Who Cares? Trust in collaboration with the Local Government Association.

Fletcher-Campbell, F. (1990) 'The education of children in care', *Educational Research* 32, pp. 186–192.

Fletcher-Campbell, F. (1997) *The Education of Children Who are Looked-After*, Slough, National Foundation for Educational Research.

Fraser, M. (ed.) (1997) *Risk and Resilience in Childhood: An ecological perspective*, Washington DC, National Association of Social Workers.

Garmezy, N. (1993) 'Vulnerability and resilience', in Funder, D.C., Parke, C., Tomlinson-Keasey, C. and Widaman, K. (eds) *Studying Lives Through Time*, Washington DC, American Psychological Association.

Gibbons, J., Conroy, S. and Bell, C. (1995) *Operating the Child Protection System: A study of child protection practices in English local authorities*, London, HMSO.

Heath, A., Colton, M.J. and Aldgate, J. (1989) 'The educational progress of children in and out of care', *British Journal of Social Work* 19, pp. 447–460.

Heath, A., Colton, M.J. and Aldgate, J. (1994) 'Failure to escape: a longitudinal study of foster children's educational attainment', *British Journal of Social Work* 24, pp. 241–259.

Holman, B. (1998) *Child Care Revisited: The children's departments 1948–1971. With a contemporary view on child care in the 1990s*, London, Institute of Childcare and Social Education UK.

Hutson, S. (1997) *Supported Housing: The experience of young care leavers*, Ilford, Barnardos.

Jackson, S. (1987) *The Education of Children in Care*, Bristol, University of Bristol School of Applied Social Studies.

Jackson, S. (1994) 'Educating children in residential and foster care: an overview', *Oxford Review of Education* 20, pp. 267–279.

Jackson, S. (1998) 'Looking after children: a new approach or just an exercise in formfilling? A response to Knight and Caveney', *British Journal of Social Work* 28, 1, pp. 45–56.

Jackson, S. (forthcoming) *Succeeding from Care*, London, Macmillan.

Jackson, S. and Martin, P.Y. (1998) 'Surviving the care system: education and resilience', *Journal of Adolescence* 21, pp. 569–583.

Jackson, S. and Thomas, N. (1999) *What Works in Creating Stability for Looked After Children?*, Ilford, Barnardo's.

Kos, A.M. (1998) 'School as psychological protection of children', in Segula, C. and Thankrai, S. (eds) *They Talk We Listen*, Ljubljana, Centre for Psychosocial Help to Refugees – Slovene Foundation, p. 248.

Maluccio, A., Abramczyk, L. and Thomlison, B. (1996) 'Family reunification of children in out-of-home care: research perspectives', *Children and Youth Services Review* 18, pp. 4–5.

National Foster Care Association (NFCA)(1997) *Foster Care in Crisis: A call to professionalise the forgotten service*, London, National Foster Care Association.

Osborn, A. and St Claire, L. (1987) 'The ability and behaviour of children who have been in care or separated from their parents', *Early Child Development and Care* 28, 3, pp. 187–354.

Russell, F. (1998) 'Lost inside – the imprisonment of teenage girls', *Criminal Justice* 16, pp. 4–5.

Rutter, M. (1987) 'Psychosocial resilience and protective mechanisms', *American Journal of Orthopsychiatry* 57, pp. 316–331.

Rutter, M. (1988) 'Longitudinal data in the study of causal processes: some uses and some pitfalls', in Rutter, M. (ed.) *Studies of Psycho-social Risk: The power of longitudinal data*, Cambridge, Cambridge University Press.

Rutter, M., Quinton, D. and Hill, J. (1990) 'Adult outcome of institution-reared children: males and females compared', in Robins, L.N. and Rutter, M. (eds) *Straight and Devious Pathways from Childhood to Adolescence*, Cambridge, Cambridge University Press.

Searle, C. (1996) 'The signal of failure: school exclusions and the market system of education', in Blyth, E. and Milner, J. (eds) *Exclusion from School: Inter-professional issues for policy and practice*, London, Routledge.

Shaw, C. (1998) *Remember My Messages: The experiences and views of 2000 children in public care in the UK*, London, Who Cares? Trust.

Sinclair, R., Grimshaw, R. and Garnett, L. (1994) 'The education of children in need, the impact of the Education Reform Act 1998, the Education Act 1993 and the Children Act 1989', *Oxford Review of Education* 20, pp. 281–292.

Social Services Inspectorate (SSI) (1997) *When Leaving Home is Also Leaving Care* (C1(97)4), London, Department of Health.

Social Services Inspectorate and Office for Standards in Education (1995) *The Education of Children who are Looked After by Local Authorities*, London, SSI/OFSTED.

Walker, T. (1990) *The Teaching Service for the Social Services Department* 1, Manchester, Manchester City Council Education Department.

Walker, T. (1994) 'Educating children in public care: a strategic approach', *Oxford Review of Education* 20, 3, pp. 339–349.

Ward, H. (ed.) (1995) *Looking After Children: Research into practice*, London, HMSO.

Werner, E. (1994) 'Overcoming the odds', *Developmental and Behavioural Pediatrics* 15, 2, pp. 131–136.

6 Social Disadvantage and Disruptive Behaviour in School

Maurice Chazan

This chapter examines the links between social disadvantage and disruptive behaviour in the classroom and school. It discusses the prevalence of disruptive behaviour among socially disadvantaged pupils; how social disadvantage may lead to disruptive behaviour; and the persistence and consequences of such behaviour. Consideration is given to factors which may protect disadvantaged children from developing maladaptive responses; measures which may prevent disruptive behaviour in school; positive strategies for intervention; and recent developments relating to exclusion from school.

Introduction

During the 1960s and 1970s the needs and difficulties of children living in conditions of social disadvantage such as poverty or poor housing were an important public issue (Silver and Silver, 1991). Since then, this concern, which was to some extent aroused by the American 'war on poverty' and such early education programmes as Head Start, has become less pronounced in Britain. However, the problems arising from social disadvantage have not gone away. Indeed, relative poverty and inequalities in the distribution of wealth in this country have increased rather than declined over the last two decades (Smith, 1995; Joseph Rowntree Foundation/LWT, 1997). Many studies have found that social disadvantage has an adverse effect on educational achievement (see Chapters 1 and 10), although some educationalists argue that poor teaching methods and ineffective schools are more to blame for educational failure than poor social circumstances (Woodhead, 1998).

Even if the relationship between social disadvantage and educational attainment is still a matter for debate, there is compelling evidence to show that factors relating to social disadvantage contribute powerfully to the causation of behaviour disorders in childhood and adolescence. As in recent years the spotlight has been turned on an apparent increase in antisocial and disruptive behaviour among schoolchildren, sometimes culminating in suspension or exclusion from school (DfE, 1992; Parsons, 1995). It is relevant to explore the links between living conditions and disruptive behaviour. This chapter sets out to discuss these links and the measures being taken or proposed to prevent or minimize disruption in school.

The complexity of the concept of social disadvantage and the many different definitions and measures which have been used by policy-makers and researchers are discussed in the Introduction to this book (Chapter 1) as well as in Chapter 10. In the present chapter, the focus will be put on the relationship between disruptive behaviour in school and social disadvantage particularly associated with material factors such as financial hardship and unsatisfactory housing conditions. These are factors which often lead to tensions and conflicts at home, and trigger off or aggravate mental health problems in the family and disturbed behaviour in the children (Fortin and Bigras, 1997).

The Nature of Disruptive Behaviour

In recent years, the term 'disruptive' has been applied to several kinds of anti-social behaviour in schools. However, it usually implies that the pupil is interfering with his or her own efficient learning or that of other pupils (Topping, 1990), and that the behaviour is highly disturbing to school staff and interrupts normal school life (Galloway et al., 1982; Badger, 1992). Gray and Richer (1988) stress that disruptive pupils tend to give less attention to work than others; to misbehave for much of the time; to ignore the teacher or flout authority in spite of efforts to relate to them or discipline them. Gray and Richer list many forms of behaviour that may be called disruptive, including rudeness; abusive language; physical attacks on teachers; shouting out; distractibility; fidgeting with materials; making unusual noises; and fighting or squabbling between pupils. Disruptive behaviour may be planned by groups within a class, and may occur outside as well as inside the class-room.

Prevalence of Disruptive Behaviour Among Socially Disadvantaged Pupils

It is difficult to be precise about the prevalence of disruptive behaviour in school among socially disadvantaged pupils, as many factors affect estimates of the extent of any form of emotional and behaviour difficulties (EBDs) in childhood and adolescence. These factors include the definitions of social disadvantage and disruption adopted by the researchers, the methods of assessment used, who carries out ratings, the location of the school, and the composition of the sample in respect of age, gender and membership of ethnic group.

Children with persistent behaviour problems come from all socio-economic groups, and by no means all socially disadvantaged pupils present EBDs. Those who do show signs of disturbance are not necessarily anti-social or disruptive. However, a variety of studies have demonstrated that behaviour problems, particularly of an externalizing kind, tend to be significantly associated with an excess of social and family background problems. For example, Rutter and Madge (1976), in their review of research on cycles of disadvantage, stressed that children from large families, especially those in overcrowded or otherwise disadvantaged homes, were much more likely than others to develop conduct disorder or become delinquent. Rutter (1973) reported a higher prevalence of 'antisocial' than 'neurotic' kinds of deviant behaviour in studies of an inner-city London borough, where much more problem behaviour was shown than on the Isle of Wight. The greater prevalence of deviant behaviour in London was associated with higher rates of disadvantage both in the children's schools and in the families (see also ILEA, 1985).

Other examples of studies pointing to an association between disadvantage and behaviour disturbance include those by Chazan and Jackson (1971, 1974), who found that, at 5 and 7 years of age, approximately 16 per cent of a sample of children living in 'deprived' areas were rated as 'somewhat' or 'very' disturbed by their teachers, as compared with about 6 per cent in 'middle-class' areas. The children in 'deprived' areas tended to display more aggressiveness and anti-social behaviour than more advantaged pupils. In a survey of a sample of 7-year-olds in New Zealand, McGee et al. (1985) found that both hyperactivity and aggressiveness, but not anxious behaviour, were related to adversities in the child's family background.

In a study of fifty 11-year-old children, who were members of socially disadvantaged families, Cox and Jones (1983) found that the anti-social items on the Rutter Child Scale B (Rutter, 1967), rated by teachers, most sharply differentiated these children from a control group coming from more advantaged families, although both groups of children were living in social priority areas. Significantly more disadvantaged group children than the controls were involved in fighting, bullying or damaging property, but did not show a markedly higher rate of worries, fears or school refusal. In their teachers' judgement, the disadvantaged sample was characterized by more disruptive types of behaviour than those of a withdrawn, anxious kind (see also Laing and Chazan, 1987).

Fergusson et al. (1994) examined the life history of a small group of New Zealand adolescents (3 per cent of a sample of 942) identified as displaying multiple problem behaviours, including conduct disorder and police contact, at age 15. The researchers found that the majority of this group were the offspring of seriously disadvantaged and disorganized home environments.

It was mentioned above that many factors affect estimates of the prevalence of disruptive behaviour in socially disadvantaged pupils. Two factors merit consideration here: (a) gender (see also Chapter 3) and (b) membership of ethnic minorities (see also Chapter 2).

Maurice Chazan

Gender

Many studies (Achenbach and Edelbrock, 1981; Stevenson et al., 1985) have shown that many more boys than girls (sometimes up to 3 or 4 times as many) are at risk of conduct disorder. Maughan and Garratt (1994) point out that the epidemiological picture is complex: rates of conduct disorder are at their height for boys in middle childhood, but the peak for girls is in the mid-teens. It is probable that different levels of social expectancy and tolerance of misbehaviour are important factors in giving rise to these findings of gender differences, but constitutional, congenital and environmental factors must all be taken into account in attempts to explain such differences.

Membership of an Ethnic Minority Group

Children from ethnic minority groups, especially boys from disadvantaged homes, tend to be over-represented in the numbers of pupils found to be disruptive or excluded from school (Garner, 1993). Rutter et al. (1974), in a total population survey of all 10-year-old children in an Inner London borough, reported that teachers rated more than twice as many pupils from families of West Indian origin as from 'non-immigrant' backgrounds as presenting EBDs. The difference between the samples was entirely confined to deviance involving disturbances of conduct in school, and did not exist for emotional or mixed types of deviance. In interpreting these findings, it is necessary to take into account that, while behaviour disturbance in the West Indian children was indeed associated with various kinds of disadvantage suffered by their families, some teachers have stereotypes of behaviour considered characteristic of certain ethnic minority groups (DES, 1985). For instance, Asian pupils are generally considered to be well-behaved in school, whereas West Indian pupils are seen by many teachers to be less well-motivated in school and more prone to behaviour problems than other children (Stone, 1981; Houlton, 1986; and see Chapter 2 for a fuller discussion of how ethnic minorities may be disadvantaged within the educational system).

How Disadvantage May Lead to Disruptive Behaviour

It is usually the case that a combination of factors, temperamental as well as environmental, rather than a single factor is at work in the causation of behaviour difficulties such as disruptiveness. Predisposing factors, for example a child's prolonged experience of stress at home, have to be considered as well as precipitating factors, such as conflict with a teacher in class. Here, the discussion will be confined to family and school factors and peer influences.

Family Factors

As previously stressed, social disadvantage, even in the form of poverty and poor housing, does not directly or necessarily result in behaviour difficulties in the children affected. However, it may well bring about or exacerbate these conditions in the family which are closely associated with behaviour difficulties. Shaw et al. (1994), for example, found that the effects of within-family factors which exert a strong influence on child behaviour, such as marital problems and lack of maternal warmth and support, were maximized in the presence of social disadvantage associated with low socio-economic status. Discordant patterns of interaction within the family, weak family relationships, inefficient supervision and discipline, and deviant models of behaviour are particularly likely to bring about conduct disorder in children (Rutter, 1985). The powerful effects of a combination of risk factors have been stressed in the research literature: when more than one stressor is present, the risk of child behaviour problems is considerably increased (Sanson et al., 1991; Blanz et al., 1991; Shaw et al., 1994).

Children in one-parent families, who often have to live in conditions of economic hardship, are at risk of developing behaviour problems, as lone parents are inclined to be vulnerable to the effects of stress and to becoming depressed (Fundudis, 1997). In two-parent families, too, where the child is unused to consistent control at home, or treated harshly, he/she may not take kindly to discipline in school and be more likely to rebel against authority. For example, a pupil subject to rejection by a parent may project his/her anger and resentment onto a figure of authority in school or onto a fellow-pupil. Adverse home conditions of the kinds listed above may result in a child bringing anxieties about the family situation into school and lead to a lack of concentration on classroom tasks and to difficulties in learning.

School Factors

Many schools in social priority areas are well-run and achieve success in spite of a considerable intake of pupils from homes suffering from various kinds of social disadvantage. However, it is not surprising if some schools in which many of the pupils are adversely affected by grossly unsatisfactory home conditions have a disproportionate number of disruptive pupils. Staff may face challenging behaviour on the part of individual pupils, or even whole classes that have lost interest in scholastic tasks and are out of control.

Schools in social priority areas may face greater problems than others in maintaining desirable standards of behaviour and achieving their academic goals. Such schools may have inadequate buildings and resources, and have difficulty in attracting and keeping teachers, so that there is a lack of continuity in teaching and low morale. Some of the key features in creating effective schools, such as having high expectations of what pupils can achieve, parental involvement and staff cohesion (Reynolds et al., 1994; Sammons et al., 1995) may be difficult to bring about in schools serving social priority areas, even with good leadership from senior staff, unless extra support and resources are provided (see Chapter 10).

Peer Influences

Particularly, but not only at the secondary school stage, pupils are readily influenced by their peers. In schools serving disadvantaged areas, pupils may be exposed to models of disruptive behaviour and a lack of interest in scholastic achievement on the part of one or more of their classmates, even among those capable of academic success. Outside school, too, there may be a peer culture tending to promote, from an early age, social life focusing on the street rather than the home or club, and perhaps encouraging truancy, substance abuse and delinquency. In cases where the influence of the family on a child is weak, peer pressures may be especially operative (see Dunn and McGuire, 1992, for a review of research on peer relationships in childhood).

Consequences of Disruptive Behaviour

Short-Term Consequences

The short-term consequences of disruptive behaviour in school are likely to be serious. Disruptive behaviour may result in physical injury to a pupil or a member of staff. It may well lead to a failure on the part of pupils concerned to keep up with the demands of the curriculum and to the loss of self-esteem, as well as possibly to the breakdown of learning in the class as a whole. In the worst cases, exclusion from school may be the outcome (see the discussion of exclusion later in this chapter). Staff having to cope with disruptive pupils may, if they cannot deal successfully with them, see themselves as failures. Where there are several classes out of control in a school, a breakdown in staff morale may result and management may become ineffective.

Often, when pupils engage in disruptive behaviour, a vicious circle develops in which matters tend to get worse unless intervention is rapid and effective. For example, a pupil is aggressive to the teacher in class; he or she is reprimanded or punished; the pupil becomes more rebellious and is sent to senior staff; the pupil remains disruptive and the class becomes difficult, if not impossible, to teach; and so suspension or exclusion from school follows.

Long-Term Consequences

A considerable body of longitudinal research has shown that externalizing behaviour problems in childhood, particularly when these are severe, are associated with a variety of difficulties and disorders in adulthood. Robins (1991), on the basis of her own research and a review of the literature, concludes that conduct disorder (which includes aggressive, destructive and disruptive behaviour) tends to be persistent over time, especially if the onset is early. While not all children presenting behaviour problems progress to anti-social personalities, conduct disorder not only predicts mental ill-health, but has a wide-ranging poor prognosis for adult life, presaging, for example, marital breakdowns, poor employment records and a failure to maintain satisfactory personal relationships.

Examples of studies testifying to the seriousness of conduct disorders in childhood include that of Farmer (1995), who found that, on the basis of data from the British National Child Development Study, boys who were classified as having externalizing behaviour problems showed significantly worse employment-related outcomes than boys who did not present such problems. Campbell (1995), too, in a review of research on behaviour difficulties in pre-school children, reports that serious externalizing problems identified at an early age often persist, particularly when the children grow up in distressed and dysfunctional families. Similar findings are reported in relation to children presenting conduct disorders in middle childhood by Fergusson et al. (1993), who affirm that these children are at considerable risk of later school failure, juvenile delinquency and other forms of social maladjustment.

Protective Factors

As previously indicated, some children succeed in life in spite of a disadvantaged background. In recent years, researchers have shown an interest in highlighting those factors which seem to protect children from the worst effects of stressful experiences. Rutter (1985) maintains that a good relationship in the midst of discord and disharmony can be a shielding influence, and that satisfying experiences at school may compensate for difficulties at home. Goodyer et al. (1990), too, point out that a close, affectionate relationship with parents significantly decreases the risk of conduct disorder, even when there are family difficulties. Problem-solving and social skills, as well as children's own beliefs about their control over situations, also act as moderators helping to protect children from the undue effects of pressures resulting from an adverse home background (Berden et al., 1990; Rossman and Rosenberg, 1992; Luthar, 1993).

Fergusson and Lynskey (1996) list the following factors as conducive to resilience in the face of childhood adversity:

1   being of higher intelligence;
2   being female (though not all studies show that girls are more resilient than boys);
3   having external interests and affiliations, e.g. a strong attachment outside the immediate family;

4 parental attachment and bonding: warm, nurturant or supportive relation-ships;

5 showing acceptable behaviour at an early age – having an 'easy' temperament; and

6 encouraging good peer relationships, which may compensate for an adverse family environment.

Prevention

As Mortimore and Whitty emphasize in Chapter 10, relatively little can be done to improve the life chances of disadvantaged children without tackling poverty and disadvantage at their roots. Even when educational initiatives such as literacy and homework support schemes have improved the absolute performance of disadvantaged pupils, the gap between these pupils and their more advantaged peers has remained wide. However, school improvement projects have shown that effective schools can make a difference to the achievements and prospects of disadvantaged children. Barber (1997) argues that both an attack on poverty and appropriate educational measures are needed to help these children.

Abrahams (1997), on the basis of research carried out for the National Children's Homes Action for Children Family Forum, lists a variety of measures needed to give support to disadvantaged families, children and young people, and to restore the social fabric and self-confidence of populations in social priority areas. Social and community measures designed to reduce poverty and help families in need will not be discussed here (but see Chapters 5 and 13). Rather the focus in the following discussion, necessarily brief, will be put on those measures primarily involving educational agencies which are likely to prevent or minimize disruptive behaviour related to social disadvantage. These measures include the early identification of children 'at risk', more educational provision in the early years, more effective schools, literacy schemes, behaviour support plans, better co-ordination of the helping services, and the setting up of education action zones by the government.

Early Identification

It is not possible to predict accurately at an early age which children are likely to be most at risk of presenting serious behaviour problems in later childhood and adolescence. However, as previously mentioned, much is now known about the factors most conducive to the development of disruptive behaviour. 'At risk' factors relating to the child include a 'difficult' temperament and early attention-deficit behaviour (Fergusson et al., 1993). 'At risk' factors relating to the family include, in addition to poverty and adverse material conditions, persistent martial disharmony, family instability and malaise, parental criminality and substance abuse, poor child-rearing practices and low commitment to the care of children (Richman et al., 1982; Fergusson et al., 1994; Campbell, 1995). All the health, social and educational agencies have a role in identifying 'at risk' children and families at the earliest possible stage, to help in preventing or minimizing the effects of adverse conditions such as those listed above. (See also Chapter 5 concerning the risk factors affecting looked-after children.)

Education in the Early Years

Sylva (1992) maintains that well-conducted early education can change the course of children's lives and result in lower involvement in anti-social and delinquent behaviour later on. According to Sylva, research studies suggest that the critical feature of early educational provision is the development by children of an early positive view of themselves as learners, setting them on the path to a 'mastering' rather than 'helpless' orientation (see also Chapter 8). However, Osborn and Milbank (1987), studying the effects of early education in Britain, report that the evidence does not support the hypothesis that pre-school education reduces the risk of behaviour problems in the long-term, though it does have a positive effect upon cognitive development and educational achievement. Evaluation research in the USA, where much effort has been expended since the 1960s in expanding early education provision for disadvantaged children, has tended to indicate that such provision results in a reduced need for special education and better employment prospects, rather than in a long-term increase in measures of intelligence or improved self-concepts (Lazar and Darlington, 1982). In general, research has shown that it is more difficult to achieve positive effects with regard to behaviour when children come from severely disadvantaged homes, and that early education provision must be of high quality and sharply focused on specific targets if it is to reduce the adverse consequences of social disadvantage on children's development.

Making Schools More Effective

School effectiveness in relation to social disadvantage is discussed in Chapter 10. Here it will suffice to stress that, although the causes of a pupil's disruptive behaviour may often lie at least partly outside the school, the ethos of the school and teachers' management of classes as well as their relationships with pupils are likely to have a bearing on the incidence of disruptive behaviour. Galloway (1987) asserts that much can be learnt about the prevention of disruptive behaviour by analysing the characteristics of successful schools, but that much can be learnt, too, from a consideration of how successful teachers operate in the classroom. Gray and Richer (1988) emphasize that disruption may be prevented by effective teaching and class control; clear and reasonable rules; avoiding threats; ensuring fairness; and providing good models of behaviour.

It is important to draw attention to the contribution that schools can make, even in difficult circumstances, to raising educational standards and maintaining reasonable behaviour in their pupils. However, it may be argued that the emphasis put by governments since the late 1980s on league tables which highlight the gap between 'successful' and 'failing' schools may not altogether achieve its purpose. Schools in general may seek to guard their reputation by refusing to admit or keep low-achieving or difficult pupils, and schools which are 'named and shamed' because of low achievement may find it hard to avoid low morale amongst pupils, parents and staff.

Literacy Schemes

The relationship between reading difficulties and conduct disorder is a complex one (Fergusson and Lynskey, 1997). However, there is evidence that children with low achievements in literacy skills, who fail to keep up with general curricular requirements and lose interest in scholastic endeavours, are in danger of developing behaviour problems in the classroom. It is also the case that disturbed children are often incapable of giving attention to work in class, and may turn to disruption (Brown and Chazan, 1989; Mandel, 1997). Well-planned schemes, therefore, aimed at promoting literacy skills in low achievers have their place in the prevention of conduct disorder.

Both the former Conservative government and the present Labour government have put an emphasis on raising children's literacy proficiency, promoting such ideas as a daily 'literacy hour' in school, summer literacy schools and the encouragement of parents to read to and with their children at home (see Chapter 7). Detailed guidance on fostering literacy as a part of a National Literacy Strategy has been sent to all primary schools.

Behaviour Support Plans

The government's Green Paper on special educational needs, published in October 1997, stresses the need to prevent and deal with emotional and behavioural difficulties by developing a programme to help primary schools tackle these difficulties at an early stage; increasing opportunities for staff to improve their skills in teaching children with EBDs; creating a national programme to offer support to EBD special schools which are experiencing problems; and expanding support for schemes aiming to increase the motivation of older pupils with EBDs.

New guidelines helping local authorities to draw up behaviour support plans for disruptive pupils came into effect in April 1998. LEAs are now required to outline the arrangements they are making to educate children with EBDs, and to make known what support services are available for schools and what alternative provision, such as pupil referral units, are available.

Better Co-ordination of the Support Services

Schools and parents are often reluctant to call upon the psychological, social and health services to help children with behaviour problems until these problems have become well-established and less amenable to modification. The support services can be most effective in preventing or minimizing behaviour disorder when they can use their expertise at an early stage, and when co-operation is forthcoming from school and family. The need for the various services to work together more effectively has been highlighted on numerous occasions in recent years (see, for example, Clark, 1988; Heflinger and Nixon, 1996). These services have not found it easy to co-operate and communicate with one another as much as is desirable, but are striving towards greater integration (NASEN S.E.N. Policy Options Group, 1996).

Education Action Zones

The government is setting up a number of education action zones in England, which are groups of about twenty primary, secondary and special schools working with local authorities, business and community groups. The aim of these zones is to encourage innovative approaches to raising standards in areas where schools need extra support, such as socially disadvantaged areas. This extra support will be given mainly through providing additional resources, helping schools in the zones to appoint high quality teaching staff, and improving information technology. Twenty-five zones should be in action by January 1999, and 100 by the year 2000. The idea of education action zones has been received with varying degrees of enthusiasm by educationists, and it remains to be seen how successful the zones will be in supporting schools in disadvantaged areas (see TES, 1998).

Intervention in School

When a pupil is disruptive the responses of the school may take the form of (a) warnings or punishment; (b) positive intervention programmes; (c) providing support for the pupil and/or (d) exclusion. Any action taken should be based on a careful assessment of the pupil's difficulties and needs as well as of the context in which disruption occurs. The family should be involved at an early stage, and help arranged as necessary.

(a) *Punishment.* Although fair and reasonable punishment does have its place in school, sanctions (such as temporary removal from the class, loss of privileges or being put on report) are often ineffective in the case of serious disruption, particularly when the pupil involved is under stress relating to his or her home circumstances (see Gilham, 1984; Docking, 1987; Wheldall and Glynn, 1989). When punishment is used, it should be combined with positive measures, and the pupil should be told the purpose of any sanctions being applied (Scherer, 1990; Cooper, 1989). Degrading or humiliating punishments, which serve to depress self-esteem when this is usually already low, should be avoided (DfE, 1994).

(b) *Individual strategies.* Positive measures aimed at improving the behaviour of disruptive pupils on an individual basis include counselling, social skills training, behaviour modification or psychotherapy. Help of these kinds may be given within the school or by outside agencies, especially the School Psychological Service (see Chapter 12 of this book and Chazan et al., 1994 for a discussion of individual strategies to help children with EBDs). Individual treatment strategies are likely to meet with formidable barriers in the case of disruptive pupils living in highly stressful home conditions. Galloway (1987), for example, considers that counselling and psychotherapy are not very successful with disruptive pupils, and that behaviour modification programmes are difficult to implement properly in schools. He asserts that responses should be institutional rather than individual in nature. Even if this may be an over-generalized judgement, the co-operation of pupil and parents may prove difficult to achieve, especially when regular attendance at a clinic or centre is required (Kazdin et al., 1997).

(c) *Support systems.* In addition to the help to schools provided by the Schools Psychological Service discussed in Chapter 12, many LEAs have established peripatetic behaviour support teams of specialist teachers. These teams aim to assist mainstream teachers to meet the needs of children with EBDs within the context of the ordinary school system, either by working with individual pupils or small groups, or by acting as consultants to teachers (Drew, 1990; Hanko, 1990; Elliott and Carter, 1992; Rennie, 1993). Peer support groups may also gain more control over their behaviour. Mosley's 'Circle Approach', for example, involves the disruptive child in working jointly with others to achieve certain behavioural targets, as well as encouraging all members of staff to participate in a variety of ways (Mosley, 1991, 1993).

(d) *Exclusion.* There are barriers to ascertaining the true extent of exclusion from school, as children may be excluded unofficially, perhaps under the façade of medical problems or by headteachers persuading parents to keep children at home while arrangements for special provision are being made (Stirling, 1992). Even so, the available evidence points to a significant increase in recent years in the number of pupils (mostly boys) being excluded from school, with even young children being excluded to a greater extent than before (Parsons and Howlett, 1996; Castle and Parsons, 1997; Hayden, 1997; Pomerantz, 1997) (but see Chapter 12, pp. 201–202). On the basis of a national survey, The Children's Society (1998) estimates that about half a million school days are lost each year as a result of exclusions.

A DfE Discussion Document (DfE, 1992) asserted that variations in the number of pupils excluded from individual schools seemed to be too great to be explained by the socio-economic nature of the schools' catchment area. However, the document acknowledges that Afro-Caribbean pupils appeared to be disproportionately represented within the excluded pupil population (see also Gillborn, 1990). Garner (1993) points out that schools with a high exclusion rate are to be found particularly in disadvantaged areas of large towns and cities. An OFSTED Report (1995) showed that many pupils admitted to Pupil Referral Units, set up by LEAs to cater for excluded pupils, faced family difficulties such as poverty, ill-health and violence.

It is generally agreed that exclusion from school should be a last resort, and if this way of dealing with disruptive pupils is used, it should be operated in as constructive a way as possible. Gersch and Nolan (1994) advocate that the views of the pupils themselves should be taken into account to a greater extent than is now usual (see also Chapter 9 of this book). Stirling (1993) goes so far as to state that withdrawal of education is inappropriate as a punishment for the child even if it has short-term advantages for the school, and proposes that every pupil, even those needing continued special provision, should be registered with a mainstream school which holds the responsibility for ensuring that appropriate education provision is secured.

The Education Act 1997, which came into force on 1 September 1998, made some changes to the law on exclusions and education otherwise than at school, including the following:

(i) headteachers may now exclude a pupil for up to 45 school days in a school year (instead of 15 days in any one term), to allow for the smooth reintegration of pupils who might otherwise have been permanently excluded;

(ii) pupils excluded for a fixed period of more than a day or two must be set school work to do at home;

(iii) headteachers should have clear arrangements for receiving pupils back into school after a fixed term exclusion;

(iv) LEAs are required to arrange 'suitable education' for excluded pupils, and to have regard to guidance from the Secretary of State in determining what arrangements to make; and

(v) LEAs must establish management committees for their Pupil Referral Units (PRUs), set up to cater for disturbed pupils, especially those excluded from school.

The Social Exclusion Unit, set up by the government, outlined plans in its first report (1998) to devote extra resources to schools receiving excluded children or doing good preventative work. The government has announced action to implement the recommendations in this report, including setting new targets for reducing exclusions, giving financial incentives to schools to prevent exclusion, and increasing provision for the education of excluded pupils (DfEE, 1998). Also LEAs can now bid for a new Standards Fund Grant (School Inclusion: Pupil Support) to provide support to schools teaching pupils with challenging behaviour.

Pupil Referral Units (PRUs) have been set up by local education authorities as a key part of their strategies to provide education for excluded pupils. The main advantages of PRUs are that they provide expertise in dealing with disturbed pupils and allow time to focus on individual behaviour and learning difficulties, but they are usually segregated from the mainstream system and have poor accommodation and facilities (OFSTED, 1995). Castle and Parsons (1997) argue that the present system of exclusions causes stress to all parties and is wasteful, asserting that most of the measures relating to exclusion in the 1997 Education Act are unhelpful or unproductive: it would be better to fund preventative schemes with support teachers and which do not deny pupils their right to full-time and appropriate education. To this end, Lovey and Cooper (1997) describe the 'Positive Alternatives to School Exclusion' (PASE) project being carried out at the University of Cambridge School of Education. This project is concerned to ascertain what schools can do to help pupils who might otherwise become excluded from school to participate positively in schooling, in ways that preclude the need for exclusion. Lovey and Cooper stress the importance of the following principles:

1   defining a clear relationship between the desired school ethos and the procedures of the school;
2   approaching conflicts through dialogue;
3   focusing on solutions as opposed to problems;
4   seeing effective classroom management as closely linked to teaching; and
5   taking account of each school's unique history and context.

Fitzherbert (1997), too, describes the work of the National Pyramid Trust to reduce exclusion by three main measures: identifying 7 and 8-year-olds at risk of social and educational failure, multi-agency consultation and action, and short-term activity group therapy to promote confidence, self-esteem and motivation (see also Robinson, 1998 and Bracher et al., 1998).

Conclusion

This chapter has shown that disruptive behaviour, especially in boys from ethnic minorities, tends to be significantly related to an excess of social and family problems. Schools in social priority areas may face formidable problems in maintaining desirable standards of discipline, and outside school the peer culture in disadvantaged areas may encourage anti-social attitudes. Both the short-term and long-term consequences of disruptive behaviour in school are likely to be serious.

Strategies designed to minimize or prevent disruptive behaviour in school include the early identification of children 'at risk', better provision of education in the early years, more effective schools, literacy and behaviour support schemes, smoother co-ordination of the helping services, and the setting up of Education Action Zones. A variety of intervention strategies in school are available on an individual or group basis, that aim at improving the behaviour of disruptive pupils and keeping them in their schools. It is to be hoped that preventative and intervention measures will succeed in reducing the number of disruptive children excluded from school.

References

Abrahams, C. (1997) *NCH Action for Children Family Forum Findings: A briefing and discussion paper*, London, National Children's Homes Action for Children.

Achenbach, T.M. and Edlebrock, C.S. (1981) *Behavioural Problems and Competencies Reported by Parents of Normal and Disturbed Children Aged four Through Sixteen*, Monographs of the Society for Research in Child Development, 46, 1, pp. 1–82.

Badger, B. (1992) 'Changing a disruptive school', in Reynolds, D. and Cuttance, P. (eds) *School Effectiveness*, London, Cassell.

Barber, M. (1997) 'Why simply tackling poverty is not enough', *Times Educational Supplement*, 12 September, p. 17.

Berden, G.F.M.G., Althaus, M. and Verhulst, F.C. (1990) 'Major life events and changes in the behavioural functioning of children', *Journal of Child Psychology and Psychiatry* 31, 6, pp. 949–960.

Blanz, B., Schmidt, M.H. and Esser, G. (1991) 'Familial adversities and child psychiatric disorders', *Journal of Child Psychology and Psychiatry* 32, 6, pp. 939–950.

Bracher, D., Hitchcock, M. and Moss, L. (1998) 'The process of permanent exclusion and implementation of "Fresh Start" programmes', *Educational Psychology in Practice* 14, 2, pp. 83–93.

Brown, R.I. and Chazan, M. (1989) *Learning Difficulties and Emotional Problems*, Calgary, Alberta, Detseling Enterprises.

Campbell, S.B. (1995) 'Behaviour problems in pre-school children: a review of recent research', *Journal of Child Psychology and Psychiatry* 36, 1, pp. 113–150.

Castle, F. and Parsons, C. (1997) 'Disruptive behaviour and exclusions from schools: redefining and responding to the problem', *Emotional and Behavioural Difficulties* 2, 3, pp. 4–11.

Chazan, M. and Jackson, S. (1971) 'Behaviour problems in the infant school', *Journal of Child Psychology and Psychiatry* 12, 3, pp. 191–210.

Chazan, M. and Jackson, S. (1974) 'Behaviour problems in the infant school: changes over two years', *Journal of Child Psychology and Psychiatry* 15, 1, pp. 33–46.

Chazan, M., Laing, A.F. and Davies, D. (1994) *Emotional and Behavioural Difficulties in Middle Childhood: Identification, assessment and intervention in school*, London, Falmer Press.

Children's Society (1998) *No Lessons Learnt*, London, The Children's Society.

Clark, M.M. (1988) *Children Under Five: Educational research and evidence*, New York, Gordon & Breach.

Cooper, P. (1989) 'Emotional and behaviour difficulties in the real world: a strategy for helping junior school teachers cope with behaviour problems', *Maladjustment and Therapeutic Education* 7, 3, pp. 178–184.

Cox, T. and Jones, G. (1983) *Disadvantaged 11-Year-Olds*, Oxford, Pergamon.

Department for Education (DfE) (1992) *Exclusions: A discussion paper*, London, DfE.

Department for Education and Employment (DfEE) (1998) *Education in Parliament*, 8–11 June, London, DfEE.

Department for Education/Department of Health (1994) *Pupil Behaviour and Discipline* (Circular DfE 8/94), Department for Education/Department of Health.

Department of Education and Science (DES) (1985) *Education For All (The Swann Report)*, London, HMSO.

Docking, J.W. (1987) 'The effects and effectiveness of punishment in schools', in Cohen, L. and Cohen, A. (eds) *Disruptive Behaviour: A source book for teachers*, London, Harper.

Drew, D. (1990) 'From tutorial unit to schools support service', *Support for Learning* 5, 1, pp. 13–21.

Dunn, J. and McGuire, S. (1992) 'Sibling and peer relationships in childhood', *Journal of Child Psychology and Psychiatry* 33, 1, pp. 67–106.

Elliott, K. and Carter, M. (1992) 'The development of the East Devon behaviour support team', *Support for Learning* 7, 1, pp. 19–24.

Farmer, E.M.Z. (1995) 'Extremity of externalizing behaviour and young adult outcomes', *Journal of Child Psychology and Psychiatry* 34, 4, pp. 617–632.

Fergusson, D.M. and Lynskey, M.T. (1996) 'Adolescent resiliency to family adversity', *Journal of Child Psychology and Psychiatry* 37, 3, pp. 281–292.

Fergusson, D.M. and Lynskey, M.T. (1997) 'Early reading difficulties and later conduct problems', *Journal of Child Psychology and Psychiatry* 38, 8, pp. 899–907.

Fergusson, D.M., Horwood, L.J. and Lynskey, M.T. (1993) 'The effect of conduct disorder and attention deficit in middle childhood on offending and scholastic ability at age 13', *Journal of Child Psychology and Psychiatry* 34, 6, pp. 899–916.

Fergusson, D.M., Horwood, L.J. and Lynskey, M.T. (1994) 'The childhoods of multiple problem adolescents: a 15-year longitudinal study', *Journal of Child Psychology and Psychiatry* 35, 6, pp. 1,123–1,140.

Fitzherbert, K. (1997) 'Promoting inclusion: the work of the Pyramid Trust', *Emotional and Behavioural Difficulties* 2, 3, pp. 30–35.

Fortin, L. and Bigras, M. (1997) 'Risk factors exposing young children to behaviour problems', *Emotional and Behavioural Difficulties* 2, 1, pp. 2–14.

Fundudis, T. (1997) 'Single parents: risk or resource', *Child Psychology and Psychiatry Review* 2, 1, pp. 2–14.

Galloway, D. (1987) 'Disruptive behaviour in school: implications for teachers and other professionals', *Educational and Child Psychology* 4, 1, pp. 29–34.

Galloway, D., Ball, T., Blomfield, D. and Seyd, R. (1982) *Schools and Disruptive Pupils*, London, Longman.

Garner, P. (1993) 'Exclusions: the challenge to schools', *Support for Learning* 8, 3, pp. 99–103.

Gersch, I.S. and Nolan, A. (1994) 'Exclusions: what the children think', *Educational Psychology in Practice* 10, 1, pp. 35–42.

Gilham, B. (1984) 'School organisation and the control of disruptive incidents', in Frude, N. and Gault, H. (eds) *Disruptive Behaviour in Schools*, Chichester, John Wiley.

Gillborn, D. (1990) *Race, Ethnicity and Education*, London, Unwin Hyman.

Goodyer, I.M, Wright, C. and Altham, P.M.E. (1990) 'Recent achievements and adversities in anxious and depressed school age children', *Journal of Child Psychology and Psychiatry* 31, 7, pp. 1,063–1,078.

Gray, J. and Richer, J. (1988) *Classroom Responses to Disruptive Behaviour*, London, Macmillan.

Hanko, G. (1990) *Special Needs in Ordinary Classrooms: Supporting teachers*, Oxford, Basil Blackwell.

Hayden, C. (1997) *Children Excluded from Primary School*, Buckingham, Open University Press.

Heflinger, C.A. and Nixon, C.T. (eds) (1996) *Families and the Mental Health System for Children and Adolescents: Policy, services and research*, Thousand Oaks, CA, Sage.

Houlton, D. (1986) *Cultural Diversity in the Primary School*, London, Batsford.

Inner London Education Authority (ILEA) (1985) *Educational Opportunities for All: Report of the Fish Committee*, London, ILEA.

Joseph Rowntree Foundation (1997) *Breadline Britain in the 1990s*, York, Joseph Rowntree Foundation and London Weekend Television.

Kazdin, A.E., Holland, L., Crowley, M. and Breton, S. (1997) 'Barriers to Treatment Participation Scale: evaluation and validation in the context of child outpatient treatment', *Journal of Child Psychology and Psychiatry* 38, 8, pp. 1,051–1,062.

Laing, A.F. and Chazan, M. (1987) *Teachers' Strategies in Coping with Behaviour Difficulties in First Year Junior School Children*, Workshop Perspectives 2, Maidstone, Association of Workers for Maladjusted Children.

Lazar, I. and Darlington, R. (1982) *Lasting Effects of Early Education: A report of the Consortium for Longitudinal Studies*, Monographs of the Society for Research in Child Development, 47 (2–3, Serial No. 195).

Lovey, J. and Cooper, P. (1997) 'Positive alternatives to school exclusion: an empirical investigation', *Emotional and Behavioural Difficulties* 2, 3, pp. 12–22.

Luthar, S.S. (1993) 'Methodological and conceptual issues in research on childhood resilience', *Journal of Child Psychology and Psychiatry* 34, 4, pp. 441–454.

McGee, R., Silva, P.A. and Williams, S. (1984) 'Behaviour problems in a population of seven-year-old children: prevalence, stability and types of disorder – a research report', *Journal of Child Psychology and Psychiatry* 25, 2, pp. 251–260.

McGee, R., Williams, S., Bradshaw, J., Chapel, J.L., Robins, A. and Silva, P.A. (1985) 'The Rutter Scale for completion by teachers: factor structure and relationships with cognitive abilities and family adversity for a sample of New Zealand children', *Journal of Child Psychology and Psychiatry* 26, 5, pp. 729–739.

Mandel, H. (1997) *Conduct Disorder and Underachievement: Risk factors, assessment, treatment and prevention*, New York, John Wiley.

Maughan, B. and Garratt, K. (1994) 'Conduct disorder: the gender gap', *Association for Child Psychology and Psychiatry Review and Newsletter* 16, 6, pp. 277–282.

Merrett, F. and Wheldall, K. (1984) 'Classroom behaviour problems which junior school teachers find most troublesome', *Educational Studies* 10, 2, pp. 67–81.

Mosley, J. (1991) 'A circular response to the Elton Report', *Maladjustment and Therapeutic Education* 9, 3, pp. 136–142.

Mosley, J. (1993) *Turn Your School Around*, Wisbech, LDA.

National Association for Special Educational Needs (NASEN) Policy Options Group (1996) *Options for Partnership Between Health, Education and Social Services* (Seminar Paper 6), Tamworth, NASEN.

Office for Standards in Education (OFSTED) (1995) *Pupil Referral Units: The first twelve inspections*, London, HMSO.

Osborn, A.F. and Milbank, J.E. (1987) *The Effects of Early Education: A report from the Child Health and Education Study*, Oxford, Clarendon Press.

Parsons, C. (1995) *National Survey of LEAs' Policies and Procedures for the Identification of and Provision for Children Who are Out of School by Reason of Exclusion or Otherwise*, London, HMSO.

Parsons, C. and Howlett, K. (1996) 'Permanent exclusion from school: a case where society is failing its children', *Support for Learning* 11, 3, pp. 109–112.

Pomerantz, M. (1997) 'Youngest exclusion ever?', *British Psychological Society Division of Educational and Child Psychology Newsletter* 77, pp. 28–29.

Rennie, E. (1993) 'Behavioural support teaching: points to ponder', *Support for Learning* 8, 1, pp. 7–10.

Reynolds, D., Creemers, B.P.M., Nesselrodt, P.S., Schaffer, E.C., Stringfield, S. and Teddie, C. (1994) *Advances in School Effectiveness: Research and practice*, Oxford, Pergamon.

Richman, N., Stevenson, J. and Graham, P.J. (1982) *Pre-School to School: A behavioural study*, London, Academic Press.

Robins, L.N. (1991) 'Conduct disorder', *Journal of Child Psychology and Psychiatry* 32, 1, pp. 193–212.

Robinson, T. (1998) 'We don't create angels: the Bristol Primary Exclusion Project', *Educational Psychology in Practice* 14, 2, pp. 75–82.

Rossman, B.R.R. and Rosenberg, M.S. (1992) 'Family stress and functioning in children: the moderating effects of children's beliefs about their control over parental conflict', *Journal of Child Psychology and Psychiatry* 33, 4, pp. 699–715.

Rutter, M. (1967) 'A children's behaviour questionnaire for completion by teachers', *Journal of Child Psychology and Psychiatry* 8, 1, pp. 1–11.

Rutter, M. (1973) 'Why are London children so disturbed?', *Proc. Roy. Soc. Med.* 66, pp. 1,221–1,225.

Rutter, M. (1985) 'Family and school influences on behavioural development', *Journal of Child Psychology and Psychiatry* 26, 3, pp. 349–368.

Rutter, M. and Madge, N. (1976) *Cycles of Disadvantage: A review of research*, London, Heinemann.

Rutter, M., Tizard, J. and Whitmore, K. (eds) (1970) *Education, Health and Behaviour*, London, Longman.

Rutter, M., Cox, A., Tupling, C., Berger, M. and Yule, W. (1975) 'Attainment and adjustment in two geographical areas: the prevalence of psychiatric disorder', *British Journal of Psychiatry* 126, pp. 493–509.

Rutter, M., Yule, N., Berger, M., Yule, B., Morton, J. and Bagley, C. (1974) 'Children of West Indian immigrants: rates of behavioural deviance and of psychiatric disorder', *Journal of Child Psychology and Psychiatry* 15, 4, pp. 241–262.

Sammons, P., Hillman, J. and Mortimore, P. (1995) *Key Characteristics of Effective Schools: A review of school effectiveness research*, London, OFSTED.

Sanson, A., Oberklaid, F., Pedlow, R. and Prior, M. (1991) 'Risk indicators: assessment of infancy predictors of pre-school behavioural maladjustment', *Journal of Child Psychology and Psychiatry* 32, 4, pp. 609–626.

Scherer, M. (1990) 'Using consequences in class', in Scherer, M., Gersch, I. and Fry, L. (eds) *Meeting Disruptive Behaviour: Assessment, intervention and partnership*, London, Macmillan.

Shaw, D.S., Vondra, J.I., Hommerding, K.D., Keenan, K. and Dunn, M. (1994) 'Chronic family adversity and early child behaviour problems: a longitudinal study of low income families', *Journal of Child Psychology and Psychiatry* 35, 6, pp. 1,109–1,122.

Silver, H. and Silver, P. (1991) *An Educational War on Poverty: American and British policy-making 1960–1980*, Cambridge, Cambridge University Press.

Smith, D.J. (1995) 'Living conditions in the twentieth century', in Rutter, M. and Smith, D.J. (eds) *Psychosocial Disorders in Young People: Time trends and their causes*, Chichester, UK, John Wiley.

Social Exclusion Unit (1998) *Truancy and School Exclusion*, London, The Stationery Office.

Stevenson, J., Richman, N. and Graham, P. (1985) 'Behaviour problems and language abilities at three years and behavioural deviance at eight years', *Journal of Child Psychology and Psychiatry* 26, 2, pp. 215–230.

Stirling, M. (1992) 'How many pupils are being excluded?' *British Journal of Special Education* 19, 4, pp. 128–130.

Stirling, M. (1993) 'Second classes for a second class?', *Special Children* 66, pp. 15–18.

Stone, M. (1981) *The Education of the Black Child in Britain: The myth of multiracial education*, London, Fontana Press.

Sylva, K. (1992) 'The impact of pre-school education on later educational motivations and attributions', *Educational and Child Psychology* 9, 2, pp. 9–16.

Times Educational Supplement (1998) 26 June, pp. 8–9.

Topping, K. (1990) 'Disruptive pupils: changes in perception and provision', in Scherer, M., Gersch, I. and Fry, L. (eds) *Meeting Disruptive Behaviour: Assessment, intervention and partnership*, London, Macmillan.

Wheldall, K. and Glynn, T. (1989) *Effective Classroom Learning*, Oxford, Basil Blackwell.

Woodhead, C. (1998) 'Where do *you* stand?', *Times Educational Supplement*, 5 June, p. 17.

Part II

Meeting the Needs of the Disadvantaged

7 Recognizing Differences: Reinterpreting Family Involvement in Early Literacy

Eve Gregory

The current interpretation of family involvement in literacy is informed by research studies showing successful early reading by children whose parents adopt school literacy practices. Official education reports over the past 30 years have stressed the importance of regular story-reading by parents from early infancy and the absence of this practice has been used by teachers and governments alike to explain early reading difficulties. This chapter argues for the need to move beyond the paradigm of *parental* involvement in children's early literacy through *the story-reading practice* which presently informs home/school reading programmes. The first part of the chapter examines the literature informing the current model showing the marked absence of studies on the different literacy practices in which children from socially disadvantaged families engage which may be very different from those of their teachers. The second part of the chapter draws upon findings from research projects investigating the home, school and community reading practices in families in East London to explore the possibilities of an alternative approach.

Introduction

Although Shabbir's parents' own reading is now limited to the occasional newspaper, they pay for him to attend Bengali classes six times a week. His mother proudly pulls down a new satchel containing carefully covered books and a new pencil-case from a similar high cupboard to that in Nazma's house. By comparison, practice in English is very brief:

'He often brings home his reading book, but when he doesn't know a word, I tell him to ask the teacher ... Look, he has more sense than I do (said laughing as he corrects an English word his mother has read)... Let's leave it, leave it to the teacher, who can help the child more, because it's too hard for us.'

(Gregory, 1996a, p. 37)

What might family involvement in early literacy mean for parents who do not feel able to initiate their children into the types of reading which count in the eyes of the school? This question is important in Britain at the approach of the millennium since the New Labour Government's promise to raise significantly literacy standards at age 11[1] will make particular and new demands upon all parents. Voluntary home/school 'partnership in reading' schemes[2] are likely to be replaced by the introduction of compulsory home/school 'contracts'[3] whereby parents will now be officially obliged to engage in specific homework activities with their children. The urgency behind these stems largely from the publication of results of national attainment tests in literacy, numeracy and science at age 11 (SATs) from 1993 which, for the first time, have given written confirmation of young children's performance and have highlighted considerable differences in their achievement in poorer and wealthier areas. The form and content of new home/school agreements or 'contracts' will, therefore, be crucial if real advances in economically disadvantaged areas are to be made.

The interaction between 6-year-old Shabbir and his mother above begins to reveal the complexity of what family involvement in early literacy actually means. Can we say that providing access to literacy in Bengali counts as 'involvement' or not? Are her reasons for leaving English literacy to the teacher in school justified? Can she be expected to help her son (the eldest child) with his English reading homework when she, herself, is unable to read or understand the text? Paradoxically, what Shabbir's mother views as active involvement in her son's reading development (like many other families, she pays for his Bengali classes) is unlikely to count as such by the school. The same may also apply to monolingual English families whose involvement in their children's literacy may take very different forms from those currently recognized by the teachers in school.[4]

A number of questions will need to be considered before official contracts for family involvement in literacy are introduced. Will only 'school literacy' count as valid or will children be recognized as members of different groups and communities with a variety of different literacies? Who will count as valid mediators of literacy in children's lives and in what contexts? Will the syncretism of home and school literacies be recognized as valid in the classroom? This chapter sets out to examine assumptions made by the currently accepted paradigm of family involvement in early literacy and then goes on to suggest a set of alternative principles and their implications for future practice.

Family Involvement in Early Literacy: The Current Paradigm

Over the past two decades numerous studies from the English speaking world point to the advantages for young children of family involvement in their literacy development. However, their emphasis has always been firmly and almost exclusively upon *parents* working with children *in specific ways* and often using particular school-sanctioned materials. Current models of *parental involvement in reading* in the UK are generally based on the following assumptions:

Assumption 1: Parents need to perform school-devised activities using school materials and teaching methods. Successful parental involvement means that school reading and learning practices should be transmitted from school to home. Existing home and community practices are consequently unimportant for involvement.

A number of studies in the UK point to the successful transmission of reading practices from school to home (see Hannon, 1995 for a summary of these). Studies on the lack of parental involvement by lower social class parents during the 1970s (Newson and Newson, 1977) coupled with evidence of unsatisfactory reading standards by their children (DES, 1975) were also used to support a transmissionist argument; that improved performance might be achieved through involvement in school practices. A number of research studies and practical classroom projects detail particularly the improved achievements of children from lower social class backgrounds when their parents learn and take over school practices (Hewison and Tizard, 1980; Tizard et al., 1982; Hannon and Weinberger, 1994). The assumption that only school reading practices count as valid is also furthered by research suggesting that a certain type of reading will be important to which 'non-school-oriented' families may not have access at home (see Assumption 4).

A transmissionist model is also informed by a number of 'family literacy' programmes taking place in the USA. These aim to target the poor literacy skills of both parent and child and often comprise workshops where parents practise how to read with their children (summarized in Nickse, 1993). Nevertheless, these have been countered by considerable evidence from longitudinal ethnographic studies detailing the *different* but nevertheless extensive literacy practices taking place in non-school-oriented families of both American (Heath, 1983; Anderson and Stokes, 1984) and immigrant origin (see Assumption 2 below). Arguing against a transmissionist approach, Auerbach (1989) has proposed a socio-contextual model where teachers ask: 'What strengths exist in the family and how can schools build upon them?'. Some studies detail practical projects conducted jointly by university and school staff which attempt this (Moll et al., 1992; Gallimore and Goldenberg, 1993). Similar projects are still unusual in the UK partly owing to the lack of tradition of collaborative work between anthropologists or other university-based staff and teachers and partly due to a lack of funding for longitudinal ethnographic studies. However, evidence emerging from studies on the Gujarati-speaking community in Leicester (Martin-Jones et al., 1995) and the Cantonese-speaking communities in Northampton and Reading (Edwards, 1995; Gregory, 1996a) shows a similar variety and wealth of practices with the difference that even *very young children* are participating in extensive formal literacy classes outside the mainstream school. The assumption, therefore, that the school has nothing to learn from these and that only school practices are valid for home reading programmes must be seriously questioned.

Assumption 2: The same home reading programmes are suitable whatever linguistic background, monolingual or bilingual, children may come from. Parents should be capable of helping their children to complete work whether or not they read English.

Researchers in the UK have generally shown a reluctance to recognize cultural differences in the learning practices of minority group families. A number of factors might be responsible for this. Since the debate on linguistic and cognitive 'deficit' or 'difference' (Bernstein, 1971; Labov, 1972), researchers and teachers have been anxious to emphasize *similarities* rather than differences in language use in the homes of different social classes (Wells, 1981; Tizard and Hughes, 1984). A second reason may well stem from the strong British tradition of *child-centredness* in early-years education which is focused on the child as *individual* rather than a member of a cultural or ethnic group. Finally, recent government policy in the UK stresses the need to promote a 'common culture' (Tate, 1995) which will iron out cultural differences between groups. This aim is practically reinforced by the English national curriculum (DfE, 1995) which fails to acknowledge the learning practices of different minority groups. 'Equality of opportunity', a promise which is made in the Education Act of 1988, is currently interpreted as 'the same' provision. In practice, this means that families not benefiting from the 'equal opportunity' provided are viewed in terms of linguistic, cognitive or cultural deficit. Such a narrow definition of culture ignores the multiple pathways to literacy shown by both adults and children from minority groups in western societies (Baynham, 1995; Luke and Kale, 1997).

As a consequence, teachers in the UK are unable to draw upon the large body of studies on the literacy and learning practices of different cultural groups as their colleagues in the USA. Here teachers benefit from a tradition of research investigating continuities and discontinuities of home and school learning practices (Scollon and Scollon, 1981; Heath, 1983; Duranti and Ochs, 1996) as well as work available on the learning styles of different cultural groups and the effect of the knowledge of these on teaching styles (Michaels, 1986). Nevertheless, some recent studies in the UK are beginning to reveal the rich variety of literacy practices of minority groups which may remain unknown to their children's teachers (Martin-Jones et al., 1996; Gregory, 1996a).

Assumption 3: Home reading programmes are for parental involvement not wider family or community participation.

Current home reading programmes assume *parental* involvement rather than involvement by the wider family or community in young children's reading. However, the role of siblings in children's learning has been the subject of various research studies; some reveal how young children learn social and emotional skills (Dunn, 1989) and cognitive skills (Cicerelli, 1976) from older siblings. Others show how in non-western societies older siblings are often culture brokers who may be as influential or more influential than parents in socializing young children (Whiting and Edwards, 1988; Rogoff, 1990). Recent studies are beginning to highlight the special role which may be played by older siblings in linguistic minority families where parents do not speak the new language (Tharp and Gallimore, 1988; Zukow, 1989; McQuillan and Tse, 1995) and to suggest that the ways in which children learn from older siblings in the home environment may have implications for school learning. The role played by grandparents in home literacy teaching may also be significant in closely-knit families (Padmore, 1994; Williams, 1997), likewise other family members, such as uncles, aunts and older cousins or friends in the widest sense. These studies problematize the notion that parents will be the exclusive caregivers and 'teachers' in families of all backgrounds.

Assumption 4: The story-reading practice between parent and young child as it takes place in western school-oriented homes provides 'enjoyment' and 'fun' and is the most valuable preparation for children's early literacy development. Although children may participate in other practices at home and in the community, these do not initiate children into crucial patterns for school success.

Official education reports since the 1970s have little doubt as to the precise material and form necessary for these early reading experiences:

> ...the best way to prepare the very young child for reading is to hold him on your lap and read aloud to him stories he likes, over and over again...We believe that a priority need is... to help parents recognize the value of sharing the experience of books with their children.
>
> (DES, 1975, p. 7.2)

The official view that 'Babies need books' and that it is the duty of parents to provide these has changed little in later decades; during the 1980s the directive states clearly that 'parents should read books with children from their earliest days, read aloud to them and talk about the stories they have enjoyed together' (DES/Welsh Office, 1989, 2.3) and very recently, we read that parents of the very youngest children should support learning through 'reading and sharing books' (SCAA, 1996, p. 7).

These official directives are drawn from findings from a number of longitudinal studies which show how a familiarity with written narrative and story-reading promote cognitive and linguistic growth as well as preparing children for school literacy (Dombey, 1983; Fox, 1988). Others go further to suggest that the early reading difficulties experienced by some children may result generally from their narrative inexperience (Wells, 1987) or, more specifically, through their lack of knowledge of when and how to provide 'what' explanations when required (Heath, 1983). Studies on the type of reading taking place during Qur'anic classes (Wagner, 1994) are not generally viewed as relevant to the British school context. However, whilst not denying the importance of experience of written narrative as a preparation for school, some researchers point to additional factors for early reading success, especially in socially disadvantaged areas. Tizard et al. (1988) maintain that children's knowledge of the alphabet at school entry is an important determinant for achievement at age 7 and Gregory (1993) argues that early success hinges on a child's ability to work out the cultural rules of classroom reading lessons.

A result of the current paradigm of *parental involvement in early literacy* means that it is generally assumed that all children should enter school in possession of the same 'cultural capital' (Bourdieu, 1977) of the English language, culture and learning styles, represented by a familiarity with written stories imparted by the parent at home. Little attention has been given to families who do not share these ways of life. Yet paradoxically, it is precisely those parents whom the government wants most to become involved in school learning. Paradoxically also, it is likely to be these parents who view formal English teaching to be the role of the teacher in school. This may be particularly true for newly arrived immigrant families. A survey conducted in 1991 by the University of Lancaster 'Bangladeshi Parents and Education in Tower Hamlets' (Tomlinson and Hutchinson, 1991) conducted with 53 families found that although 93 per cent of the parents they interviewed reported receiving books home from school, only 40 per cent of mothers and 50 per cent of fathers said they felt able to use these with their children. Their reasons for not doing so fell into two categories:

1   an inability to speak English: 'My English is not good enough … We can't do this, it is too difficult.' (p. 21)
2   the belief that it is the teacher's job to teach the children to read in English – especially knowing how little English they spoke (71 per cent judged their oral English to be either non-existent or poor and only 33 per cent claimed they were able to read or write in English as opposed to 80 per cent who were literate in Bengali).

One reason explaining the lack of involvement by parents may have been the stress placed upon *parents reading to children* which has meant that children are likely to take home books which depend upon the ability of the parent to understand and read the English text to the child. Coupled with the assumption that everyone should understand both the theory and practice of story-reading, teachers may well be asking many monolingual English and limited English speaking parents to do the impossible without actually explaining how and why they should do it. It is, therefore, understandable that parents may feel both disempowered or resentful of what is requested of them (Gregory et al., 1993).

In what ways might this discussion inform future literacy contracts? The second part of this chapter outlines key principles behind an alternative paradigm of family involvement in literacy and their implications for practitioners in devising home/school literacy programmes.

Recognizing Differences: Some Key Principles

The second part of this chapter outlines principles and practical implications for future family literacy involvement which stress the recognition of *diversity and contrasts* through experience of a number of different reading practices (involving different purposes, materials and methods), taking place with a variety of *guiding lights* (Padmore, 1994) or *mediators* of literacy and a *dynamism and syncretism* of home and school learning practices. Evidence upon which these principles are based are drawn from development projects and research studies taking place in the USA (Heath, 1983; Moll et al., 1992; Au, 1993; Duranti and Ochs, 1996; Volk, 1998), Australia (Freebody et al., 1995; Cairney and Ruge, 1998) and particularly from an ongoing research and development project taking place in Spitalfields, East London (Gregory et al., 1996; Gregory and Williams, forthcoming).[5] Each of the above projects provide detailed insights into the literacy practices taking place in different communities of economically disadvantaged groups together with accounts of classroom practice showing ways in which family involvement might take this knowledge as a starting-point. Data from the Spitalfields project is used to illustrate the practical implications of each principle below.

Principle 1: Recognize and acknowledge the variety of literacies and 'funds of knowledge' in the lives of children's and their families as practised through home and community activities.

Hasna:	… I didn't read *Winnie-the-Pooh* or *The Jungle Book* or anything like that. You know, if I speak to a lot of my white friends, they were really into *Winnie-the-Pooh*. It was an integral part of their bed-time stories. You know, the concept of a bed-time story didn't exist in my family.
Interviewer:	Would you have Bengali stories read to you?
Hasna:	No. It depends on the dynamics of your family unit. Some families do, some don't. It's got nothing to do with the nationality of a family. And I didn't have any *Winnie-the-Pooh* stories or their Bengali equivalent. So Enid Blyton I read …

(Hasna, aged 23 who grew up and was educated
in Spitalfields, East London and who has since gained
a higher degree from London University)

The absence of bedtime story-reading is a common factor uniting participants in ethnographic studies on economically disadvantaged communities across the USA (Heath, 1983; Anderson and Stokes, 1984; Duranti and Ochs, 1996), Australia (Freebody et al., 1995; Cairney and Rouge, 1998) and the UK (Minns, 1990; Gregory, 1996b). Nevertheless, families in all these studies took part in a wide range of reading practices. Table 7.1 reveals the scope and nature of reading in the lives of thirteen 5 year old children (6 monolingual English and seven bilingual Bangladeshi British children) in two adjacent schools in Spitalfields, East London. These show clearly how the nature of the reading activities differed in the groups as well as between both groups and the school.

However, in spite of differences between the monolingual English and the Bangladeshi British community, there were a number of common factors. Significantly, both groups of children spent considerably longer engaged in 'non-homework' reading activities at home and in the community than in work specifically sent from school. Both viewed reading primarily as a group rather than an individual activity (this was particularly so for the Bangladeshi British children). Both viewed formal 'homework' (community language or religious class or work sent from school) as a serious activity which involved repetition, practice and (for the Bangladeshi British children) a test before it was judged to have been satisfactorily carried out.

Insight into the literacy practices of individual school communities is important for practitioners if a principal aim is to build upon the strengths of families rather than exploiting their weaknesses. Evidence from the Spitalfields project shows that, for this community, 'school-type reading' and *homework* are serious rather than 'fun'. This has been reflected by readers from different generations: 'I used my reading for learning. I went to evening classes. Then I had to pass exams for gardening ... ' (Annie, 82); ' ... I worked out that if you read a lot of books it improves your learning anyway. And it did ... ' (Hasna, 23).

Recognition of home and community literacies means deciding whether a variety of literacy materials in different languages which are available to children will be considered 'valid' or will be used in home or school reading programmes. Further, it means looking carefully at the availability and cost of certain reading materials, whether or not families prefer to buy or borrow, as well as examining how far both content and language are accessible to parents with limited skills in written English. It also means examining different learning styles and patterns of interaction used as families 'teach' young children. Some parents in the Spitalfields project looked back on very different methods from those used currently in English schools: 'The teacher would show us how to write letters and make sounds. We also had a private tutor and he would guide our hand with his to help our handwriting ... ' (Louthfer's mother in Gregory, 1996a, p. 40).

Finally, and highlighted by the experience of Louthfer's mother, it means understanding that *parents* may not always consider themselves equipped to

Table 7.1 Children's out of school literacy activities

(a) Bangledeshi British children

Type of practice	Context	Participants	Purpose	Scope	Materials	Role of child
Qur'anic class	Formal: in classrooms or someone's living room	Group of up to 30 mixed age-range	Religious: to read and learn the Qur'an	Approx. 7 hours per week	Raiel (wooden book stand). Preparatory primers or Qur'an	Child listens and repeats (individually or as group). Practises and is tested
Bengali class	Formal: in classrooms or someone's living room	Group of mixed age range. Can be children of one family up to group of 30	Cultural: to learn to read, understand and write standard Bengali	Approx. 6 hours per week	Primers, exercise books, pens	Child listens and repeats (individually or as group). Practises and is tested
Reading with older siblings	Informal: at home	Dyad: child and older sibling	'Homework': to learn to speak and read English	Approx. 3 hours per week	English school books	Child repeats, echoes, predicts and finally answers comprehension questions
Videos/Televsion	Informal: at home	Family group	Pleasure/entertain-ment		TV in English. Videos (often in Hindi)	Child watches and listens. Often listens to and joins in discussions. Sings songs from films

Table 7.1 (continued)

(b) English monolingual children

Type of practice	Context	Participants	Purpose	Scope	Materials	Role of Child
Playing school	Informal: at home	Group or individual	Play		Blackboard, books, writing materials	Child imitates teacher and/or pupils
PACT (parents and children together: home reading scheme	Informal: at home	Dyad: parent/child	Homework: to improve child's reading		School reading book	Child reads and is corrected by parent using 'scaffolding' or 'modelling' strategies
Comics, fiction, non-fiction	Informal: at home	Individual or dyad (parent or grandparent/child)	Pleasure		Variety of comics, fiction, non-fiction books	Child as 'expert' with comics or books; as interested learner reading adult non-fiction, magazines etc.
Drama class	Formal	Group	Pleasure and to learn skill	2 hours per week	Books: poetry and plays	Child performs in group; recites as individual
Computers	Informal	Individual or in dyad with friend or sibling	Pleasure		Computer games	Child as expert
Video/Television	Informal	Family group or entertainment	Pleasure/enter-tainment		TV/videos	Child as questioner

Source: Gregory and Williams, 1998

teach their children this particular skill and prefer to look to other mediators of literacy in the community for guidance and help.

Principle 2: Understand and Support the Value of Different Mediators of Literacy or 'Guiding Lights' in Children's Literacy Development.

> Like many of the children he (Louthfer) rocks to and fro to the sound of the voices. Children do this because they are encouraged to develop a harmonious voice; they are told Allah listens to His servants and is pleased if time is taken to make the verse sound meaningful. The old man's wife takes the children who have already started the Qu'ran into a separate room, so she can hear the recitations clearly. She comments, 'English is very important for this life. But Arabic is required for the life hereafter, which is eternal. Therefore, it must be given greatest importance ... Or else, how can our children know?'
>
> (Gregory, 1996a, p. 41)

In contrast with the current emphasis on the responsibility of the *parent* as story-provider and reader, childhood initiation into literacy may be seen by many families as a *collaborative group activity* whereby the cultural knowledge of generations is passed on through a whole variety of mediators and methods. Mediators may be within the family as grandparents (Padmore, 1994; Luke and Kale, 1997; Williams, 1997) or siblings (Volk, 1997; Gregory, 1997); or in the wider community as friends (Long, 1997) or aunts (Duranti and Ochs, 1996), clubs and libraries (Gregory, 1999) or religious and community classes (Wagner, 1994).

Mediators in the Community

Perhaps the most significant mediator of childhood literacy in the outside school lives of both young Bangladeshi British and older Jewish participants in the Spitalfields project were their community and religious classes. For the former group, this meant up to twelve hours per week spent at Bengali and/or Qur'anic classes. Although the role of religious classes on the literacy development of children has generally received little attention, studies undertaken (see Zinsser, 1986 and Gregory, 1994) detail ways in which children learn to read different scripts using a variety of methods plus a set of procedural rules (Street and Street, 1995) on how to behave during literacy events.

Methods of teaching during classes conform strictly to the pattern 'Demonstration, Practice, Test'. A typical excerpt shows what this might look like in practice as five-year-old Shuma reads at her Qur'anic class which takes place at her neighbour's house:

Teacher:	Read this, Shuma
Shuma:	Alif, bah, tah, sayh, hae ...
Teacher:	What was that? Say it again.
Shuma:	Alif, bah, tah, sayh, jim
Teacher:	Um, that's it, now carry on.
Shuma:	Jim – jim, hae, kae, d- (hesitates),
Teacher:	Dal – dal, *remember it and repeat.*
Shuma:	Dal, zal, rae, zae, sin, shin, swad, dwad,
Teacher:	(nods), What's next? Thoy, zoy,
Shuma:	Zoy, thoy,
Teacher:	No, no, *listen carefully.* Thoy, zoy,
Shuma:	(repeats)
Teacher:	Okay. Say it again from the beginning ...

(Gregory et al., 1996, Appendix 2)

Similar patterns of interaction occur during Bengali classes, drama, choral and other music lessons where accuracy is considered important. By contrast, some community mediators, such as librarians and other social club leaders may allow autonomy and encourage work in pairs where individuals, themselves, take the initiative. Such work corresponds more closely to reading which may take place with mediators other than parents at home.

Mediators of Literacy at Home

Various studies show young children reading with different family members who may have more time or may be better able to initiate children into school reading practices. Although an under-researched group, we know that grandparents play an important role in handing down cultural and linguistic knowledge of both the family and community through literacy practices (Luke and Kale, 1997; Williams, 1997). Friends at home may also be important for children entering a new linguistic community (Long, 1997). For first and second generation immigrants, older siblings are likely to become crucial mediators of literacy who play a substitute but very different role from that which parents may take in monolingual households. The Spitalfields project highlights ways in which siblings engage in extensive *homework activities* with young children (Gregory, 1998). Teaching strategies are characterized by a finely-tuned 'scaffolding' which is only very gradually removed. This scaffolding syncretizes strategies learned during Qur'anic and English classes. The older child at first allows repetition or echoing of one word (gave/gave; her/her; fishy/fishy; gifts/gifts) resulting in a very high number of fast and smooth exchanges; this 'scaffold' is gradually removed to allow prediction and text-based questions built more upon school-based strategies.

Teachers devising home/school agreements will need to consider carefully whether and in what ways homework schemes will take account of existing mediators of literacies in children's lives. If the role of older siblings is to be recognized, should they be asked to adopt school teaching strategies or remain as cultural and linguistic 'bridges' between children's different lives? How far do children's clubs and activities 'count' as valid *homework* if it is out of control of the school? What might be the role of *homework clubs* as a literacy domain?

Principle 3: Recognize the syncretism between home/community and school learning in classrooms and school homework clubs.

> I went to drama club … It was brilliant … It was the beginning … 'cos I went into entertainment. One of our teachers is a famous producer now … I did my first play when I was 10 and a half. It was called *The Italian Straw Hat*. It's a very old Italian play. I'd been there only three months and I was saying 'I can do that. No problem … '
>
> (Andrew, now aged 40, reflecting on living in
> Spitalfields as a child in Gregory, 1999).

Clubs, community classes, libraries and siblings are all recalled by participants in the Spitalfields research as 'bridges' between home and school learning. Interaction between siblings in linguistic minority families reveals a syncretism whereby familiar strategies from both community and school reading classes are blended to form a dynamic literacy practice presently regarded as *homework* by the children. Studies from the USA (Au, 1993; Heath, 1983; Moll et al., 1992) and Australia (Cairney and Ruge, 1998) show how home/school literacy schemes are most successful when teachers are knowledgeable about the strengths of their communities and encourage a syncretism of practices in their classrooms. In a study of innovative home/school partnerships in four multi-ethnic schools in Australia, Cairney and Ruge (1998) discuss the role of children themselves as mediators between home and school. Bruner (1986) has referred to the 'joint culture creation' needed for learning which recognizes that every classroom community will be different and, as a consequence, every homework scheme will reflect this difference. Teachers in Britain might well consider the role of homework clubs in literacy development. Are they viewed as creating a dynamic new culture of learning which syncretizes home/school practices rather than seeking to recreate the established practices of classrooms? A practical classroom project describing one school's approach to family literacy involvement can be found in Gregory (1996b).

Summary and Conclusion

One also hears the claim, 'All children should be treated alike. There should be no discrimination.' It must be conceded that to overlook individual differences and cultural differences and to treat everyone as though they were the same, does, indeed, involve a lack of discrimination. Think about it. It certainly is not in the child's interest.

(Duquette, 1992, p. 14)

The term 'equality of opportunity' is at the core of the Education Reform Act passed in Britain in 1988 and is central to the various documents emerging from it. It is reflected in the National Curriculum Council's initial promise (NCC, 1988, p. 4) that it 'will be taking account of ethnic and cultural diversity and ensuring that the curriculum provides equal opportunities for all pupils, regardless of ethnic origin or gender'. The question addressed in this chapter has been: 'In what ways might equality of opportunity be provided for pupils whose parents are not familiar with school literacy practices?' Do we start by 'teaching' parents school literacy 'rules' (e.g. storybook-sharing etc.) or do we begin by learning about children's existing outside-school literacy knowledge and skills? Obviously, it is crucial that all young children become members of school literacies as early as possible; but may it be that these are best introduced explicitly by teachers within the culture of each individual classroom?

Seminal work during the early 1980s in Liberia was revolutionary in showing through tests how cognitive skills are clearly linked to a familiarity with specific cultural practices (Scribner and Cole, 1981). This chapter argues that if real equality is to be promoted, we surely need to know which cultural practices young children know about both before and outside school. An approach which takes this knowledge by practitioners as a starting-point means reinterpreting family involvement in early literacy to take account of existing literacy knowledge in families, to recognize the vital role played by other mediators of literacy than parents and to be excited by the syncretism as children blend languages and literacies from home, community and school. Only then can we lay some claim to attempting to provide the equality which has been promised.

Acknowledgements

This research was supported by the Economic and Social Research Council, 1994–1995 (R000 22 1186) and a Leverhulme Research Fellowship in 1997. I should like to acknowledge the help of Ann Williams and Nasima Rashid, research officers on the ESRC project for the data collected as well as the families and teachers participating in the Spitalfields project.

Notes

1   Through a policy of 'nil tolerance of failure' the government aims to ensure that 80 per cent of all 11-year-olds achieve a level 4 or above in national literacy tests (average or above) before passing to secondary education before the end of their current term of office.
2   See Hannon (1995) for an overview of schemes currently taking place in the UK.

3   There is a feeling amongst some LEAs in socially disadvantaged areas (e.g. Tower Hamlets in East London) that the term 'agreement' is more appropriate.
4   See Williams (1997) and Williams and Gregory (forthcoming) for examples of family involvement in literacy in monolingual families in East London.
5   This research aims to investigate the question: 'How have young children in Spitalfields throughout the twentieth century set about learning to read in their homes, schools and communities?' Separate phases of this study have addressed different issues: Phases 1 and 2 (1992–1996) (funded by Goldsmiths College, The Paul Hamlyn Foundation and the Economic and Social Research Council) examined the literacy histories and current reading practices in seven Bangladeshi British and six monolingual English families whose 5-year-old children attended two neighbouring schools. The questions investigated were: 'What is the scope and nature of reading practices taking place in the children's lives, and how far do children transfer learning strategies from home to school and vice versa?'

References

Anderson, A.B. and Stokes, S.J. (1984) 'Social and institutional influences on the development and practice of literacy', in Goelman, H., Oberg, A. and Smith, F. (eds) *Awakening to Literacy*, London, Heinemann Educational.

Au, K. (1993) *Literacy Instruction in Multicultural Settings*, Fort Worth, Harcourt Brace.

Auerbach, E.R. (1989) 'Toward a social contextual approach to family literacy', *Harvard Educational Review* 59, 2, pp. 165–181.

Baynham, M. (1995) *Literacy Practices: Investigating literacy in social contexts*, London, Longman.

Bernstein, B. (1971) 'A socio-linguistic approach to socialisation with some reference to educability', in Hymes, D. and Gumperz, J. (eds) *Directions in Sociolinguistics*, New York, Rinehart & Winston.

Bourdieu, P. (1977) *Outline of a Theory of Practice*, Cambridge, Cambridge University Press.

Bruner, J. (1986) *Actual Minds, Possible Worlds*, Cambridge, MA, Harvard University Press.

Cairney, T. and Rouge, J. (1998) *Community Literacy Practices and Schooling: Toward effective support for students*, University of Western Sydney Nepean, Department of Employment, Education, Training and Youth Affairs

Cicerelli, V.G. (1976) 'Mother–child and sibling–sibling interactions on a problem solving task', *Child Development* 47, pp. 588–596.

Department for Education (DfE) (1995) *English in the National Curriculum*, London, HMSO.

Department of Education and Science (DES) (1975) *A Language for Life: Report of the committee of inquiry appointed by the Secretary of State for Education and Science under the chairmanship of Sir Alan Bullock*, London, HMSO (The Bullock Report).

Department of Education and Science (DES)/Welsh Office (1989) *English for Ages 5–16. Proposals of the Secretary of State for Education and Science and the Secretary of State for Wales*, London, Central Office for Information (The Cox Report).

Dombey, H. (1983) 'Learning the language of books' in Meek, M. (ed.) *Opening Moves*, Bedford Way Papers 17, Institute of Education, University of London.

Dunn, J. (1989) 'The family as an educational environment in the pre-school years' in Desforges, C.W. (ed.) *Early Childhood Education*, The British Journal of Educational Psychology Monograph Series no. 4, Scottish Academic Press.

Duquette, G. (1992) 'The home culture of minority children in the assessment and development of their first language', *Language, Culture and Curriculum* 51, pp. 11–23.

Duranti, A. and Ochs, E. (1996) 'Syncretic literacy in a Samoan American family' in Resnick, L., Saljo, R. and Pontecorvo, C. (eds) *Discourse, Tools and Reasoning*, Berlin, Springer Verlag.

Edwards, V. (1995) *Reading in Multilingual Classrooms*, Reading and Language Information Centre, Reading, University of Reading.

Fox, C. (1988) 'Poppies will make them grant' in Meek, M. and Mills, C. (eds) *Language and Literacy in the Primary School*, Lewes, Falmer Press.

Freebody, P., Ludwig, C. and Gunn, S. (1995) *Everyday Literacy Practices in and Out of Schools in Low Socio-Economic Status Urban Communities: A descriptive and interpretive research program*, unpublished draft report.

Gallimore, R. and Goldenberg, C. (1993) 'Activity settings of early literacy: Home and school factors in children's emergent literacy' in Forman, E., Minick, N. and Stone, C.A. (eds) *Contexts for Learning*, New York, Oxford University Press.

Gregory, E. (1993) 'What counts as reading in the early years' classroom?', *British Journal of Educational Psychology* 63, pp. 213–229.

Gregory, E. (1994) 'Cultural assumptions and early years pedagogy: the effect of the home culture on children's reading in school', *Language, Culture and Curriculum* 7, 2, pp. 1–14.

Gregory, E. (1996a) *Making Sense of a New World: Learning to read in a second language*, London, Sage/Paul Chapman.

Gregory, E. (1996b) 'Learning from the community: a family literacy project in East London' in Wolfendale, S. and Topping, K. (eds) *Family Involvement in Literacy: Effective partnerships in education*, London, Cassell.

Gregory, E. (Ed) (1997) *One Child, Many Worlds: Early learning in multicultural communities*, London, Fulton.

Gregory, E. (1998) 'Siblings as Mediators of Literacy in Linguistic Minority Communities', *Language and Education: An international journal* 11,1, pp. 33–55.

Gregory, E. (1999) 'Myths of illiteracy: childhood memories of reading in London's East End', *Written Language and Literacies,* 12, 1, pp. 89–111.

Gregory, E. and Williams, A. (1998) 'Family literacy and children's learning strategies at home and at school', in Walford, G. and Massey, A. (eds) *Studies in Educational Ethnography*, vol. 1, Connecticut, JAI Press.

Gregory, E. and Williams, A. (forthcoming) *City Literacies: Learning to read across languages and cultures*, London, Routledge.

Gregory, E., Lathwell, J., Mace, J. and Rashid, N. (1993) *Literacy at Home and at School*, Literacy Research Group, Goldsmiths' College.

Gregory, E., Mace, J., Rashid, N. and Williams, A. (1996) *Family Literacy History and Children's Learning Strategies at Home and in School*, ESRC Final Report R 000 221186.

Hannon, P. (1995) *Literacy, Home and School: Research and practice in teaching literacy with parents*, London, Falmer Press.

Hannon, P. and Weinberger, J. (1994) 'Sharing ideas about pre-literacy with parents: working with parents to involve children in reading and writing at home in Sheffield' in Dombey, H. and Meek-Spencer, M. (eds) *First Steps Together: Home–school literacy in European contexts*, Stoke-on-Trent, Trentham Books.

Heath, S.B. (1983) *Ways With Words: Language, life and work in communities and class-rooms*, Cambridge, Cambridge University Press.

Hewison, J. and Tizard, J. (1980) 'Parental involvement and reading attainment', *British Journal of Educational Psychology* 50, pp. 209–215.

Labov, W. (1972) *Sociolinguistic Patterns*, Philadelphia, University of Philadelphia.

Long, S. (1997) 'Friends as teachers: the impact of peer interaction on the acquisition of a new language', in Gregory, E. (ed.) *One Child, Many Worlds: Early learning in multicultural communities*, London, Fulton.

Luke, A. and Kale, J. (1997) 'Learning through difference: cultural differences in early learning socialisation', in Gregory, E. (ed.) *One Child, Many Worlds: Early learning in multicultural communities*, London, Fulton.

Martin-Jones, M., Barton, D. and Saxena, M. (1996) *Multilingual Literacy Practices: Home, community and school*, ESRC Final Report, R 000 23 3833.

McQuillan, J. and Tse, L. (1995) 'Child language brokering in linguistic minority communities', *Language and Education* 9, 3, pp. 195–215.

Michaels, S. (1986) 'Narrative presentations: an oral preparation for literacy with 1st. graders', in Cook-Gumperz, J. (ed.) *The Social Construction of Literacy*, Cambridge, Cambridge University Press.

Minns, H. (1990) *Read It To Me Now!*, London, Virago Press.

Moll, L., Amanti, C., Neff, D. and Gonzalez, N. (1992) 'Funds of knowledge for teaching: using a qualitative approach to connect homes and classrooms', *Theory into Practice* 31, 2, pp. 132–141.

National Curriculum Council (1988) *Introducing the National Curriculum Council*, London, National Curriculum Council.

Newson, J. and Newson, E. (1977) *Perspectives on School at Seven Years Old*, London, Allen & Unwin.

Nickse, R. (1993) 'A typology of family and intergenerational literacy programmes: implications for evaluation', *Viewpoints* 15, pp. 34–40.

Padmore, S. (1994) 'Guiding Lights' in Hamilton, M., Barton, D. and Ivanic, R. (eds) *Worlds of Literacy*, Clevedon, Multilingual Matters.

Rashid, N. and Gregory, E. (1997) 'Learning to read, reading to learn: the importance of siblings in the language development of young bilingual children' in Gregory, E. (ed.) *One Child, Many Worlds: Early learning in multicultural communities*, London, Fulton.

Rogoff, B. (1990) *Apprenticeship in Thinking: Cognitive development in social contexts*, Oxford, Oxford University Press.

School Curriculum and Assessment Authority (SCAA) (1996) *Desirable Outcomes for Children's Learning on Entering Compulsory Education*, London, HMSO.

Scollon, R. and Scollon, B.K. (1981) *Narrative, Literacy and Face in Interethnic Communication*, Norwood, NJ, Ablex Publications.

Scribner, S. and Cole, M. (1981) *The Psychology of Literacy*, Cambridge, MA, Harvard University Press.

Street, B. and Street, J. (1995) 'The schooling of literacy' in Murphy, P., Selinger, M., Bourne, J. and Briggs, M. (eds) *Subject Learning in the Primary Curriculum*, London, Routledge.

Tate, N. (1995) Summing up speech at the International Conference on Teaching English as an Additional Language (SCAA) London, April 1995.

Tharp, R. and Gallimore, R. (1988) *Rousing Minds to Life: Teaching, learning and schooling in social context*, Cambridge, Cambridge University Press.

Tizard, B. and Hughes, M. (1984) *Young Children Learning*, London, Fontana.

Tizard, J, Schofield, W. and Hewison, J. (1982) 'Collaboration between teachers and parents in assisting children's reading', *British Journal of Educational Psychology* 52, pp. 1–15.

Tizard, B., Blatchford, P., Burke, J., Farquhar, C. and Plewis, I. (1988) *Young Children at School in the Inner-City*, London, Lawrence Erlbaum Ass.

Tomlinson, S. and Hutchinson, S. (1991) *Bangladeshi Parents and Education in Tower Hamlets*, Research Report, Advisory Centre for Education, University of Lancaster.

Volk, D. (1997) 'Continuities and Discontinuities: teaching and learning in the home and school of a Puerto-Rican five-year-old' in Gregory, E. (ed.) *One Child, Many Worlds: Early learning in multicultural communities*, London, Fulton.

Wagner, D.A. (1994) *Literacy, Culture and Development: Becoming literate in Morocco*, Cambridge, Cambridge University Press.

Wells, G. (1981) *Learning Through Interaction*, Cambridge, Cambridge University Press.

Wells, G. (1987) *The Meaning Makers*, London, Hodder & Stoughton.

Whiting, B. and Edwards, C. (1988) *Children of Different Worlds: The formation of social behaviour*, Harvard University Press.

Williams, A. (1997) 'Investigating literacy in London: three generations of readers in an East End family' in Gregory, E. (ed.) *One Child, Many Worlds: Early learning in multicultural communities*, London, Fulton.

Williams, A. and Gregory, E. (1999) 'London literacies: home and school reading practices in two East London communities' in Leung, C. and Tosi, A. (eds) *Rethinking Language Education*, London, CILT.

Zinsser, S. (1986) 'For the Bible tells me so: teaching children in a fundamentalist church' in Schieffelin, B. and Gilmore, P. (eds) *The Acquisition of Literacy: Ethnographic perspectives*, New Jersey, Ablex Publications.

Zukow, P.G. (1989) 'Siblings as effective socialising agents: evidence from central Mexico' in Zukow, P.G. (ed.) *Sibling Interactions Across Cultures: Theoretical and methodological issues*, New York, Springer Verlag.

8 Early Childhood Education to Ensure a 'Fair Start' for All

Kathy Sylva

Research evidence is mounting which shows that early intervention in the lives of young children and families living in disadvantaged communities can prevent later school failure, social exclusion and delinquency. In many rigorous research studies early childhood programmes which are of high quality have been shown to prevent children falling behind at school and taking up deviant pathways. Research from the US and Europe is described which demonstrates that pre-school education (in the period 3–6 years) can provide a firm foundation for later school learning. It also shows that the curriculum of early childhood programmes makes a difference: children who attend formal didactic programmes in their pre-school years enter school at a disadvantage, with lower self-esteem, more anxiety and a poorer preparation for literacy. Moreover, children whose pre-school curriculum was very formal are more likely to become anti-social adults, with poor educational and employment records. It is concluded that early childhood education can help prevent academic failure and social problems – but only if it is based on 'informal, play-based' pedagogy. Active curricula provide the intellectual foundation for later learning while at the same time promoting the child's commitment to the classroom community.

Introduction

Schools are the natural environment for preventing disadvantage; the vast majority of children attend schools and it is within them that they develop the skills and attitudes which propel them to their eventual 'life destinations'. Research evidence is now accumulating which suggests that early intervention against disadvantage and exclusion is more successful than later intervention and certainly more effective than hoping for 'reversal' at the end of primary school or even adolescence (Durlak, 1995; Barnett and Escobar, 1990).

It is argued in this chapter that early childhood education, if it is of high quality, can prevent the school failure and problems of adjustment which are associated with social disadvantage. 'Prevention is a multidisciplinary science that draws upon basic and applied research conducted in many fields, such as public health, epidemiology, education, medicine, and community development'

(Durlak, 1995). Primary prevention consists of intervention with normal populations to avoid the development of the problem, such as low school attainment or even school drop-out. Secondary prevention consists of interventions during the early development of the difficulties before they turn into full-blown failures or disorders. The aim of tertiary prevention is to reduce the prevalence of failure or disorder. When early education, defined here as education before and immediately after the start of statutory schooling, lessens the risk of failure in disadvantaged groups then it functions as primary prevention.

Who is at Risk of School Failure and What Can be Done About it?

> The best single predictor of academic performance before a child reaches elementary school is the family's socioeconomic level, with many more children from the lowest income levels doing poorly. Once in elementary school, however, academic performance becomes a better predictor of subsequent performance. Retention at grade at any time between kindergarten and eighth grade is associated with later poor academic and personal/social outcomes regardless of a child's gender, race, or socioeconomic status. (Meisels and Liaw, 1993) The presence of early academic performance predicts not only later learning problems but also subsequent behavioural and social difficulties, special education placement, and dropping out of school. Although not all pupils display the same developmental sequence, the progression of serious academic problems often proceeds through a four-stage sequence: from early academic problems, to grade retention, to special education placement, to dropping out of school or graduation with low levels of academic achievement.
>
> (Durlak, 1995, p. 44)

Despite parental hopes, many children do not outgrow their learning difficulties. Once children begin to fall behind academically, they rarely catch up with their peers. The longer learning problems are ignored, the more difficult it is to reverse them and only intense and sustained interventions like Reading Recovery can get the child back on course (see Slavin, 1995; Sylva and Hurry, 1995). For reasons reviewed elsewhere in this volume (see Chapters 1 and 10 in this book) it is widely agreed that children from low income homes are at a disadvantage compared to wealthier peers in their capacity to adjust to and master the curriculum of primary school. There have been hundreds of educational interventions before the start of schooling and the vast majority of these have been aimed at children from low income families. This chapter begins by reviewing the research literature on early childhood interventions before going on to speculate on the reasons successful programmes 'work' and the implications of such effectiveness for the early childhood curriculum in the UK.

Evidence from Meta-Analysis in the US

There is general agreement about the immediate effects of early childhood programmes such as Head Start. Head Start is a community-based pre-school programme which features parental involvement. In many (but not all) research studies children's participation in Head Start immediately before school had a significant short-term positive impact on academic and social development (McKey et al., 1985; Lazar and Darlington, 1982a). The major doubts about the efficacy of Head Start do not concern short-term effects early in school but rather the long-term impact. Although many authors praise the parental and community involvement which is so central to Head Start (Zigler and Styfco, 1993) Head Start programmes vary in quality from state to state and even city to city. In the face of such diversity, few large scale research studies have found lasting, positive outcomes.

A series of meta-analyses carried out on 'experimental' early childhood interventions provides a more optimistic picture. A meta-analysis of the effects of a small group of pre-school programmes which were of excellent quality was carried out by Lazar and Darlington (1982b). The authors limited their selective meta-analysis to pre-school programmes planned from the start as evaluation studies. Each individual project had an adequate sample size, used norm-referenced assessment tests to establish outcomes, assessed outcomes for comparison/control groups, and follow up of children well beyond school entry. By these strict criteria the results of eleven carefully monitored programmes were subjected to meta-analysis, a statistical exercise which enables researchers to compare the size of effect across many different studies. These early intervention programmes represent a wide variety of interventions, almost all aimed at disadvantaged children and all of high quality and often on a small-scale. Lazar and his colleagues compiled information on education and employment of more than 2,000 individuals who had participated in early intervention programmes when they were young. In addition, the researchers carried out interviews with the young adults at age 19 and their families. Results from the meta-analysis showed that participation in excellent, cognitively oriented pre-school programmes was associated with later school competence and avoidance of assignment to 'special' education. Interviews revealed that the individuals who had participated in the intervention programme talked to their parents more about 'life in school' (including homework) and the parents themselves developed higher aspirations for employment of their children. This research suggested that the long-term effects of early childhood education lay not with IQ gains but with children remaining in mainstream education and developing positive views of themselves and their futures. Note however that these high quality programmes were set up for 'demonstration' and 'research' – making generalization to all early childhood programmes impossible.

In 1990 Barnett and Escobar published a review of early interventions. They added to the original eleven studies cited in Lazar and Darlington six further studies on large-scale, public pre-school programmes, with follow-up periods ranging from 3 to 12 years. They also came to the conclusion that early childhood interventions had significant long-term effects on the following outcomes: assignment to special needs education, retention at grade and school drop-out. Across the 17 programmes reviewed by Barnett and Escobar, 48.5 per cent fewer 'intervention' children were placed in special education classes, 32 per cent fewer were retained in grade, and there were 26 per cent fewer drop-outs.

The effects of early childhood programmes on school grades are not so clear. Barnett and Escobar (1990) and Sylva (1994) argue that the long-term impact of early childhood education is not easily found in school grades but in outcomes in which cognitive and social/emotional characteristics interact in their contribution to judgements made by professionals, such as assignment to special needs provision.

Slavin and his colleagues (Slavin et al., 1994) took a different analytic strategy to those who carried out the two meta-analyses described above. Using 'best evidence synthesis' they identified successful programmes which included those identified above but added some new ones as well. These include the Milwaukee Project, the Carolina Abecedarian Project, the Family Development Research Programme, and the Parent–Child Development Center. From this large list of research studies, including many aimed at very young children, Slavin concluded that high quality early childhood intervention was effective at preparing disadvantaged children for school entry. In addition he found that the more successful programmes were interventions that combined several 'strands' of intervention, involved intensive participation by children and families and lasted for a substantial number of years. It was particularly important to carry out the intervention close to school entry, or, for interventions aimed at very young children, to implement 'top-up' near to school entry.

The High/Scope Research: Comparing 'Intervention' Children to a Control Group

The most carefully controlled of all early intervention research was the Perry Pre-School Project, later called High/Scope. This curriculum is based on Piagetian theory, but also includes intensive parent participation. The prog-ramme has been subjected to careful evaluation for almost 30 years and has consistently shown striking social and economic benefits (Berrueta-Clement et al., 1984; Schweinhart et al., 1993). The study is one of the few pre-school evaluations following an experimental design with random assignment of children to the 'treatment' (i.e. early childhood education) or 'control' (i.e. home) groups. The results showed an initial IQ advantage for pre-school graduates which disappeared by secondary school. The High/Scope evaluators widened their outcome measures to include social and economic behaviours in adulthood. They found startling differences in social adjustment, community participation, and crime between the individuals who attended the programme as pre-schoolers and the control group who had remained at home.

Results from follow-up at age 27 appear in Figure 8.1. This broad range of positive outcomes is confirmed in other research, especially with regard to delinquency, by Larry et al. (1988) who found that pre-school attendance lowered the rate of anti-social behaviour.

Schweinhart et al., (1993) carried out a cost-benefit analysis of the High/Scope programme and found that for every $1,000 that was invested in the pre-school programme, at least $7,160 (after adjustment for inflation) had been or will be saved by society. These calculations were based on the financial cost to society of crime, remedial education, income support, and joblessness – set against the running costs of an excellent pre-school programme. The economic analysis also estimated the return to society of taxes from the higher paid individuals who had attended pre-school centres.

There have been two other cost-benefit analyses carried out on pre-school interventions, both in the US. Barnett and Escobar (1990) present data from a pre-school language intervention curriculum studied by Weiss and a comprehensive early day care programme for disadvantaged families studied by Seitz. Both studies showed that the costs of the early childhood programmes were more than offset by the savings later on in the children's schooling and medical care.

Figure 8.1 Perry Pre-School (High/Scope) outcomes

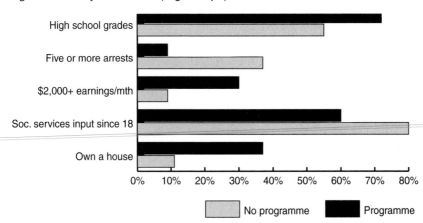

Source: adapted by the present author form data provided in Schweinhart et al., 1993

Comparing the Effects of Different Curricula (Including High/Scope)

It is clear that some, but certainly not all, pre-school interventions put children on the path to greater school adjustment, better jobs and lower rates of anti-social behaviour. In a later study, Schweinhart et al., (1986) compared the effects of three different curricula: High/Scope (the 'active learning' curriculum used in the Perry Pre-School Project), formal skills (direct instruction) and traditional nursery (curriculum centred on free play). At the point of entry to school, they found that children from all three programmes had increased IQs. However, follow-up at the age of 15 showed that children who had attended the formal programme had higher rates of anti-social behaviour and had lower adjustment to school than those who attended the two programmes based on active learning and play. Only the children who experienced play-based programmes before school retained the advantage of their early education, an advantage they demonstrated by pro-social behaviour and higher confidence when interviewed as adolescents.

A later follow up of the same cohort at age 23 (Schweinhart and Weikart, 1997) investigated the impact of the three different curricula on adult social and economic outcomes. Table 8.1 shows that the individuals who had participated in the formal, direct instruction programme had poorer psychological adjustment in secondary school and poorer grades throughout their secondary school careers. These differences were statistically significant.

By the age of 23 the graduates of High/Scope and the traditional nursery programmes were better off in important ways compared to those whose pre-school education was formal in the Direct Instruction group. Those who had experienced the direct instruction programme had been arrested more often (over the lifetime), both for felonies and misdemeanours (see Figure 8.2), had more years of special education and less adult involvement in community activities. More of the graduates of the 'play' programmes (High/Scope and nursery school) were living with a spouse and had fewer suspensions from work for discipline problems. Intriguingly, Figure 8.3 shows the results of in-depth interviews revealing that the High/Scope graduates reported

Table 8.1 Selected outcomes at age 23 by curricula

	Direct instruction	High/Scope	Nursery school	Probability (p)
Years of identified emotional impairment or disturbance	1.1	0.1	0.1	0.004
Total number of subjects failed in secondary school	9.6	5.0	4.9	0.050
Living with spouse (%)	0%	31%	18%	0.045

Source: Schweinhart and Weikart (1997, pp. 40, 42)

significantly fewer instances of 'daily irritation'. They were particularly less likely to report that friends or family were 'giving them a hard time', suggesting a more positive view of their immediate social environment. Thus children who had experienced a formal, instruction-orientated programme before entering school grew up to be hostile to authority and also towards their family and peers. Conversely children who had participated in 'active learning' pre-school programmes had similar outcomes to those in the original High/Scope research reported above. This second High/Scope study gives confidence in the results of the first since it too used experimental methods and similar analytic strategies.

This rigorous longitudinal study with random assignment supports the claim that early childhood curricula in which children initiate their own learning are superior to programmes of didactic instruction. It is possible that play enables children to learn to direct and control their own behaviour, especially impulsiveness, when they attend 'active learning' pre-schools which provide opportunity for collaborative and exploratory play. Alternatively it may be that the social skills they developed during the freer programmes were useful later on.

European Research on the Effects of Three Contrasting Curricula

A direct replication of Schweinhart and Weikart (1997) was carried out in Portugal (Nabuco, 1996; Nabuco and Sylva, 1995). Nabuco investigated the effects of the three approaches to pre-school curriculum on children's academic and social development at the start and end of first grade in the

Figure 8.2 Effects of curriculum on arrests

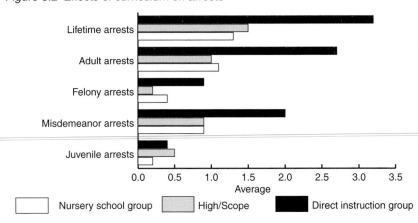

Source: Schweinhart and Weikart (1997, p. 52)

Figure 8.3 Effects of curriculum on 'irritation'

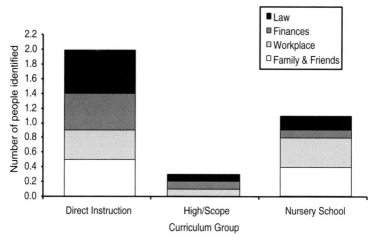

Source: Schweinhart and Weikart (1997, p. 49)

Lisbon area. The pre-school curricula included High/Scope, a Formal Skills curriculum and a Progressive Nursery programme, all similar to those studied by Schweinhart and Weikart (1997). Each curriculum was represented by five pre-school centres in Portugal, all chosen as 'good examples of the curricular model'. When children transferred at age 6 to primary school, control children with no experience of pre-school were recruited from the same first-grade classes. In this design, children's academic and social progress over the first year in school was measured by comparing control children (classmates) who had not attended pre-school with children who had attended pre-school centres implementing different curricula.

The results of this short-term longitudinal study are in complete agreement with those of Schweinhart and Weikart (1997). Children who had attended the High/Scope programme while in pre-school showed significantly higher educational attainment (reading and writing), higher self-esteem (on the Harter Assessment of Perceived Competence and Acceptance), and lower anxiety than matched control children. When compared to children in the Formal Skills group, the High/Scope children performed better on literacy tests, better on self-esteem and showed significantly less anxiety than children from the Formal Skills group. When compared with the children in the traditional nursery, the High/Scope children showed better outcomes, although their superiority was relatively less than that in comparison with the Formal Skills group.

The effects of the three different curricular approaches are presented in Figures 8.4, 8.5, 8.6 and 8.7. Each quasi-experiment consisted of children entering primary school from one of the three curricular pre-school groups. Their progress over the first year is compared with that of a matched group of

Figure 8.4 Effects of pre-school curriculum on reading

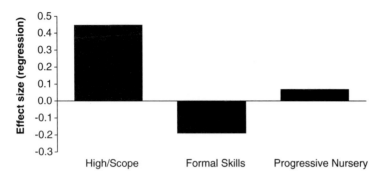

Source: Nabuco (1996)

Figure 8.5 Effects of pre-school curriculum on writing

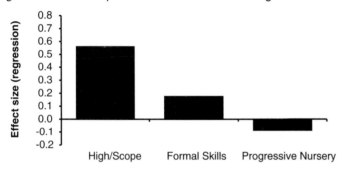

Source: Nabuco (1996)

children who entered direct from home. The Figures therefore show the effect sizes for the three separate comparisons between pre-school and home children in each of the quasi-experiments. It can be seen that the High/Scope programme, balanced between guided and free play, led to higher educational attainment and self-esteem in primary school along with better emotional development. Of these three approaches to pedagogy which were studied in Portugal, High/Scope led to improved child outcomes while Formal Skills led to lower academic attainment and social adjustment.

Sylva (1997a) emphasized the contribution of Nabuco's research to the emerging 'consistent pattern of findings across settings and countries'. The results from Nabuco's larger study support the findings from the more rigorous but smaller study carried out by Schweinhart and Weikart (15 pre-schools in Portugal compared to 1 pre-school in the US; 219 children in Portugal compared to 65 in the US). The findings from these two linked studies make convincing arguments about the power of early childhood

Figure 8.6 Effects of pre-school curriculum on anxiety

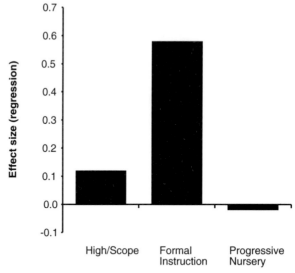

Source: Nabuco (1996)

Figure 8.7 Effects of pre-school curriculum on self-esteem

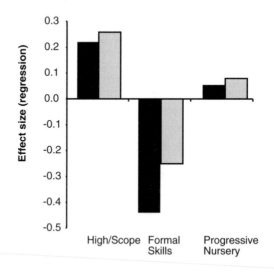

Source: Nabuco (1996)

education to boost achievement in primary school and the risks of an overly formal pre-school curriculum.

Evidence from the UK

There has been insufficient large-scale, systematic research in the UK on the effects of early childhood education. The 'Start Right' Enquiry (Ball, 1994) reviewed the evidence and concluded that small-scale studies suggested a positive impact but that large-scale research was inconclusive. Longitudinal studies with baseline measures are needed so that the 'value added' by pre-school education can be established.

Sylva et al. (1996) are carrying out a five-year longitudinal study on more than 3,000 children to answer the following questions: Are some pre-school centres more effective than others in promoting academic competence and social skills? If so, what are their characteristics? What are the effects on child outcomes of differing curricula, management, parent involvement and resourcing? Recruitment and base line assessments have been completed at age 3, there will be interim assessments at school entry, and final outcomes will be measured at age 7 via standardized tests of reading and maths, national curriculum SAT scores, rigorous assessment of social and emotional adjustment and self-report on pupil's attitudes towards learning and school. The complex design is based upon multi-level modelling and will lead to conclusions at three levels:

- the institutional level – to compare the effects on children's progress of attendance at various types of early education
- the centre level – to identify individual centres which have led to positive or negative developmental outcomes for children, and then to describe their 'quality' through use of qualitative case studies
- the child level – to look for characteristics of children (including their social background) which influence later development and may interact with the type and quality of educational provision.

Each of these levels can be looked at independently, e.g. which type of children benefit most from early education; which type of programme is most effective for sub-groups of children, especially those from disadvantaged backgrounds. Such designs require extensive large samples and precise levels of measurement. Detailed information is required on child attainment, social skill and family background. This large government-funded study will end in 2001. The final results will show if and how differences in early childhood provision in the UK lead to different outcomes for children, especially those from disadvantaged backgrounds.

Explaining the Long-Term Effects

In 1985, Michael Rutter reviewed the literature on the effects of education on children's development and concluded that the long-term educational benefits stemmed not from what children are specifically taught but from effects on children's attitudes to learning, on their self-esteem and on their task orientation. 'Learning how to learn may be as important as the specifics of what is learned' (p. 700). More than a decade later we can summarize the evidence unavailable when Rutter wrote his classic review. The most important effects of early childhood education include children's aspirations, motivations and self-concept. These are moulded through active learning experiences in the pre-school centre which enable children to make a good start to their school careers and to meet (at least) the minimal academic requirements. The evidence from early interventions in disadvantaged communities is especially strong.

The longitudinal studies, especially from the US, gave fresh inspiration because they showed that the 'successful graduates' from early childhood programmes such as High/Scope not only had better cognitive performance in primary school but – even more importantly – they became better citizens in their communities. Personal and motivational factors were as important outcomes of early education as academic skills (Sylva, 1994). The many benefits from good early childhood education include (1) pupil's self-concept as learner, (2) self-esteem, (3) 'disposition to learn' and (4) motivation centred on 'mastery' rather than 'performance' aspiration (see Ball, 1994). Learners characterized as 'mastery' rather than 'helpless' oriented will be resilient when solutions don't come easily, situations encountered all too frequently in disadvantaged communities.

So far the chapter has concentrated on the fruits of early childhood education which are individual attributes inside the child: self-esteem, disposition to learn and mastery motivation. If we are to understand the long-term impact of the interventions reviewed earlier we must postulate one further legacy of pre-school education. 'Social commitment' is a transactional outcome rather than a personal one and it is this which bonds the individual child to his or her learning community. Social commitment keeps the ten year old from joining his peers in vandalizing the school and prompts a child to volunteer as peer counsellor in the school's anti-bullying campaign. There are three distinct outcomes from early education, *cognitive* skills which underpin academic learning, *personal attributes* which give a child confidence, curiosity and perseverance, and *social commitment* which bonds the child to the community.

Why do longitudinal studies of High/Scope graduates show that they get better jobs, experience fewer 'irritations' and avoid adult crime? Why indeed are High/Scope graduates more likely to be living with a spouse, to vote in elections and read a newspaper? These must be the consequence of their acquiring social commitment as well as personal attributes. Perhaps having a trusting relationship with a 'best friend' at nursery can be a first step towards choosing a marriage partner. Certainly taking responsibility for cleaning up the classroom may lead eventually to voting for local government officials!

The High/Scope curriculum has changed considerably in 25 years. Its earliest version was pure Piaget, with 'key experiences' carefully planned so that children could acquire classification, seriation, representation – all Piagetian operations. However, in the most recent version, alongside the key cognitive experiences are now to be found planned experiences for children and staff aimed at the development of social skills and social cohesion. Daily activities are described in the new curricular guidelines to promote sharing, respect for one another, skill at avoiding and resolving peer conflict, and thinking-before-acting. If the original High/Scope curriculum was 'cool' and cognitive, the new one is 'hot' and very social.

In England and Wales over the last 25 years there has been a progressive move towards more formal learning, especially of early literacy and numeracy skills. This chapter closes by recommending a shift in 'Desirable Outcomes' (the UK pre-school curriculum, DfEE, 1996) towards a more social curriculum. We cannot leave these matters to chance; children must trust, care for others, concentrate on group goals, give and take opinions, work collaboratively to create and maintain a healthy environment. They must learn to control both attention and impulse, things they won't do easily without the rewards of group ownership and group achievement. Young children will rise to these challenges; it's up to curriculum, assessment, inspection and training to work together to support them. It has been suggested elsewhere (Sylva, 1997b) that the government revision to the Early Years curriculum should aim at the promotion of social commitment alongside disposition to learn and the foundations of literacy and numeracy.

In Conclusion

If we were to make evidence-based policy for preventing educational and behaviour problems in children from disadvantaged communities, we would recommend universal early childhood education. And on the basis of evidence presented here, curriculum and pedagogy would shift away from the current stress in the UK on formal academic preparation and towards the development of social skills and commitment to the learning community.

Acknowledgements

The expert assistance of Paul Colman and Emma Evans in compiling figures and checking references is gratefully acknowledged. Some parts of this chapter were drawn from a lecture at the Royal Society of Arts on 'Handing on the Education Baton' (21 October 1998).

References

Ball, C. (1994) *Start Right: The importance of early learning*, London, Royal Society of the Arts, Manufacturing and Commerce.

Barnett, W.S. and Escobar, C.M. (1990) 'Economic costs and benefits of early intervention', in Meisels, S.J. and Shonkoff, J.P. (eds) *Handbook of Early Childhood Intervention*, Cambridge, Cambridge University Press.

Berrueta-Clement, J.R., Schweinhart, L.J., Barnett, W.S., Epstein, A.S. and Weikart, D.P. (1984) *Changed Lives: The effects of the Perry Pre-School Program on youths through age 19*, Ypsilanti, MI, High/Scope Press.

Department for Education and Employment (DfEE) (1996) *Nursery Education Scheme: The next steps and desirable outcomes for children's learning*, London, DfEE/SCAA.

Durlak, J.A. (1995) *School-Based Prevention Programs for Children and Adolescents*, London, Sage Publications.

Larry, J.R., Mangione, P.L. and Honig, A.S. (1988) 'Long-term impact of an early intervention with low-income children and their families', in Powell, D.R. (Ed) vol. 4, *Parent Education as Early Childhood Intervention: Emerging directions in theory, research and practice*, Hillsdale, NJ, Ablex.

Lazar, I. and Darlington, R. (1982a) 'Does Head-Start work? A 1-year follow up comparison of disadvantaged children attending Head-Start, no pre-school, and other pre-school programmes', *Developmental Psychology* 24, 2, pp. 210–222.

Lazar, I. and Darlington, R. (1982b) *The Lasting Effects of Early Education: A report from the Consortium for Longitudinal Studies*, Monographs of the Society for Research in Child Development, 47, pp. 2–3, serial no. 195.

McKey, H.R., Condelli, L., Ganson, H., Barrett, B., McConkey, C. and Plantz, M. (1985) *The Impact of Head Start on Children, Families and Communities*, the Head Start Bureau, Administration for Children, Youth and Families, Office of Human Development Services, Washington, DC, CSR Incorporated.

Nabuco, M.E.M. (1996) *The Effects of Three Early Childhood Curricula in Portugal on Children's Progress in the First Year of Primary School*, Ph.D thesis, Institute of Education, University of London.

Nabuco, M.E.M. and Sylva, K. (1995) 'Comparisons between ECERS ratings of individual pre-school centres and the results of Target Child Observations: do they match or do they differ?', *Paper presented at 5th European Conference on the Quality of Early Childhood Education*, Paris.

Rutter, M. (1985) 'Family and school influences on cognitive development', *Journal of Child Psychology and Psychiatry* 26, 5, pp. 683–704.

Schweinhart, L.J. and Weikart, D.P. (1997) *Lasting Differences: The High/Scope Preschool Curriculum comparison through age 23*, Ypsilanti, MI, High/Scope Press.

Schweinhart, L.J., Barnes, H.V. and Weikart, D.P., (1993) *Significant Benefits: The High/Scope Perry Pre-School Study through age 27*, Ypsilanti, MI, High/Scope Press.

Schweinhart, L.J., Weikart, D. and Larner, M. (1986) 'Consequences of three preschool curriculum models through age 15', *Early Childhood Research Quarterly* 1, 1, pp. 15–45.

Slavin, R. E. (1995) 'Best evidence synthesis: an intelligent alternative to meta-analysis', *Journal of Clinical Epidemiology* 48, pp. 9–18.

Slavin, R.E., Karweit, N.L. and Wasik, B.A. (1994) *Preventing Early School Failure*, Needham Heights, MA, Allyn & Bacon.

Sylva, K. (1994) 'School influences on children's development', *Journal of Child Psychology and Psychiatry* 35, 1, pp. 135–170.

Sylva, K. (1997a) 'The quest for quality in curriculum', in Schweinhart, L. and Weikart, D., *Lasting Differences: The High/Scope pre-school curriculum comparison study through age 23, monographs of High/Scope Educational Research Foundation* 12, Ypsilanti, MI, High/Scope Press.

Sylva, K. (1997b) 'The early years curriculum: evidence based proposals', in *Developing the Primary School Curriculum: The next steps*, London, School Curriculum and Assessment Authority (SCAA).

Sylva, K. and Hurry, J. (1995) *The Effectiveness of Reading Recovery and Phonological Training for Children with Reading Problems*, London, School Curriculum and Assessment Authority (SCAA).

Sylva, K., Melhuish, E.C., Sammons, P. and Siraj Blatchford, I. (1996) *The Effective Provision of Pre-School Education*, Institute of Education, University of London, unpublished report.

Zigler, E. and Styfco, S.J. (1993) 'Using research and theory to justify and inform Head Start expansion', SRCD, *Social Policy Report* 7, 2.

9 Pupils' Perspectives on their Education

Theo Cox

Drawing upon a variety of research studies, this chapter first explores the question of whether the attitudes to school and to learning of socially disadvantaged pupils are any different from those of other pupils, and examines how such attitudes are related to pupils' behaviour and scholastic attainment. It then goes on to describe the views of selected samples of secondary school pupils on the goals of education and on particular aspects of their received education, and their ideas for improving the quality of their learning. The chapter concludes by stressing the importance of developing favourable attitudes to learning in all pupils and discusses possible ways in which this might be achieved.

Introduction

The present government's vigorous campaign to raise the general standards of school attainment, particularly in the basic skills, is laudable but less emphasis seems to be placed upon the development of positive attitudes toward learning in all pupils, but especially those from disadvantaged backgrounds. The present statutory national curriculum subject orders are predominantly concerned with skills and knowledge and even the 'Desirable Outcomes' for children's learning on entry to compulsory education (SCAA, 1996) includes only one reference to attitudes to learning. This is under the heading of personal and social development and refers to children ' … being eager to explore new learning and show the ability to initiate ideas and to solve simple practical problems' (SCAA, 1996, p. 9).

Although, as discussed later in this chapter, there is an important distinction between pupils' attitudes to school and learning and their actual behaviour and application in school, it is surely desirable as an educational goal that all pupils should be helped to develop a positive attitude to learning which will sustain their motivation both at school and in life beyond (see Chapter 15). This is certainly a central tenet of the philosophy of play based learning espoused by many early years educators (see Chapter 8). It is equally important for children to be helped to develop positive attitudes to themselves as learners, i.e. in terms of their self-concepts, self-esteem, and their levels of aspiration in learning, so that they can approach the challenges of learning with confidence.

On the premise that the development of positive attitudes to learning and to the self as learner are vitally important in the education of children it is incumbent on all those involved in the education process to monitor the development of such attitudes. Equally it is important for them to be aware of pupils' views on a range of educational topics and questions which directly concern them, particularly within the context of school improvement programmes. As Davie and Galloway (1996) point out, the pragmatic benefits of listening to children, such as their greater readiness to co-operate in situations where they feel that they have a voice, should not obscure the moral and educational arguments for doing so. The United Nations Convention on the Rights of the Child (Article 12) states the right of children to express their views upon all matters affecting them and for their views to be given due weight in accordance with their age and maturity. In the view of Davie and Galloway the educational service has, to date, been relatively slow to provide the necessary opportunities and contexts in which children can exercise these rights, particularly in comparison with the Social Services, following the 1989 Children Act, which explicitly embodied the principle of listening to children.

More recently the Education White Paper produced by the present government (DfEE, 1997a) makes virtually no reference to the importance of seeking pupils' views on various aspects of education covered in the proposed reforms. The topics on which it would have been highly relevant to have sought pupils' views include:

> home-school contracts;
> information on pupils' reports, school prospectuses and annual reports;
> a national framework for motivating pupils outside the classroom; and
> programmes for citizenship and parenting skills, including teenage pregnancies, smoking and drug/alcohol abuse.

Rudduck et al. (1997) discuss the traditional exclusion of young people from the consultative process, which they argue is founded upon an outmoded view of childhood which fails to acknowledge children's capacity to reflect on issues concerning their lives. They go on to assert that teachers and researchers find that 'Young people *are* observant, *are* often capable of analytic and constructive comment, and usually respond well to the responsibility, seriously entrusted to them, of helping to identify aspects of schooling that strengthen and that get in the way of their learning (Rudduck et al., 1997, p. 4). Rudduck's own pioneering work on eliciting the views of secondary school pupils upon aspects of their educational experiences is described in the second part of this chapter. The first part examines the research on the pupils' attitudes to school and learning.

137

Pupils' Attitudes to Learning

The *Concise Oxford Dictionary* provides several definitions of attitude, one of which is 'a settled opinion or way of thinking'. It is useful to make at least a relative distinction between generalized attitudes on the one hand, and views or opinions on the other. In relation to attitudes, opinions or views tend to be expressed with regard to fairly narrow or specific points or questions, and a person's expressed opinions on a number of related questions may allow us to infer the existence of a more general underlying attitude (Oppenheim, 1992). For this reason the measurement of attitudes for research purposes, ideally, makes use of composite attitude scales which sample the respondent's views/opinions on a range of related matters, but, in practice, as we shall see, some studies rely upon the use of only one or two specific questions or statements in order to measure attitudes. In this part of the chapter research studies on the attitudes of pupils towards school and learning are presented, particularly those of pupils from disadvantaged backgrounds.

The Attitudes to School/Learning of Socially Disadvantaged Pupils

Given the well researched link between social class and social disadvantage and educational attainment (see Chapters 1 and 10), it might be predicted that a similar correlation would exist between these factors and pupil attitudes to school and learning. In fact the association is somewhat weaker. As part of the National Child Development Study (NCDS) (1958 Cohort), in 1974, a sample of over eight thousand 16 year old pupils were asked to respond to the question 'I feel school is largely a waste of time.' Eighty per cent of the pupils rejected this view but a breakdown of the responses by social class showed that a higher proportion of pupils from non-manual (professional) backgrounds (84–89 per cent) did so, compared with pupils from manual (working-class) backgrounds (70–77 per cent). It was also found that pupils who were doing well in school, as judged by their reading test scores, were more likely to take a positive view of school whatever their social background (Fogelman, 1983).

The NCDS finding was in line with the results of a longitudinal study of disadvantaged pupils carried out by the present writer. This followed the school progress of approximately fifty children from homes judged to be disadvantaged on a number of related measures, and compared it with that of a group of children chosen to be comparable in age, sex and non-verbal reasoning ability, and who attended the same schools as their disadvantaged peers but came from homes judged to be more favourable to their educational progress. All of the schools in the study were judged to be serving socially disadvantaged areas in England and Wales. In a second follow-up phase of the study, the pupils, who were then aged 15+ years, were asked to complete a written attitude to school scale, as well as scales designed to measure their self-concepts and self-esteem. The disadvantaged pupils scored significantly lower as a group on all of these measures than their more advantaged peers but the differences between the mean scores of the two groups were not as pronounced as on the measures of the pupils' academic attainments in reading, writing and mathematics. Thus the disadvantaged children in this study showed less positive general attitudes to school and learning, and lower levels of academic self-concept and self-esteem than their more advantaged peers, but these between-group differences were not as great as might have been expected on the basis of the achievement gap between the two groups at age 16 (Cox, 1983).

In another longitudinal study the school attitudes and views of pupils attending schools serving inner city, largely working-class areas in the former Inner London Education Authority were explored by Blatchford (1996). No attempt was made to assess the home backgrounds of these pupils but the author describes the catchment areas they lived in as predominantly disadvantaged. The sample comprised British black (Afro-Caribbean) and white pupils, who were interviewed about their views on the value and interest of school work and related matters. At age 16 the pupils were also asked to complete a short attitude to school scale and a self-description scale. At ages 11 and 16 almost all pupils felt that it was important to do well at school but there was a trend for the number of pupils who claimed to find school work interesting to decline between the two ages. Despite this broad endorsement of the importance of schooling however, at age 16 years, white pupils had lower scores on the attitude to school scale than black pupils. For example they were more likely to agree with the statement that school work was a waste of time, and to agree that they did not want to come to school, and fewer of them judged that their parents thought it was important for them to come to school. They also had lower scores than black pupils on the measures of general and academic self-concepts, being more likely to agree that they were too stupid to go to university and stupid at most subjects. In contrast to these marked ethnic differences, however, the study found few significant differences between boys and girls in their school views and attitudes. Also there were few significant associations between the pupils' attitudes and their school attainments, for example, between how interesting they found school, mathematics or reading at age 7 years and their attainments in English at age 16 years.

In discussing possible reasons for the markedly less positive attitudes to school and school work of white pupils at age 16, compared with those of black pupils, Blatchford suggests that one might be that the attitudes to school work of white working-class parents may be less positive than those of other parents. Linked with this is the possibility that white working-class parents in this study may have offered less active support to their children during their learning of the basic skills during their early years, compared to that received by children of the black parents. A similar difference in favour of ethnic minority pupils was found in a survey of school attitudes carried out in the

London Borough of Tower Hamlets (Tower Hamlets Education Strategy Group, undated). Over one thousand pupils aged 13 to 17 years completed a questionnaire concerning their views on a range of educational questions. The majority of the sample were Bangladeshi or white pupils, with a small proportion of black pupils. While the majority of all pupils expressed satisfaction with their education, Bangladeshi pupils, especially girls, expressed greater satisfaction than white pupils and white UK boys had the lowest positive response rate on this question. These ethnic minority pupils also reported better attendance records than their white peers, and were more likely to report finding homework useful for their studies.

As in Blatchford's study, no attempt was made to assess the socio-economic level of the homes and the level of educational support they provided, but it is well known that there is a relatively very high level of social and material disadvantage in this particular borough. Here also it may have been the case that the ethnic minority parents in this sample provided a higher level of support for their children than did the parents of the white pupils. In support of this interpretation the study found very marked differences between the ethnic minority and white pupils in their use of public libraries and also in their reported reading habits, with three quarters of Bangladeshi girls and half of the Bangladeshi boys claiming to read regularly, compared to only 1 in 5 white boys and 2 in 5 white girls. As with all surveys of this type one makes the assumption that respondents are providing honest answers to the questions, but if these reported differences in reading habits were valid, it seems very likely that they were at least an indirect reflection of the degree of parental support received by the different groups of children.

A major national study of the school attitudes of secondary school pupils in Year 7 (11–12) and Year 9 (13–14) age groups provides only qualified support for the association between social disadvantage and attitudes to school and learning (Keys and Fernandes, 1993). This survey was commissioned by the National Commission on Education and carried out in 1992. There were approximately one thousand students in each age group which constituted a nationally representative sample. A major aim of the study was to identify factors associated with motivation towards school and school learning and to hypothesize causes for hostility towards school. The inquiry was based on written attitude questionnaires completed by the pupils. It was found that the majority of students in both age groups, but particularly in the younger group, expressed positive attitudes towards the value of school and school learning, with lower proportions of pupils expressing a liking for school or judging school work to be interesting. Most of the pupils appeared to believe that their parents were interested in their schooling.

The only home background measure used in this study was an estimate by the pupils themselves of the number of books in their homes. The results of statistical analyses carried out on the data showed that factors significantly associated with positive attitudes to school included a high level of perceived parental support by the pupils in the sample. The cultural level of the home, based upon the pupils' estimates of the number of books at home, was only weakly related to measured school attitude, as was the type of catchment area served by the school, i.e. pupils in schools serving disadvantaged areas did not show markedly less positive school attitudes than those in schools serving more favoured areas. In fact most of the variation in measured school attitudes was due to differences between pupils *within* schools, with only a small amount attributable to differences between schools. This finding of limited between-school variation was in line with previous research reviewed by these authors.

The evidence from the studies reviewed above appears to show that pupils from socially disadvantaged backgrounds may not have markedly poorer attitudes to school and learning than those from more favoured backgrounds and this is encouraging. On the other hand a recent MORI survey of attitudes to learning amongst a nationally representative sample of over 1,000 adults and young people, aged 16 years and above, in England and Wales, found that those from lower social class households, the retired, and those with no qualifications were less likely to be currently involved in learning, or to express a desire to be involved in learning in the future. They were also less likely to feel that learning was important or enjoyable (Campaign for Learning, 1998). This is a worrying finding since it does suggest a clear link between social disadvantage and attitudes to learning among adults from as young as age 16. This survey also sampled the views about learning of over 4,000 pupils in England and Wales and, while they found that, encouragingly, only a minority of them found learning at school unenjoyable (22 per cent), their enquiry did not enable them to break down the responses by social class or any other home background measure. Had they been able to do so it is possible that social group differences might have emerged, as in their adult sample.

Although the research evidence for a link between social disadvantage and attitude to learning is inconclusive at this stage, there is strong evidence that the school behaviour and academic attainment of these pupils is related strongly to socio-economic factors, as shown in Chapters 1 and 10. This was also clearly shown in the present writer's own study of disadvantaged pupils (Cox, 1982), whose GCSE examination performance and school attendance in their fourth and fifth secondary school years were markedly poorer than those of their more advantaged peers. This raises the question of how attitudes to school relate to academic achievement and motivation and to school behaviour. These relationships may be complex. Blatchford (1996), for example, found no significant association between certain school attainments and pupils' feelings about school and concluded that the lack of any clear-cut relationship between the two still left open the possibility of an indirect influence of attitudes on academic performance (and probably vice versa). On the basis of reviewing the research literature, Keys and Fernandes (1993) argue that the direction and strength of the relationship depends on the attitude dimension under consideration. Liking for school, for example, shows only a weak relationship with attainment, but attitude to school work, educational aspirations and self-esteem show low but significant associations. In a survey of secondary school pupils' attitudes carried out at Keele University it was found that, while over 90 per cent of pupils appeared to regard school work as important, as many as 40 per cent showed a general lack of school motivation (Barber, 1996).

More research needs to be done to clarify the interplay between attitude, motivation and performance. Even so there is already enough evidence to show that attitudes to learning, or certain aspects of them, do have some bearing upon academic achievement, quite apart from their importance in the personal development of pupils.

Disaffected Pupils

Although the evidence reviewed here suggests that, in general, social disadvantage may not be strongly related to attitudes to learning among children, studies of selected groups of disaffected and underachieving pupils show a much clearer link between negative school attitudes and disadvantaging factors, including a lack of educational support at home. Keys and Fernandes (1993), for example, list the following student-home related factors which tend to be associated with early school leaving and dropout, based on their review of the literature:

> disillusionment with and dislike of school;
> belief that school would not improve their career prospects;
> low educational aspirations;
> lack of interest and effort in class and less time spent on homework;
> disruptive behaviour and resentment of rules;
> poor academic achievement;
> poor attendance and truancy;
> lack of parental interest and support; and
> low socio-economic status.
>
> (Keys and Fernandes, 1993, pp.II–5)

In their own attitude survey Keys and Fernandes found that pupils expressing negative attitudes to school were more likely than other pupils to have negative views of their own abilities and perseverance, to behave badly in school and to judge that they received lower levels of support from their parents. In their exploration of the school views of 12 to 14 year-old-pupils Rudduck et al. (1996) found that, compared with other pupils, students who were judged by their teachers to be disengaged from their school work differed in the way they perceived themselves as learners and in the way they tackled their work. In particular they showed lower self-esteem and poor self-concepts, poor strategies for coping with school work and poorer relations with their teachers and their peers. Despite this they still expressed the desire to do well in school.

Rudduck et al.'s exploration of the views on their education of a sample of pupils aged from 12 to 16 years offers insights into the additional factors which may lead particular pupils downwards on the path to disaffection with school. One of these is a failure to realise how learning in the early secondary school years provides the foundation for more advanced, examination-oriented work in Years 10 and 11. In consequence, such pupils may fail to establish the skills, knowledge and ways of working that would equip them to cope with the multiple demands of the later school years. Rudduck et al. (1997) describe how some pupils, who had not worked steadily in their early secondary school years, looked back from Year 11 'with regret and a sad sense of powerlessness'.

A second disadvantaging factor mentioned by Rudduck is that of peer labelling, Particularly during Year 8. Pupils showing a strong academic motivation may be castigated by their less committed peers as 'swots, boffs or keenos'. In contrast other pupils may come to be labelled as non-academic 'thickos', partly perhaps as a result of policies of grouping by ability within the school which can lead to such negative labelling by other pupils and even teachers. As Rudduck et al. (1997) points out, such pupils may come to identify themselves with their negative labels since, for a time at least, they accord them a certain status with their peers. However, once such self-accepted labelling becomes fixed, unproductive behaviours are reinforced and it becomes very difficult for these pupils to escape from their stereotypes, with the result that they may reject school and its values.

Intercultural Comparisons

The studies by Blatchford (1996) and Tower Hamlets (undated) described earlier found that the attitudes to school and learning of ethnic minority children in their research samples were distinctly more positive than those of white children. There is also supporting evidence for this from a more recent MORI survey of the attitudes to learning of a sample of British schoolchildren, carried out on behalf of the Campaign for Learning (1998). This found that black and minority ethnic group pupils were more likely to express an enjoyment of learning than white boys.

On the basis of these studies at least, it seems that ethnic minority group children in Britain tend to have more positive attitudes to school and learning than their white British peers. It also appears that French primary pupils have more positive attitudes than their British counterparts, according to an ongoing cross-cultural study being carried out at Bristol University and Christ College Canterbury, entitled 'Quality in Experiences of Schooling Transnationally' (QUEST). As part of a larger study written questionnaires were given to 800 children in the top two years of primary school in England and France during 1996. The sample schools were chosen to represent a geographic and socio-economic mix and were drawn from two contrasting regions in each country, a socially disadvantaged and a more affluent area respectively. On the basis of their written responses the French pupils appeared to be more highly motivated to learn and to succeed than their English peers, 86 per cent, compared with only 66 per cent expressing the strong desire to do well in school. The authors concluded that the importance of hard work and the work ethic was more firmly entrenched in French schools and was accepted as necessary by the pupils (Osborn et al., 1997, 1998).

The QUEST study found few significant differences in attitude between high and low social status pupils within England and France respectively but, in contrast, large differences between French and English pupils in their attitude to teachers and to being at school, regardless of social status, in favour of the former. After studying their data the authors concluded that there were important differences between the educational cultures of England and France. In their view, in England, a culture unsupportive to the notion of intrinsic and lifelong learning appears to be thriving more strongly, both inside school from the existence of pupil counter cultures, and outside school from an emphasis on instrumental, rather than intrinsic reasons for learning (Osborn et al.,1997). They surmise that the combination of school ethos and wider familial and cultural values are more mutually supportive of positive attitudes to education and academic motivation in French society, in comparison with that in England. This cultural difference appears to extend even to socially disadvantaged children, for the study found that the low socio-economic status French children showed significantly more positive school attitudes and motivation than the equivalent English children. The authors attributed this difference to the French system's ideological emphasis on equal entitlement, in contrast with the English system's emphasis upon differentiation of curriculum and task according to ability.

Support for the Quest findings comes from an international comparison of the educational attitudes, motivation and school behaviour of samples of pupils from Russia (St Petersburg), the USA (Kentucky), and Britain (Sunderland) by Elliott et al., 1999. They found that the British and American pupils showed less positive attitudes than their Russian peers and held a more instrumental view of their education. The authors concluded that the academic motivation of the British and American students was negatively influenced by an anti-work climate in many classrooms.

Gender Differences

Without citing any supporting evidence, the annual report of HM Chief Inspector of Schools for England for 1996–1997 (OFSTED, 1998), reporting the poorer academic achievement of boys than girls, particularly in GCSE examinations, comments that this is often linked to weaknesses in their basic skills and their lack of commitment to school. The report urges secondary schools to make every effort to combat the 'anti-achievement culture' which can develop at Key Stage 3, alienating some boys from academic work. The research evidence for gender differences in pupils' attitudes to learning is, however, not conclusive.

In their review of the previous literature on pupil attitudes Keys and Fernandes (1993) state that many studies found that girls tend to hold more positive attitudes to school than boys, although boys, on average tend to show higher self esteem. Despite this however their own major study of the attitudes of Year 7 and Year 9 pupils found only a slight tendency for girls to show more positive attitudes than boys. Similarly Blatchford's (1996) study of the attitudes of secondary aged, mainly working-class pupils in inner London found relatively few differences between the sexes in their attitudes to school and school work, in contrast with their finding of marked ethnic differences. As against this, a large study of secondary school pupils' school attitudes carried out at Keele University found that girls showed more positive attitudes than boys and appeared to be better motivated (Barber, 1996). Also a recent MORI survey of 4,000 pupils aged 11 to 16 found that boys had significantly more negative attitudes to learning than girls, with over a quarter of them finding learning 'boring', compared with fewer than 1 in 6 girls. This difference was more pronounced among the older age groups. However, this study, which was commissioned by the Campaign for Learning (1998), did not make use of specially constructed attitude scales, unlike the studies by Keys and Fernandes and Blatchford, but relied upon the pupils' responses to specific questions such as 'School is boring'. Possible reasons why white working-class children, especially boys, may develop negative attitudes to academic learning are explored by Lucey and Walkerdine in Chapter 3 of this book.

Pupils' Views on their Education and How it Can be Improved

As well as assessing and monitoring children's general attitudes towards school and learning it is equally important to listen to their views on particular aspects of their education so that these can be taken into account when improvements are planned, whether at a national, local authority or school level. The views of pupils drawn from a selection of research studies will be presented under the headings 'Purposes of Schooling' and 'Teaching and Learning in School'.

Purposes of Schooling

A number of studies have explored pupils' views on the goals of school education. In the present author's own study of disadvantaged children, carried out at the second follow-up stage, when aged 15 plus years, the pupils were asked to assess the importance of 20 selected possible objectives of school education. These were then ranked in order of their perceived impor-tance according to the number of pupils endorsing each one as 'very important'. The resulting sets of rankings for the disadvantaged pupils and their more advantaged peers respectively were so close that they were combined into one composite set, as shown in Figure 9.1 (Cox, 1983).

It is clear from Figure 9.1 that the children overwhelmingly endorsed the importance of schools preparing them for examinations, and a correspond-ingly low rating to the importance of developing an interest in non-examination subjects. It is equally clear that the children accorded the highest importance to career-related objectives, including the passing of examinations. Objectives relating to the teaching of everyday skills, including numeracy, literacy and oracy, and the fostering of personal development received middle rankings, while those concerning general interest and aware-ness received the lowest rankings on the whole. Perhaps surprisingly the objective that school should 'make sure that you have an education so inter-esting, useful and enjoyable that you will be keen to continue it into adult life' received only a middle ranking of importance, supporting the proposition, discussed earlier in this chapter, that British pupils may have a strongly, extrinsic, instrumental view of the purposes of schooling.

This general pattern of results showed some concordance with the attitude survey carried out by Keys and Fernandes (1993) with Year 7 and Year 9 pupils. As part of this study five statements which focused on the students' perceptions of the purposes of school were presented. It was found that all of them appeared to believe in the utilitarian purposes of school. The vast majority (around 90 per cent in both groups) strongly agreed or agreed that schools should help them to do well in exams, teach them things which would be useful when they got jobs, and to be independent. Although couched in a different way the MORI survey of pupils' views on learning commissioned by the Campaign for Learning (1998) produced a similar finding. Ninety six per cent of the sample agreed that 'learning will help me to get a good job'. On the other hand only 39 per cent of them agreed with the view that 'I only learn in order to get qualifications', with a further 24 per cent neither agreeing nor disagreeing. Blatchford's (1996) study of mainly working-class pupils in disadvantaged areas of London provided further evidence of pupils' utilitarian views. It found that the vast majority of pupils at age 11 and 16 years judged that it was important to do well at school, the main reasons for this, at age 16, being 'in order to get a good job' (52 per cent), 'to get good grades' (31 per cent), and 'to do well in life' (23 per cent). Blatchford emphasized the constant concern shown by these pupils, even at entry into their secondary schools, with future employment and careers, and their awareness of the importance of school work in getting a job. In this they may of course simply be reflecting an emphasis upon such instrumental goals by both their teachers and their parents.

Figure 9.1 Percentages of children saying that various school objectives were very important (control and disadvantaged groups combined) (n=92)

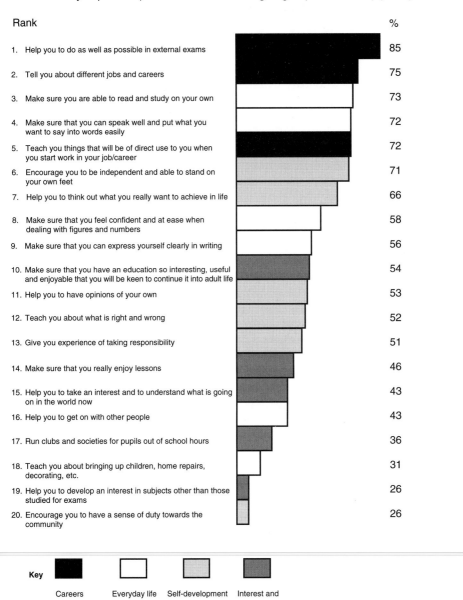

Rank — %

1. Help you to do as well as possible in external exams — 85
2. Tell you about different jobs and careers — 75
3. Make sure you are able to read and study on your own — 73
4. Make sure that you can speak well and put what you want to say into words easily — 72
5. Teach you things that will be of direct use to you when you start work in your job/career — 72
6. Encourage you to be independent and able to stand on your own feet — 71
7. Help you to think out what you really want to achieve in life — 66
8. Make sure that you feel confident and at ease when dealing with figures and numbers — 58
9. Make sure that you can express yourself clearly in writing — 56
10. Make sure that you have an education so interesting, useful and enjoyable that you will be keen to continue it into adult life — 54
11. Help you to have opinions of your own — 53
12. Teach you about what is right and wrong — 52
13. Give you experience of taking responsibility — 51
14. Make sure that you really enjoy lessons — 46
15. Help you to take an interest and to understand what is going on in the world now — 43
16. Help you to get on with other people — 43
17. Run clubs and societies for pupils out of school hours — 36
18. Teach you about bringing up children, home repairs, decorating, etc. — 31
19. Help you to develop an interest in subjects other than those studied for exams — 26
20. Encourage you to have a sense of duty towards the community — 26

Key

Careers   Everyday life   Self-development   Interest and awareness

Source: Cox (1983, p. 75)

Teaching and Learning

Teachers' behaviour and attitudes towards their pupils, and their expectations regarding them, are likely to have a powerful influence upon children's academic motivation and progress. Given the salience of teachers in their lives at school it is not surprising to find that pupils are very ready to articulate their views on what makes for good teachers and good teaching. Rudduck's interviews with secondary school pupils yielded a range of teacher behaviours judged by their pupils to be most likely to increase their commitment to learning. These included teachers who:

> enjoy teaching their subject;
> enjoy teaching their students;
> make their lessons interesting and link them to life outside school;
> will have a laugh but know how to keep order;
> are fair;
> explain things and go through things students don't understand without making them feel small; and
> don't give up on students.

> (Rudduck et al.,1997)

The students aged 15 plus in the present writer's own study of disadvantaged pupils referred to a similar range of desired qualities or behaviour in their teachers to these, including:

> approachability, so that pupils do not feel scared to ask for help;
> helpfulness, e.g. 'He helps us with our work if we are stuck and if we are falling behind he will drive us until we catch up.';
> treating pupils with respect, e.g. 'Teachers who treat you more like adults than children.'

Conversely pupils were critical of teachers who failed to keep discipline, with the consequent disruption of learning. Other sources of dissatisfaction from pupils in this study were favouritism and unfairness on the part of teachers. One pupil, for example, criticized the tendency of teachers to favour compliant, well-performing students:

> If you are the type who has 100 for this and 100 for that they love you. They say it's a pleasure to teach you. They don't think about the girl in the back years who wants to learn but got a problem and can't.

Also the understandable desire of students for acknowledgement of their work and effort was reflected in the finding of Keys and Fernandes (1993) that only half of the sample of pupils said that teachers praised them for good work. Their further finding that nearly one-quarter of the pupils felt that their teachers were easily satisfied with their work suggests that pupils probably appreciate work which challenges them appropriately.

As part of the MORI attitude survey of 11 to 16-year-old pupils commissioned by the Campaign for Learning (1998), the pupils were asked to identify, from a list, factors which impeded their learning. A high proportion, particularly of older pupils, selected poor teaching, feeling unhappy, and 'having teachers who do not understand how children learn' as such factors. They were also asked questions relating to their preferred learning styles. Over half of them expressed a preference for learning in groups, but there were gender differences, with boys preferring to learn by doing practical things, by using computers, and also by learning alone. The most frequently endorsed changes they wished to see made to their schools were more visits to places of interest, being allowed to concentrate on things they were good at, more work experience placements, and being helped to plan for their own futures.

Although pupils appear to be well aware of teacher behaviours which either facilitate or impede their learning they also show a readiness to acknowledge their own responsibilities in the learning process. A large majority of the 16-year-old students in Blatchford's (1996) study of pupil attitudes felt that they were not doing as well as they would like academically. (These pupils were drawn from working-class area schools whose GCSE results were well below average.) The main reasons they offered for their self-perceived underperformance were that they were lazy or made no effort, that they could work harder and that there was too much pressure of work. There were no ethnic or gender differences in this respect. When asked how teachers and pupils could help in this situation they emphasized pupil strategies such as doing more work and applying themselves more to homework and revision, and organizing themselves to work better, e.g. through meeting deadlines and pacing their work better. The main ways that teachers could help were by giving more help and attention, by pushing and encouraging them more, explaining things better and making work more challenging and interesting.

Blatchford concluded that, at 16, these pupils took the prime responsibility for their school progress themselves and that, apart from their own level of ability, the internal factors bearing upon their academic performance which they identified were ones over which they had some control. However, he questioned the extent to which the pupils were being truly objective in their self-appraisal since, during adolescence, they may have been more inclined to blame themselves when they did badly. Moreover, as Blatchford points out, the analysis of external factors influencing their performance relating to school organization and structure requires a certain maturity (which, by implication, they may not have achieved at that stage).

Rudduck's study of pupils making their way through secondary school identified a number of these school-related factors. The study was conducted in three English secondary comprehensive schools and followed a core group of pupils in each school from ages 12 to 16, using interviews supplemented with data gathered from teachers and from analyses of school documents and records. One of the schools served a predominantly disadvantaged, ethnically mixed community. On the basis of this study Rudduck et al. (1997) offered a number of suggestions for school improvement, including the following:

> Giving each year of secondary schooling a distinct identity that might motivate students as they look ahead and that offers progress in terms of autonomy and responsibility.
> Creating time for dialogue about learning so that students develop a language for thinking about learning and about themselves as learners.
> Making time for teachers to talk to individual students about problems with school work and legitimizing such discussion so that students do not feel that talking about their work is not 'cool'.
> Helping students to manage the multiple demands of homework, course work and revision.
> Formalizing opportunities to support one another in learning.
> Responding to the problem of catching up for students who have missed work.

An interesting study by de Pear (1997) illustrates the apparent benefits for some pupils of one or more of the strategies recommended above. She interviewed a sample of secondary aged pupils who had been excluded from their mainstream schools and placed in one of two special schools. Prior to exclusion they had all been identified as having special educational needs. The author hypothesized that these pupils wanted to be accepted socially in school and wanted to take some responsibility for their own learning, but, as a result of having been labelled and marginalized by their learning difficulties, their inherent fear of failure kept them distanced from others and induced in them a feeling of incompetence as pupils. She speculated that these pupils might have been helped, prior to their exclusion, if they had been given a chance to express their views regarding their preferred learning style and the teaching style that would best serve their needs. The Code of Practice for special educational needs (DfE, 1994) allows pupil advocacy as part of the review strategy and, in the context of her work as a secondary school special educational needs co-ordinator (SENCO), de Pear observed how much more the pupils with SEN were achieving after they were brought into the process of negotiating their learning targets and discussing barriers to learning. She concluded that these vulnerable pupils need to feel valued, that what they have to say about their learning is important, and that future planning of their education should be a negotiated process in which they feel some ownership. These principles surely apply to students in general.

Conclusions

Although, like their more advantaged peers, socially disadvantaged pupils, in general, endorse the value of school education in principle, and acknowledge the importance of doing well in school examinations in order to get a good job, this awareness is not, in many cases, translated into a personal commitment to learning which can sustain these pupils' effort and motivation during their secondary school careers. The more disadvantaged the pupil's personal circumstances, within home, school and community, the greater the risk that she/he will become steadily more disillusioned with school learning and will then opt out of it either actively or passively. Even among the wider population of British secondary aged pupils surveys have shown that attitudes towards school learning become more negative between the ages of 11 and 16, particularly among boys, and it also appears that white pupils, again, especially boys, tend to have less positive attitudes and motivation to learn than ethnic minority children in Britain. There is some limited evidence too that, compared with French and Russian pupils, British primary pupils have a more instrumental attitude to learning, regarding it as more of a means to an end than as an inherently worthwhile and fulfilling experience. Such a view, if coupled with a peer group culture which is antithetical to learning, will act as a real barrier to the development of a personal commitment to learning.

On the positive side, the evidence from the limited research available to date suggests that, on the whole, the attitudes of many socially disadvantaged children in Britain do not appear to be markedly poorer than those of their more advantaged peers, and this gives grounds for hope that, if we take the right measures, these pupils can be helped to become more highly motivated to learn, not only within school but beyond it.

Certainly more research is needed into the process by which attitudes to learning develop through the school years, and into the influences which most powerfully shape their development. More research is also needed into the evidently complex and indirect relationships between attitudes to learning and motivation and scholastic achievement. Given the urgency of the challenge posed by the under-achievement of many socially disadvantaged pupils, however, we cannot afford simply to wait upon the future outcome of such research, important though it is. A multi-pronged strategy is urgently needed if the attitudes and academic motivation of disadvantaged pupils are to be significantly improved. Such a strategy, based upon our existing research knowledge and good practice should include the following aims:

to raise the status of learning among disadvantaged children;
to raise the level of involvement of parents in their children's learning and their perception of the importance of education; and
to raise the level of involvement of pupils in the shaping of their school education.

Raising the Status of Learning

The more that our society proclaims its belief in the importance of learning and gives a tangible demonstration of that belief, the more likely it will be that children will maintain throughout their lives the drive and enthusiasm for learning which characterizes their early years. In its Education White Paper the present British Government states its goal of achieving a greater awareness across society of the importance of education and increased expectations of what can be achieved (DfEE, 1997a). Osborn et al. (1998), in discussing how British pupils can be helped to develop a more intrinsic form of learning motivation, proposes that the media should be harnessed in a concerted effort to combat negative peer group attitudes to learning and to improve attitudes to learning in wider society. The latter is precisely the aim of the recently formed Campaign for Learning, a sponsored charity whose vision is of 'an inclusive society in which learning is valued, understood and widely available. A society in which every individual and every organisation is actively involved in learning' (Campaign for Learning, 1998, back cover). This campaign is targeted particularly upon those in our society who have negative experiences of learning in the past and may even have developed a deep rooted hostility to it. Further suggestions as to how the national status of learning could be enhanced are made by Barber (1996).

Raising the Level of Involvement of Parents in their Children's Education

If a nationwide campaign to raise the status of learning in Britain does succeed this will positively influence both parents and children, especially the disadvantaged. Nevertheless, given their key role in their children's education, such parents need to be directly informed, encouraged and supported in their exercise of this role. In their survey of secondary pupils' attitudes to learning Keys and Fernandes (1993) reported that most of the students believed that their parents were interested in their educational progress, were supportive and held high aspirations for them. These authors stated their belief that there was a pool of parental interest waiting to be tapped but more research was needed to map the extent and type of such interest and to yield recommendations on ways in which secondary schools can involve parents more fully and effectively.

The Government's recently launched Education Action Zones (EAZs) offer real possibilities for the enhanced involvement of parents in their children's education in socially disadvantaged areas, for example, through early excellence centres and literacy summer schools which will feature in them. Indeed one of the expected characteristics of successful local partnerships bidding for EAZ funding is the ' ... shared responsibility for learning by parents and their families with full participation in school life and support for its aims' (DfEE, 1997b, p. 12) (see also Chapter 16).

Raising the Level of Involvement of Pupils in the Shaping of their Education

Rudduck and her co-workers have consistently argued that the views of pupils themselves should be seriously and systematically taken into account by schools and teachers in the general drive to improve the quality of their education and learning. Their work, referred to earlier in this chapter, has yielded practical suggestions for school improvement based upon pupils' views and experiences. Currently they are engaged in an action research project entitled 'Improving Learning: the Pupils' Agenda', which is based jointly at the universities of Cambridge and Keele, and supported by the Nuffield Foundation. The project aims to support both primary and secondary schools in enhancing pupils' achievement by documenting and disseminating good educational practice in relation to three themes: 'Creating a Learning Culture', 'Catching Up and Keeping Up' and 'Pupils Helping Other Pupils in their Learning'.

Under the first of these themes the project has sought schools which have changed the pupils' attitudes to learning in significant ways, particularly where teachers have successfully combated a strong anti-work culture among peer groups. It is hoped that the project studies will help teachers to understand and take account of pupils' views about factors which either help or hinder their learning.

In addition to the work of Rudduck and her co-workers there have been a number of other significant developments in the provision of structured opportunities for students' voices to be heard on relevant educational matters. MacBeath et al. (1998) describe a European project involving 101 schools in 18 countries entitled 'Evaluating Quality in School Education'. Each participating school completes a self-evaluation profile following a rigorous analytic process involving pupils, teachers, parents and governing bodies, all coming to the exercise as equal partners with an equal right to be heard. Also the Government's Advisory Group for Citizenship and Democracy in Schools, under the chairmanship of Professor Bernard Crick, seems likely to press strongly for pupils to be given meaningful opportunities to contribute to discussions concerning their lives within their schools and their local communities (TES, 1998). In the present book Jackson (Chapter 5) describes a project in which looked-after children are being actively involved in educational and other decisions concerning them.

Acknowledgements

The writer would like to thank Professor Jean Rudduck of Homerton College Cambridge, Dr Marilyn Osborn of the University of Bristol School of Education, and Professor Julian Elliott of the University of Sunderland for their helpfulness in making copies of their publications available.

References

Barber, M. (1996) *The Learning Game: Arguments for an education revolution*, London, Victor Gollanz.

Blatchford, P. (1996) 'Pupils' views on school work and school from 7 to 16 years', *Research Papers in Education* 11, pp. 263–288.

Campaign for Learning (1998) *Attitudes to Learning 98. MORI State of the Nation Survey: Summary report*, London, Campaign for Learning.

Cox, T. (1982) 'Disadvantaged fifteen-year-olds: initial findings from a longitudinal study', *Educational Studies* 8, pp. 1–13.

Cox, T. (1983) 'The educational attitudes and views about school of a sample of disadvantaged fifteen-year-olds', *Educational Studies* 9, pp. 69–79.

Davie, R. and Galloway, D. (1996) *Listening to the Voice of the Child in Education*, London, David Fulton.

Department for Education (DfE) (1994) *Code of Practice on the Identification and Assessment of Special Educational Needs*, London, DfE.

Department for Education and Employment (DfEE) (1997a) *Excellence in Schools* (Education White Paper), London, The Stationery Office.

Department for Education and Employment (DfEE) (1997b) *Education Action Zones: An introduction*, London, DfEE.

Elliott, J., Hutton, N., Hildreth, A. and Illusin, L. (1999) 'Factors influencing educational motivation: a study of attitudes, expectations and behaviour of children in Sunderland, Kentucky, and St Petersburg', *British Educational Research Journal* 25, pp. 75–94.

Fogelman, K. (Ed) (1983) *Growing Up in Great Britain: Collected papers from the National Child Development Study*, London, Macmillan.

Keys W. and Fernandes, C. (1993) *What Do Students Think About School? Research into factors associated with positive and negative attitudes towards school and education*, Slough, National Foundation for Educational Research.

MacBeath, J., Meuret, D., Jakobsen, L. and Schratz, M. (1998) 'Evaluating quality in school education', *Paper Delivered at the American Educational Research Association*, San Diego, April 1998.

Office for Standards in Education (OFSTED) (1998) *The Annual Report of Her Majesty's Chief Inspector of Schools in England. Standards and Quality in Education 1996/97*, London, The Stationery Office.

Oppenheim, A.N. (1992) *Questionnaire Design and Attitude Measurement*, 2nd edn, London, Pinter.

Osborn, M., Broadfoot, P., Planel, C. and Pollard, A. (1997) 'Social class, educational opportunity and equal entitlement: dilemmas of schooling in England and France', *Comparative Education* 33, pp. 375–393.

Osborn, M., Broadfoot, P., Planel, C., Sharpe, K. and Ward, B. (1998) 'Being a pupil in England and France: Findings from a Comparative Study', in Kazamias, A.M. and Spillane, M.G. (Eds) *Education and the Structuring of the European Space*, Seirios Editions, Athens, Greece and the Greek Comparative Education Society, for the Comparative Education Society in Europe (CESE).

Pear, S. de (1997) 'Excluded pupils' views of their educational needs and experiences', *Support for Learning* 12, pp. 19–22.

Rudduck, J., Chaplain, R. and Wallace, G. (1996) *School Improvement: What can pupils tell us?*, London, David Fulton.

Rudduck, J., Wallace, G. and Day, J. (1997) 'Students' perspectives on school improvement', in Hargreaves, A. (ed.) *Rethinking Educational Change with Heart and Mind. ASCD Yearbook*, Vancouver, ASCD.

School Curriculum and Assessment Authority (SCAA) (1996) *Nursery Education: Desirable Outcomes of Children's Learning on Entering Compulsory Education*, London, SCAA.

Times Educational Supplement (TES) (1998) 27 March, p. 17.

Tower Hamlets Education Strategy Group (undated) *Living in Tower Hamlets: A survey of the attitudes of secondary school pupils*, London, Tower Hamlets Education Strategy Group.

10 Can School Improvement Overcome the Effects of Disadvantage?

Peter Mortimore and Geoff Whitty

The relationship between pupils' backgrounds and their school achievement has received little attention in education discussions which, for the last ten years, has been dominated by markets and league tables. Yet the correlation between disadvantaged family background and low achievement persists. This chapter considers what disadvantage can mean for pupils, discusses some of the strategies that have been adopted to combat it and evaluates their efficacy. We argue that efforts to compensate at school for disadvantage at home have been too limited in scope. We endorse school improvement work which has established mechanisms for whole-school change but we fear that claims for its significance may have been exaggerated. In our view, the publicity given to league tables, and the attention being paid to the need for school success defined in such crude terms, may mean that school improvement actually works against the disadvantaged. We consider that, if the achievement gap between the advantaged and their disadvantaged peers is to be closed, the new government must – in addition to its work on school improvement – better co-ordinate initiatives that seek, more directly, to help the disadvantaged, maintain those interventions which have proved to have positive effects and extend the opportunities for post-school learning.

This chapter is an amended and updated version of an earlier publication by the authors (Mortimore and Whitty, 1997).

Background

Despite the Thatcher and Major governments' refusal to acknowledge the importance of the relationship between social disadvantage and educational achievement, stark differences in the lives of pupils with different family backgrounds have not gone away, nor has the problem of knowing how best to deal with them. According to some commentators, this topic has been 'almost a taboo subject in public policy debate in recent years' (Smith and Noble, 1995, p. 133). Teachers who have dared to mention the subject have been branded defeatist or patronizing for even considering that social background can make a difference. Although some members of the Blair government have shown an alarming tendency to perpetuate such attitudes, the change of government could provide an opportunity to re-open this important public policy debate.

In schools – especially in those with high proportions of disadvantaged pupils – the issue is of crucial importance although many of us, including teachers and governors, are unclear about the best approach to adopt. If the problem in the past has been low expectations, should we now ignore disadvantage, in the hope that pupils themselves will find the necessary strengths to overcome their problems? Should we rely on adopting, and trying to instil, high expectations for pupils' achievement or are such 'hands off' approaches doomed to failure – no matter how genuinely they are intended to help disadvantaged pupils?

The lessons of history are not hopeful. Whilst some outstanding individuals have achieved the highest levels despite (or, in some cases, motivated by) their inauspicious home backgrounds, most formal education systems have failed pupils whose families are disadvantaged (Douglas, 1964; Davie et al., 1972; Essen and Wedge, 1982; Mortimore and Mortimore, 1986; Osborne and Milbank, 1987; Gorman and Fernandes, 1992; OECD, 1995). Paradoxically, those who have had most to gain from education have often been the least able to do so.

In recent years the problem has been exacerbated by the introduction of a requirement to publish examination and test results which have been turned, by the press, into crude league tables. Parents have been encouraged to use these results to judge the quality of schools, despite the absence of any relevant information about the background or prior achievement of pupils as they enter the schools. It is thus in schools' interests to avoid admitting disadvantaged pupils who – in the absence of extra resources – would be likely to perform poorly and thus worsen the position of the school in the league tables. Such 'hard to teach' pupils are often only welcome in schools which are undersubscribed and which are desperate for extra pupils to increase their financial viability. Unfortunately, many such schools are already coping with problems to do with the low morale of staff and pupils and are not – other than in exceptional cases – in a strong position to 'lift' the achievement of disadvantaged pupils.

Meanwhile, our society appears to be deeply confused about the relationship of disadvantage to patterns of achievement. In particular, there is confusion over how much underachievement is due to the actions of individuals and how much to the influence of the school or the attitudes of the wider society. In this chapter, we will try to clarify some of the issues by exploring what we do know about disadvantage and the impact it can have on the life of school pupils. We will also evaluate some of the remedies that have been adopted in attempts to try to change patterns of disadvantage. Finally we will outline other approaches that appear prima facie to offer hope for this group of pupils and discuss both their advantages and their limitations.

Social Disadvantage

More than fifteen years ago Mortimore and Blackstone (1982) commented that 'The concept of social disadvantage is not easy to define partly because it is a relative concept, tied to the social context of time and place.' (1982, p. 3). Townsend (1996) sees poverty in the same relative way, as '... the absence or inadequacy of those diets, amenities, standards, services and activities which are common or customary in society'. In an attempt to provide objective measures, studies carried out by the National Children's Bureau on the effects of disadvantage adopted three 'hard' criteria: membership of a large or a single parent family; being in receipt of a low family income; and living in poor quality housing (Essen and Wedge, 1982). The Organization for Economic Co-operation and Development draws attention not only to the multiplicative effects of such factors (with one form of disadvantage often leading to the experience of other forms) but also to the fact that much of the impact is felt disproportionately by women (OECD, 1995).

A graphic account of what being poor is actually like has been reported by Oppenheim (1993):

> Poverty means going short materially, socially and emotionally. It means spending less on food, on heating and on clothing ... Poverty means staying at home, often being bored, not seeing friends ... not being able to take the children out for a treat or a holiday. ...
>
> (1993, p. 4)

Despite the general improvement over recent years in most people's living standards, conditions have worsened for a significant minority. According to Walker and Walker (1997), the number of people living in poverty (50 per cent of average national earnings or less) has shown a threefold increase since 1979 and now stands at one quarter of the population. Our country has been exceptional in that the difference between the 'haves' and the 'have nots' seems to have resulted from official policies designed to lift the constraints affecting the rich. These policies have also sought to penalize the poor in the interests of freeing them from a so-called 'dependency culture'. 'Britain stands out internationally in having experienced the largest percentage increase in income inequality between 1967 and 1992' (Dennehy et al., 1997, p. 280) (see also Chapter 1).

The proportion of children living in poor households is now 32 per cent compared to the European Union average of 20 per cent (Eurostat, 1997). Researchers from the Thomas Coram Research Unit estimate that about one third of children now live in households with no full-time earner (Brannen et al., 1997). For many such children, life is grim:

> Children from poor homes have lower life expectancy and are more likely to die in infancy or childhood; they have a greater likelihood of

poor health ... a greater risk of unemployment, a higher probability of involvement in crime and enduring homelessness.

(Holtermann, 1997, p. 26)

What Impact Does Social Disadvantage Have on Children's Educational Opportunities?

Almost by definition, children from disadvantaged backgrounds are more likely than other children to live in a worse environment. Of course disadvantage exists in rural areas, as it does in estates on the fringes of many of our cities, but it is often in the inner city that the worst problems are found in this country. High density living is not, in itself, a bad thing – many people choose to live in this way – but it tends to mean living in greater proximity to crime and drugs and it frequently means living in poor quality housing. As noted by Holtermann (1997), social disadvantage is also frequently associated with poorer health. Children tend to be physically weaker and have less energy for learning than their peers. They are also more likely to be emotionally upset by the tensions in their lives. Finally, they are less likely to have the opportunity for study and for educational help at home. These are just the conditions in which children will be vulnerable to low levels of self efficacy: 'an inability to exert influence over things that adversely affect one's life, which breeds apprehension, apathy, or despair' (Bandura, 1995, p. 1). They, in turn, will work against children's development as effective school learners and, ultimately, according to Wilkinson (1997), their chance of a long healthy life.

Whether the impact of disadvantage on a particular child's education is lasting or not will depend on their own resilience as well as on how much their parents are able to shield them from the effects of disadvantaging circumstances. We know from studies of educational priority programmes that the effects of disadvantage are cumulative. Each new factor adds to the problem. This became starkly evident in a recent study of the educational consequences of homelessness with which one of us was involved (Power et al., 1995).

Remedies Already Tried

There have been a number of distinct approaches to the amelioration of the effects of poverty on educational opportunities. We will focus, for the time being, on education-centred measures, although we shall point later to the limitations of these. One approach rests on the concept of meritocracy. First taken seriously with the introduction of public examinations for officials in the mid-nineteenth century, the concept has subsequently underpinned the widely held assumption that those with talents would rise to the top through public competition. It was used to justify the scholarship ladder introduced at the turn of the century, formed the basis of the 11-plus selection procedure and, most recently, the assisted places scheme. It has also informed the thinking behind public examinations generally. The evidence from studies of social mobility shows that such a meritocratic approach does help overcome the effects of disadvantage by promoting some individuals with outstanding talents. What such studies also show, however, is that, although this works for some, it fails to do so for many more (Brown et al., 1997). The philosophy of 'plucking embers from the ashes' of inner city deprivation (cited in Edwards et al., 1989) does nothing to improve the standard of education for those left behind. The Conservative governments introduced choice and competition strategies with an avowed aim of equalizing opportunities for all families regardless of where they lived. Too often, however, these strategies seem only to have polarized provision even further (Whitty et al., 1998).

The second approach has been characterized by the use of compensatory mechanisms. These include individual benefits, such as free school meals, uniform grants and other special measures for low income families. The problems with individual benefits are that the levels of funding have always been relatively modest and have thus been unable to compensate for the major differences in the conditions of children's lives (Smith and Noble, 1995). Compensatory mechanisms have also included the allocation of additional resources to schools, such as in the Educational Priority Area programmes of the 1960s and 1970s, when extra payments were made to schools with high proportions of disadvantaged pupils (Halsey, 1972; Smith, 1987). One drawback of school-wide schemes is that targeting is necessarily inefficient: some advantaged pupils will gain access to extra resources within the chosen schools, whilst many disadvantaged pupils, in other schools, will fail to do so (Acland, 1973; Plewis, 1997). However, there may still be cost-effective benefits, as work concerned with the development of 'at risk' registers of birth disorders, carried out over 20 years ago, shows (Alberman and Goldstein, 1970). Later versions of this idea, adopted by the (former) Inner London Education Authority, provided extra resources on a sliding scale rather than on an all or-nothing basis (Sammons et al., 1983). The local management formulae for schools approved by governments over the last few years, however, allow little scope for radical positive discrimination.

The third approach to combating disadvantage involves the creation of intervention projects, potentially open to all pupils, but which have mainly been used with the disadvantaged with a view to accelerating their educational development. Such projects include: in the United States, the High/ Scope programme which promoted active child learning (Weikart, 1972; Schweinhart and Weikart, 1997); the Comer Approach – which addresses children's health and social as well as their educational, needs (Comer, 1980); and Success for All (Slavin et al., 1993) – seen as one of the most promising approaches to overcoming the educational effects of disadvantage (Herman and Stringfield, 1995) (see Chapters 8 and 4 for a fuller account of these and other programmes). In New Zealand, Clay has developed the Reading

Recovery Programme, a structured approach to overcoming early reading failure which has been shown to be effective for disadvantaged pupils (Clay, 1982; Rowe, 1995). In Latin America, there has been a number of initiatives based on the work of the late Paulo Freire (see de Figueiredo-Cowen and Gastaldo, 1995). There has also been an interest in capitalizing on research which demonstrates that intellectual tasks can be found in the everyday activities of disadvantaged children (see, for instance, Nunes et al. 1993). In the United Kingdom, the Early Years Nursery Study, which focused on ways of increasing children's capacity to learn (Athey, 1995) has also claimed some success; a series of British parent involvement schemes designed to encourage children and parents to read together (see, for example, Tizard et al., 1982) has been shown to have positive effects; and a Scottish project on the use of homework has demonstrated gains in disadvantaged areas (MacBeath and Turner, 1990).

Despite the enthusiastic support of teachers and local authorities in the UK for each of these projects, official support and hence widespread implementation has been strictly limited. The Reading Recovery Programme, for instance, was trialed in an English LEA and introduced more widely in a highly systematic way. It had £14 million spent on it through government grants and obtained positive evaluations from a carefully controlled experiment (Sylva and Hurry, 1995; Hobsbaum, 1995). Nevertheless it was dropped from government priorities after three years, just as its impact was beginning to be felt. Furthermore, the Early Years Study by Athey has never been promoted more widely despite some evidence that its application might even lessen the gap between disadvantaged and other pupils. These interventions have the ability to change pupil outcomes but their potential benefits have not been exploited, nor have the limits to their efficacy been properly investigated. In particular, we need to know whether these approaches are especially advantageous with disadvantaged pupils to the extent that they would help close the achievement gap even if used with all pupils.

Although these approaches can clearly combat the individual consequences of disadvantage to some degree, they have so far failed significantly to alter the established differential patterns of achievement in this country. There remains a strong negative correlation between most measures of social disadvantage and school achievement, as even a cursory glance at the league tables of school by school results demonstrates (Smith and Noble, 1995). Why is this so? First, there is the obvious fact that what has been done in compensatory and supplementary activity remains slight in comparison with the impact of the cumulative benefits of growing up in an advantaged home. It would be odd if having warmer, more spacious accommodation, more nutritious food, better health, greater access to books, educational toys and stimulating experiences, and more informed knowledge about how the system works, did not confer considerable advantage in any tests or examinations.

Second, it should not be forgotten that measures of educational achievement are determined by competition within the tradition of a meritocracy.

Thus even though there has been a rise in achievement, as recorded by the General Certificate of Secondary Education results (from 22 per cent in 1980 to 44.5 per cent in 1996 gaining the five high grades usually deemed the mark of success), more than half the age group still does not succeed at this level (DfEE, 1996a). Given this reality and the factors noted earlier, it would surely be surprising if those with disadvantaged backgrounds succeeded in equal proportions to their more advantaged peers (see also Chapter 3).

Examination success is not, of course, rationed and the official examination boards would be quick to refute any suggestion that they work within strict norms, but it would be naïve to think that expectations established over many years could be set aside other than by a slow incremental progression. The annual chorus of 'more must mean worse' ensures that the scope for disadvantaged candidates to join the successful group is likely to remain strictly limited, whatever improvements are made to their absolute levels of achievement.

The Report *Learning Works: Widening participation in further education* (Kennedy, 1997a) has drawn attention to the evidence that it is those who are already well qualified who go on to earn more and to demand and get more learning.

So there remains a need to do a great deal more if an often-declared goal of our education system – to help every child, regardless of family background, achieve up to the limits of his or her potential – is to be realized.

What Else Can be Done?

Two possible avenues forward are often seen as mutually exclusive alternatives. One builds on the work in school improvement that has been pioneered as a result of research into school effectiveness. The other is more fundamental and demands change not only to the nature of educational practice but also to the broader social and cultural contexts within which education takes place. We believe that an effective strategy for tackling disadvantage requires movement on both fronts.

Change Through School Improvement

The roots of school improvement lie in 20 years of research into school effectiveness carried out mainly in England, the Netherlands and the United States (Hopkins et al., 1994). The central tenet of school improvement is that the responsibility for change must lie in the hands of the school itself (Stoll and Fink, 1996). In contrast to centrally driven projects, those working in school improvement believe that the head teacher, staff and school governing body – having listened to the views and advice of school inspectors, consultants or researchers – are well placed to decide how best to improve their own institutions (Mortimore, 1996).

Evaluations of established improvement projects show that they tend to have a common pattern (Stoll and Fink, 1996). Initially, the school improvement team carry out an audit of the current state of the school: the pupils' outcomes (including behaviour as well as attainment), the curriculum, the pedagogy, the management of learning, behaviour and resources, and the state of the premises. In the light of such investigations, the team draws up an action plan to enhance the good and repair the bad. Although problems are sometimes obvious, it is often difficult precisely to diagnose their cause. The team has to make a series of hypotheses about what has probably caused which outcome, and what might – if changed – produce a different result. This is far from being an exact science and in the third stage – the evaluation – the team may discover that many outcomes are the result of a complex web of influences and, furthermore, that some changes have produced unintended negative results.

School improvers know they cannot create a recipe book – schools are far too complex for such an approach (Stoll and Myers, forthcoming). They have sought, rather, to identify and make use of the underlying processes of change. Writers such as Fullan (1991), Huberman (1992) and Louis and Miles (1990) have identified a number of facilitating or inhibiting factors that affect the process. Fullan, for instance, lists a number of warnings about change that he urges school head teachers to heed: that change is not easy, that conflict and disagreement will be inevitable and that not all colleagues will embrace it. Fullan stresses that heads should expect these outcomes and not be caught unawares if they occur in reaction to change efforts.

Two questions arise from this brief review of improvement strategies: can school improvement help schools that have high proportions of disadvantaged pupils and can it help individual disadvantaged pupils?

Can Improvement Projects Help Schools with High Proportions of Disadvantaged Pupils?

The National Commission on Education (NCE, 1996) undertook a project designed to uncover how some schools with disadvantaged pupils had improved and succeeded against the odds. Eleven teams (each consisting of an educational researcher and two representatives from the business world or the community) carried out fieldwork to identify why particular schools were successful in the face of disadvantage. In the school case study carried out by one of us (Mortimore et al., 1996), we were particularly impressed with the quality of the leadership team and the way it had trusted the majority of the staff to create a set of school aims around the idea of achievement. Pupils were committed to learning and staff held high expectations about examination performance and social behaviour. The confidence of the teachers in the good sense of the pupils – even to the radical point of encouraging them to draw up a code of what they expected of the staff – was impressive.

Maden's and Hillman's (1996) discussion of the findings from all the case studies in the project emphasizes the importance of a leadership stance which builds on and develops a team approach; a vision of success which includes a view of how the school can improve; the careful use of targets; the improvement of the physical environment; common expectations about pupils' behaviour and success; and an investment in good relations with parents and the community. They note how a crisis in the life of the school can become a catalyst for successful change.

What the project demonstrates is that committed and talented heads and teachers can improve schools even if such schools contain a proportion of disadvantaged pupils. In order to achieve improvement, however, such schools have to exceed what could be termed 'normal' efforts. Members of staff have to be more committed and work harder than their peers elsewhere. What is more, they have to maintain the effort so as to sustain the improvement. There can be no switching on the 'automatic pilot' if schools are aiming to buck the trend. We must, however, be aware of the dangers of basing a national strategy for change on the efforts of outstanding individuals working in exceptional circumstances.

Further evidence about the ability of schools with disadvantaged pupils to improve comes from the first tranche of case studies published by the DfEE (DfEE, 1997a). These studies describe some of the ways in which improvement was brought about in schools that had failed their OFSTED inspections. In contrast to much of the rhetoric about resources not mattering, what stands out is the impact of the extra resources invested by the LEAs in their efforts to turn the schools round.

Can School Improvement Projects Help Individual Disadvantaged Pupils?

Evidence from a recent study of the 'value added' results from one local authority shows that some schools are able – once all background factors have been taken into account – to 'lift' the GCSE results by the equivalent of a change from seven grade Ds to seven grade Bs (Thomas and Mortimore, 1996). MacGilchrist (1997) also argues forcefully that some of the special interventions (noted earlier) which have been mounted to support the learning of pupils with special difficulties – and, in many cases, disadvantaged backgrounds – demonstrate that more schools, given adequate support, could help such pupils. She notes, however, that these opportunities have not been sufficiently exploited.

In theory, researchers should be able to estimate fairly precisely how many individual pupils have been helped by their schools to overcome the effects of personal disadvantage. By addressing the GCSE results of secondary schools and noting their intake information from five years before (for example, what was pupil attainment at the end of primary schooling and how many pupils were eligible for free school meals) it should be possible to estimate some 'value added' scores for their schools in relation to other institutions. Those that had raised the achievement of their 'disadvantaged pupils' significantly beyond what had been achieved by similar pupils in other schools could be assumed to have helped, especially, this group of pupils. The results could then be aggregated to provide an estimate of the likely total number of disadvantaged pupils that have been helped by the efforts of school improvement. Retrospective investigations could then attempt to explore how the schools had helped these pupils and, in particular, whether improvement had been the result of a planned programme or whether it had occurred seemingly spontaneously. Other information, such as whether the 'disadvantaged' group had been a particularly high or low proportion of the total, could also be collected so as to inform us about the importance of the educational context in which a pupil learns.

Unfortunately, such an investigation remains a theoretical possibility because not only would it be difficult to ensure that one really was 'comparing like with like' but also because there is not a suitable national database which brings together accurate intake and examination outcome data. It is worth noting, anyway, that attributing causal effects to particular initiatives in complex organizations such as schools is always likely to be difficult. Analysis of American statistical evidence suggests that achievement gains are often too readily attributed to a particular initiative when there may well be entirely different explanations, such as a change of intake (Henig, 1994). Without appropriate data and suitably robust analytical techniques, therefore, the evidence for the ability of schools to help individual disadvantaged pupils has to rest on theory and on the historical evidence of those institutions which, in the absence of alternative explanations, do appear to have bucked the trend.

Cultural and Structural Change

Sociologists of education have frequently been critical of work on school effectiveness and school improvement. For example, Angus criticizes it for failing 'to explore the relationship of specific practices to wider social and cultural constructions and political and economic interests' (1993, p. 335). He argues that it 'shifts attention away from the nature of knowledge, the culture of schooling and, most importantly, the question of for whom and in whose interests schools are to be effective' (p. 342). Hatcher (1996) sees school improvement as downplaying the significance of social class, with similar consequences. In this context, even the very term 'disadvantage' can serve to hide the structured inequalities of class and race and actually contribute to the 'colour-blindness' of recent education policy (Gillborn, 1997) (see also Chapters 2 and 3).

Can Changes in Curriculum and Assessment Help?

Angus' questions suggest that the curriculum itself may be implicated in perpetuating disadvantage by marginalizing the culture of the least powerful groups in society. There is certainly a case for broadening the scope of what counts as legitimate knowledge in schools (Comer, 1980; Whitty, 1985). Some of the national curriculum orders have been criticized for adopting an unduly narrow view of worthwhile knowledge and ignoring the pluralism and multi-culturalism of late twentieth-century Britain (Ball, 1993).

Although some of these issues will need to be addressed by the new government, individual schools can also play some part in the way they choose to interpret the national curriculum and they need to be mindful of this opportunity to help the disadvantaged. Trying to counter the cultural bias of current curricular arrangements and making schools more 'inclusive' of diverse communities is sometimes seen as a watering down of standards. Yet schools that are successful with pupils from a variety of backgrounds recognize that high standards can be achieved in a number of ways. While some learning goals need to be tackled by all pupils in the same way, others can be achieved through a variety of routes that take account of different back-grounds. This is not the same as adjusting standards to the lowest common denominator. That is an unacceptable option, especially in the light of the increasing globalization of labour and the need to ensure that young people from the United Kingdom can compete with their peers from elsewhere in the world.

Nevertheless, such considerations also demand that we find ways to ensure that a greater proportion of our pupils can succeed. This may require a restructuring of the assessment system. Can we design a progression system so that a much higher proportion of candidates reaches the currently accepted level of success? The experience of assessing the progress of pupils through the national curriculum is not very promising and efforts to combine a pupil's need for diagnostic assessment with a system need for certification and moni-toring have generally proved unsatisfactory for each of these needs. There are a number of ways in which our national approach to assessment could be improved: the standards set for performance could be better defined; feedback could be more positive; a range of performance tasks and modes could be provided (Gipps, 1994). It has to be borne in mind, however, that such improvements would be more likely to lift overall standards than specifically help the disadvantaged. This would be helpful to our national standards of achievement and is to be greatly encouraged, but clearly does not address the particular problem of the disadvantaged.

It is sometimes suggested that the print-based culture of schools is in itself an obstacle for disadvantaged pupils and that this might be overcome by the new information technologies (IT). It is too early to know whether these will provide dramatic new opportunities. So far few schools have had the resources to invest in adequate equipment and too few teachers have been fully trained in its use. Experiments in particular schools in the United States and in Australia need to be evaluated before we know whether the technology will provide radically more powerful ways of learning. But while it is possible that IT may help, particularly, pupils from disadvantaged backgrounds, we have to remember that IT is shaped by the same social forces as other more obviously social phenomena. For example, any potential benefits for disadvantaged pupils may be offset by the fact that those from advantaged families are more likely to have access to IT equipment in the home and thus to develop the relevant 'know how' sooner. Furthermore, the Internet, often proclaimed as a democratic medium which eradicates social distinctions, is actually used mainly by white middle-class males and this has consequences for the material available on it (Kenway, 1996).

Addressing the Impact of the Wider Society

Whatever changes occur in the curriculum and means of assessment, it seems inevitable that schools will be affected by their role within a wider society that still maintains social divisions and a powerful sense of hierarchy. A particular criticism of school improvement work is that it has tended to exaggerate the extent to which individual schools can challenge such structural inequalities. Whilst some schools can succeed against the odds, the possibility of them all doing so, year in and year out, still appears remote given that the long-term patterning of educational inequality has been strikingly consistent throughout the history of public education in most countries.

Doubts have recently even been cast on whether Sweden, usually seen as a shining exception, has actually succeeded in bucking this particular trend in recent years (Erikson and Jonsson, 1996). Although there are different theories about how the social and cultural patterning of educational outcomes occurs (Goldthorpe, 1996), these patterns reflect quite closely the relative chances of different groups entering different segments of the labour market. Accordingly, whilst it might be possible, for example, for the ethos of a particular school to help transform the aspirations of a particular group of pupils within it, it seems highly unlikely that all schools could do this in the absence of more substantial social changes.

As noted earlier, one of the depressing findings is that the relative performance of the disadvantaged has remained similar even when the absolute performance of such groups has improved. Just as poverty is a relative concept, we are faced with a situation in which educational success also appears to be partly relative. A large-scale longitudinal study of primary schools carried out by one of us (Mortimore et al., 1988) found that no school reversed the usual 'within school' pattern of advantaged pupils performing better than the disadvantaged. However, some of the disadvantaged pupils in the most effective schools made more progress than their advantaged peers in the least effective schools and even did better in absolute terms. Yet, encouraging as this is, it would appear that, if all primary schools were to improve so that they performed at the level of the most effective, the difference between the overall achievement of the most advantaged social groups and that of the disadvantaged might actually increase.

At secondary level, schools only rarely overcome the relative differences between the performance of different social groups, as the latest evidence on differential school effects demonstrates (Thomas et al., 1997). Moreover, despite the optimism of some school improvement literature, it is still difficult to counter the conclusion to be drawn from a reading of the pioneering *Fifteen Thousand Hours* research (Rutter et al., 1979) that, if all schools performed as well as the best schools, the stratification of achievement by social class would be even more stark than it is now. This would happen because socially advantaged children in highly effective schools would achieve even more than they might do in a less conducive environment and the gap between them and their less advantaged peers would increase.

The initial report of the Literacy Task Force (Literacy Task Force, 1997) seemed to recognize the existence of such problems but underestimated the resource implications of overcoming them. However, New Labour's subsequent literacy strategy, which grew out of the work of that group, does propose a modest redistribution of resources. Nevertheless, the problems and dilemmas facing schools with large numbers of disadvantaged pupils, compared with those with advantaged intakes, are much greater than even current policies recognize (Proudford and Baker, 1995; Thrupp, 1995, 1997). This suggests a continuing need for positive discrimination and the effective targeting of human and material resources. Smith et al. (1997) recommend three sets of actions to support schools in disadvantaged areas. They argue that, because of the competitive market that has been created, education in poor areas must not be considered in isolation. Given the existence of this competitive market between schools, they recommend a stronger interventionist role for the LEA. They suggest that 'choice' is too blunt an instrument for improvement and recommend the targeting of resources to schools in disadvantaged areas and possibly a transfer of resources from inspection to school improvement.

Robinson claims that educational measures are unlikely to alleviate the impact of disadvantage. He rightly sees the tackling of social and economic disadvantage as more likely to succeed, arguing that 'a serious programme to alleviate child poverty might do far more for boosting attainment and literacy than any modest intervention in schooling' (Robinson, 1997, p. 17). Unlike Robinson, however, we believe more up to date evidence shows that schools can make some difference. Schools with disadvantaged pupils can lift achievement levels, provided those who work in them invest the energy and the dedication to maintain momentum even while working against the grain. Within any school, however, the powerful factors associated with a more advantaged home background appear, in general, to be paramount and this is even more evident when we look across the education system as a whole. It is, therefore, important for government, LEAs and school governors to set challenging goals but it is also important to be clear about the limits of school-based actions. Setting unrealistic goals and adopting a strategy of 'shame and blame' will lead only to cynicism and a lowering of morale amongst those teachers at the heart of the struggle to raise the achievement of disadvantaged pupils.

Tackling Disadvantage Beyond the School

Grace has argued that too many urban education reformers have been guilty of 'producing naïve school-centred solutions with no sense of the structural, the political and the historical as constraints' (Grace, 1984, p. xii). If schools alone are unable to close the gap between the disadvantaged and their peers, are there other institutions or agencies that can do so? Clearly, if disadvantage has multiple causes, tackling it requires strategies that bring together multiple agencies that more usually work in isolation. There have, of course, been a number of initiatives that have sought to do this in targeted areas (see Wilmott and Hutchinson, 1992, and also Chapter 13), but the recent 'marketization' of housing, health and education appears to have provided disadvantaged families with less rather than more co-ordination of services (Power et al., 1995). A major priority for the new government must surely be to provide incentives for effective multi-agency work to counter disadvantage.

This is not just a matter of ensuring greater efficiency in the delivery of public services, important as that is. Considerable concern has been expressed recently about a decline in 'social capital' in modern societies, with an alleged breakdown in relationships of trust and supportive social networks. Furthermore, there is growing evidence of the damaging effects of vast differences in social capital between different communities (Wilkinson, 1996). Hall (1997, p. 35) suggests that Britain is becoming increasingly divided between 'a well-connected and active group of citizens and another whose associational life ... is very limited'. Arguably, the situation has been made worse by policies that treat education as a consumer right rather than a citizen right and thereby undermine the notion that education is a public good and the responsibility of the whole community (Whitty, 1997). Yet Coleman's analysis (Coleman, 1988) suggests that the social capital of a community, as well as that of families and schools, can have an important bearing on the educational achievement of its children. Policies that may appear to have little to do with education, such as community development or the building of 'healthy alliances', might therefore actually contribute to the raising of achievement in schools. Thus, statutory agencies could usefully assist voluntary associations in developing networks within the wider community that support the work of schools at the same time as bringing other benefits to the community. The Healthy Schools Initiative, recently launched by the Department of Health and the Department for Education and Employment, is an example of this and it will be important to evaluate its impact on school effectiveness in disadvantaged areas.

The enhancement of social and cultural capital in disadvantaged areas also requires that more be done to provide opportunities for learning beyond the years of compulsory schooling. Traditionally this has been one of the tasks of further education colleges and adult institutes committed to continuing life-long learning but these institutions and their clientele have too often been marginalized within the system as a whole.

The previous government's *Lifetime Learning* (DfEE, 1996b) tried to focus public debate on the importance of lifelong education and training but there are other ways in which, in our view, the government could help disadvan-taged people extend their education. These include: a radical revision of its approach to studying whilst unemployed; an extension of tax exemptions for all in post-compulsory training; an equalization of treatment of part-time and full-time students; support for a national credit-based education and training framework; and the provision of increased child care to support learning opportunities for part-time and temporary workers.

The Kennedy Report (Kennedy, 1997a) lists a number of detailed recom-mendations for government, the Training and Enterprise Councils and individual further education colleges. These include the launching of a lottery-funded government campaign for the creation of a learning nation; the redistribution of public resources towards those with less success in earlier learning; the encouragement of company-funded learning centres for adult workers; and the creation of a unitized system for recognizing achievement (the Pathways to Learning Project).

In a comment on the Report, Kennedy argues (Kennedy, 1997b, p. 3) that drawing more people into the community of learning is not only central to economic prosperity but also 'one of the most effective ways of tackling social exclusion'. She claims that 'we have been seeing the most terrible separation between rich and poor over the past decades and education has a vital role in redressing the consequences of that division'. This requires 'a redistribution of public resources towards those with less success in earlier learning'. It is not yet clear how far the new government is prepared to move in this direction.

Changes such as those proposed above would ease the financial costs for those who needed to make up in their own time for an unsatisfactory experi-ence of schooling. Such opportunities are necessary if more people are to continue their education and, in particular, if the disadvantaged are to play any part in the formation of a learning society. They are only likely to succeed, however, in the context of a culture – as well as a structure – of inclusiveness. Yet much of our previous history of education has been built on a culture of exclusiveness. It is how to change this culture that probably represents the new government's greatest challenge, as has been recognized through the establishment of a Social Exclusion Unit based at the heart of government.

One of the ways to alter this culture is to invent new approaches that bring together partners from across society rather than seeing problems as being solely in the realm of the education service. A commitment to doing this is evident in one of the few New Labour education initiatives that signals a clear break with the policies of the recent past. The government is establishing a pilot programme of up to 25 Education Action Zones in areas with a mix of underperforming schools and the highest levels of disadvantage (DfEE, 1997b). Such Action Zones will have at their centre a forum of local parents and representatives from local business and community interests in which an action plan and targets will be formulated, implemented and monitored. It remains to be seen how these develop and whether their existence does indeed channel more help and energy into the target areas whilst avoiding the pitfalls of the old Educational Priority Areas. Nevertheless, the idea seems worth pursuing, provided each zone's forum includes and values the contribution of all relevant constituencies and provided there really is a significant redistribution of resources into these areas (see Chapter 16 for a further discussion of these zones).

Conclusions

In this chapter we have spelled out our interpretation of the educational problem faced by pupils from disadvantaged families in our society. We have found – with some notable exceptions – that school pupils with such backgrounds do less well than their peers, hardly a surprising finding in a competitive system. We have also shown that previous governments have failed to exploit what knowledge there is about how to combat the problem. In particular, we have described how a number of the co-ordinating initiatives and intervention strategies that appear to have had some success in other countries have been ignored. Furthermore, some of those that have been adopted and shown to have benefits have inexplicably been allowed to wither. Meanwhile, the advantaged have sometimes gained even more than the disadvantaged from those initiatives that have been pursued. The effect is that the advantaged become more so and the disadvantaged – without the help and support of focused extra help – slip further behind. Thus the conventional pattern of outcomes is maintained – with the advantaged at the top and the disadvantaged (with some exceptions) at the bottom. So can there be a solution to this set of problems?

The re-engineering of the educational system, so that disadvantaged groups can succeed, will not be easy. As Bernstein (1970) noted nearly 30 years ago, 'Education cannot compensate for society'. Nor is education's role in helping to change society well understood. Probably the single most significant factor that currently distinguishes the most academically successful schools (even if not the most 'effective' ones in value-added terms) is that only a small proportion of their pupils come from disadvantaged homes. To that extent, policies which tackle poverty and related aspects of disadvantage at their roots are likely to be more successful than purely educational interventions in influencing overall patterns of educational inequality. Yet if dynamic school improvement strategies can be developed as one aspect of a broader social policy, then they will have an important role to play on behalf of individual schools and their pupils.

What we have been concerned to stress in this chapter is that society needs to be clearer about what schools can and cannot be expected to do. As we have tried to demonstrate, the relationship between individuals, institutions and society is complex and blaming schools for the problems of society is unfair and unproductive. Nevertheless, demonstrating that opportunities for some disadvantaged pupils can be changed in particularly effective schools – even if the disadvantaged as a group still remain behind their peers – can itself help to transform a culture of inertia or despair. It is this transformation that those who work in the field of school improvement are seeking. Schools with high proportions of disadvantaged pupils need extra support. Teachers who choose to work in these schools – because they want to help the disadvantaged – need their commitment recognized and supported rather than being 'blamed', as has happened so shamefully in the past.

In short, we do not consider that there is any single factor that could reverse longstanding patterns of disadvantage but neither do we regard them as an unchangeable fact of life. We believe that our society must – through government actions as well as grass roots initiatives – begin to adjust the balance between individuals' opportunities and their social responsibilities so as to develop a more equal society. Society should not have to cope with what Wilkinson terms the 'corrosive effects of inequality' (Wilkinson, 1996).

With such a perspective, we consider four clusters of immediate action to be vital:

- better co-ordination of the work of the support agencies by the government and by local authorities;
- early interventions that provide additional educational opportunities for the disadvantaged, funded from an increased education budget;
- reconsideration of the approaches to learning and teaching used with disadvantaged pupils;
- extra support for pupils with disadvantaged backgrounds in school improvement programmes.

Even with these actions we accept that there is unlikely to be a sudden reversal of long-established patterns of disadvantage or any significant long-term change in the absence of concurrent strategies to tackle poverty and disadvantage at their roots. We do consider, however, that the current waste of human resources caused by the educational failure of those with disadvantaged backgrounds is unacceptable in a modern society. We urge the government to make a fresh start. We believe that, if it could focus its energy on this problem and set a new tone by working with local authorities, the teaching and other caring professions, it would have a better chance of achieving change than previous governments. Future generations of school pupils from disadvantaged families would stand to benefit but the real gain would be the creation of a better educated society more likely to surmount the challenges of the twenty-first century.

References

Acland, H. (1973) 'Social determinants of educational achievement: an evaluation and criticism of research', Ph.D. thesis, University of Oxford.

Alberman, E.D. and Goldstein, H. (1970) 'The "at risk" register: a statistical evaluation', *British Journal of Preventative Medicine* 24, 3, pp. 129–135.

Angus, L. (1993) 'The sociology of school effectiveness', *British Journal of Sociology of Education* 14, 3, pp. 333–345.

Athey, C. (1990) *Extending Thought in Young Children*, London, Paul Chapman Publishing.

Ball, S.J. (1993) 'Education, Majorism and "the curriculum of the dead"', *Curriculum Studies* 1, 2, pp. 195–214.

Bandura, A. (1995) 'Exercise of personal and collective efficacy in changing societies', in Bandura, A. (ed.) *Self Efficacy in Changing Societies*, Cambridge, Cambridge University Press.

Bernstein, B. (1970) 'Education cannot compensate for society', *New Society* 387, pp. 344–347.

Brannen, J., Moss, P., Owen, C. and Wale, C. (1997) *Mothers, Fathers and Employment: Parents and the labour market in Britain 1984–1994*, London, DfEE/Institute of Education.

Brown, P., Halsey, A.H., Lauder, H. and Wells, A. (1997) 'The transformation of education and society: an introduction' in Halsey, A.H., Lauder, H., Brown, P. and Wells, A. (eds) *Education: Culture, economy and society*, Oxford, Oxford University Press.

Clay, M.M. (1982) *Observing Young Readers*, New Hampshire, Heinemann.

Coleman, J. (1988) 'Social capital in the creation of human capital', *American Journal of Sociology* 94, Supplement, pp. 95–120.

Comer, J.P. (1980) *School Power: Implication of an intervention project*, New York, Free Press.

Davie, R., Butler, N. and Goldstein, H. (1972) *From Birth to Seven*, Harlow, Longman.

Dennehy, A., Smith, L. and Harker, P. (1997) 'Not to be ignored: young people, poverty and health', in Walker, A. and Walker, C. (eds) *Britain Divided: The growth of social exclusion in the 1980s and 1990s*, London, CPAG.

Department for Education and Employment (DfEE) (1996a) *Education Statistics*, London, HMSO.

Department for Education and Employment (DfEE) (1996b) *Lifetime Learning: A policy framework*, DfEE.

Department for Education and Employment (DfEE) (1997a) *The Road to Success*, London, Institute of Education/DfEE.

Department for Education and Employment (DfEE) (1997b) *Excellence in Schools*, Cm 3681, London, HMSO.

Douglas, J.W.B. (1964) *The Home and the School*, London, MacGibbon & Kee.

Edwards, T., Fitz, J. and Whitty, G. (1989) *The State and Private Education: An evaluation of the assisted places scheme*, Lewes, Falmer Press.

Erikson, R. and Jonsson, J.O. (eds) (1996) *Can Education be Equalized? The Swedish case in comparative perspective*, Boulder, CO, Westview Press.

Essen, J. and Wedge, P. (1982) *Continuities in Childhood Disadvantage*, London, Heinemann.

Eurostat (1997) Reported in the *Guardian* 28 April.

Figueiredo-Cowen, M. de and Gastaldo, D. (eds) (1995) *Paulo Freire at the Institute*, London, Institute of Education, University of London.

Fullan, M. (1991) *The New Meaning of Educational Change*, London, Cassell.

Gillborn, D. (1997) 'Young, black and failed by school: the market, education reform and black students', *Journal of Inclusive Education* 1, 1, pp. 65–87.

Gipps, C. (1994) *Beyond Testing: Towards a theory of educational assessment*, London, Falmer Press.

Goldthorpe, J.H. (1996) 'Class analysis and the reorientation of class theory: the case of persisting differentials in educational attainment', *British Journal of Sociology* 47, 3, pp. 482–505.

Gorman, T. and Fernandes, C. (1992) *Reading in Recession*, Slough, NFER.

Grace, G. (1984) *Education in the City*, London, Routledge & Kegan Paul.

Hall, P.A. (1997) 'Social capital: a fragile asset' in Christie, I. and Perry, H. (eds) *The Wealth and Poverty of Networks: Tackling social exclusion*, London, Demos.

Halsey, A.H. (ed) (1972) *Educational Priority, E.P.A. Problems and Policies* 1, London, HMSO.

Hatcher, R. (1996) 'The limitations of the new social democratic agendas', in Hatcher, R. and Jones, K. (eds) *Education after the Conservatives*, Stoke-on-Trent, Trentham Books.

Henig, J.R. (1994) *Rethinking School Choice: Limits of the market metaphor*, Princeton, NJ, Princeton University Press.

Herman, R. and Stringfield, S. (1995) *Ten Promising Programmes for Educating Disadvantaged Students*, Baltimore, Johns Hopkins University Press.

Hobsbaum, A. (1995) 'Reading Recovery in England', *Literacy, Teaching and Learning* 1, 2, pp. 21–39.

Holtermann, S. (1997) 'All our futures: the impact of public expenditure and fiscal policies on children and young people', in Walker, A. and Walker, C. (eds) *Britain Divided: The growth of social exclusion in the 1980s and 1990s*, London, CPAG.

Hopkins, D., Ainscow, M. and West, M. (1994) *School Improvement in an Era of Change*, London, Cassell.

Huberman, M. (1992) Critical introduction to Fullan, M., *Successful School Improvement*, Buckingham, Open University Press.

Kennedy, H. (1997a) *Learning Works: Widening participation in further education*, London, FEFC.

Kennedy, H. (1997b) 'The Report', *Guardian Education* 1 July, p. 2–3.

Kenway, J. (1996) 'The information superhighway and post-modernity: the social promise and the social price', *Comparative Education* 32, 2, pp. 217–231.

Literacy Task Force (1997) *A Reading Revolution: How we can teach every child to read well*, London, Literacy Task Force.

Louis, K. and Miles, M. (1990) *Improving the Urban High School*, New York, Teachers' College Press.

MacBeath, J. and Turner, M. (1990) *Learning Out of School: Homework, policy and practice*, a research study commissioned by the Scottish Education Department, Glasgow, Jordanhill College.

MacGilchrist, B. (1997) 'Reading and achievement', *Research Papers in Education*, 12, 2, 157–176.

Maden, M. and Hillman, J. (1996) 'Lessons in success', in National Commission on Education, *Success Against the Odds*, London, Routledge.

Mortimore, P. (1996) 'Partnership and co-operation in school improvement', *Paper Presented at the Association for Teacher Education in Europe Conference*, Glasgow, Scotland, September.

Mortimore, J. and Blackstone, T. (1982) *Education and Disadvantage*, London, Heinemann.

Mortimore, P. and Mortimore, J. (1986) 'Education and social class', in Rogers, R. (ed.) *Education and Social Class*, Lewes, Falmer Press.

Mortimore, P. and Whitty, G. (1997) *Can School Improvement Overcome the Effects of Disadvantage?*, London, Institute of Education, University of London.

Mortimore, P., Davies, H. and Portway, S. (1996) 'Burntwood School: a case study', in National Commission on Education, *Success Against the Odds*, London, Routledge.

Mortimore, P., Sammons, P., Stoll, L., Lewis, D. and Ecob, R. (1988) 'The effects of school membership on pupils' educational outcomes', *Research Papers in Education* 3, 1, pp. 3–26.

National Commission on Education (NCE) (1996) *Success Against the Odds: Effective Schools in Disadvantaged Areas*, London, Routledge.

Nunes, T., Schliemann, A.D. and Carraher, D.W. (1993) *Street Mathematics and School Mathematics*, Cambridge, Cambridge University Press.

Oppenheim, C. (1993) *Poverty: The facts*, London, CPAG.

Organization for Economic Co-operation and Development (OECD) (1995) *Our Children at Risk*, Paris, OECD.

Osborne, A.F. and Milbank, J.E. (1987) *The Effects of Early Education*, Oxford, Clarendon Press.

Plewis, I. (1997) Letter to the *Times Educational Supplement*, 9 May, p. 19.

Power, S., Whitty, G. and Youdell, D. (1995) *No Place to Learn: Homelessness and education*, London, Shelter.

Proudford, C. and Baker, R. (1995) 'Schools that make a difference: a sociological perspective on effective schooling', *British Journal of Sociology of Education* 16, 3, pp. 277–292.

Robinson, P. (1997) *Literacy, Numeracy and Economic Performance*, London, CEP/London School of Economics.

Rowe, K.J. (1995) 'Factors affecting students' progress in reading: key findings from a longitudinal study in literacy', *Teaching and Learning, an International Journal of Early Literacy* 1, 2, pp. 57–110.

Rutter, M., Maughan, B., Mortimore, P. and Ouston, J. (1979) *Fifteen Thousand Hours*, London, Paul Chapman Publishing.

Sammons, P., Kysel, F. and Mortimore, P. (1983) 'Educational priority indices: a new perspective', *British Educational Research Journal* 9, 1, pp. 27–40.

Schweinhart, L.J. and Weikart, D.P. (1997) 'Lasting differences: the High/Scope Pre-School Curriculum Comparison Study through age 23', *Early Childhood Research Quarterly* 12, pp. 117–143.

Slavin, R.E., Karweit, N.L., Dolan, L.J., Wasik, B.A. and Madden, N.A. (1993) ' "Success for all": longitudinal effects of a restructuring program for inner city elementary schools', *American Educational Research Journal* 30, pp. 123–148.

Smith, G. (1987) 'Whatever happened to educational priority areas?', *Oxford Review of Education* 13, 1, pp. 23–38.

Smith, T. and Noble, M. (1995) *Education Divides: Poverty and schooling in the 1990s*, London, CPAG.

Smith, G., Smith, T. and Wright, G. (1997) 'Poverty and schooling: choice, diversity or division?' in Walker, A. and Walker, C. (eds) *Britain Divided: The growth of social exclusion in the 1980s and 1990s*, London, CPAG.

Stoll, L. and Fink, D. (1996) *Changing our Schools*, Buckingham, Open University Press.

Stoll, L. and Myers, K. (forthcoming) *No Quick Fixes: Perspectives on schools in difficulty*, London, Falmer Press.

Sylva, K. and Hurry, J. (1995) 'The Effectiveness of Reading Recovery and Phonological Training for Children with Reading Problems', full report prepared for the School Curriculum and Assessment Authority, London, Thomas Coram Research Unit, University of London, Institute of Education.

Thomas, S. and Mortimore, P. (1996) 'Comparison of value added models for secondary school effectiveness', *Research Papers in Education* 11, 1, pp. 5–33.

Thomas, S., Sammons, P., Mortimore, P. and Smees, R. (1997) 'Differential secondary school effectiveness: comparing the performance of different pupil groups', *British Educational Research Journal* 23, 4, pp. 451–469.

Thrupp, M. (1995) 'The school mix effect: the history of an enduring problem in educational research, policy and practice', *British Journal of Sociology of Education* 16, pp. 183–203.

Thrupp, M. (1997) 'The art of the possible: organizing and managing high and low socio-economic schools', paper presented to the annual meeting of the American Educational Research Association, Chicago, 24–28 March.

Tizard, J., Schofield, W. and Hewison, J. (1982) 'Symposium: reading-collaboration between teachers and parents in assisting children's reading', *British Journal of Educational Psychology* 52, 1, pp. 1–15.

Townsend, P. (1996) Comment quoted in Richards, H., 'Perspectives', *Times Higher Education Supplement* 30 August, p. 13.

Walker, A. and Walker, C. (eds) (1997) *Britain Divided: The growth of social exclusion in the 1980s and 1990s*, London, CPAG.

Weikart, D.P. (1972) 'Relationship of curriculum, teaching and learning in pre-school education', in Stanley, J.C. (ed.) *Preschool Programs for the Disadvantaged*, Baltimore, MD, Johns Hopkins University Press.

Whitty, G. (1985) *Sociology and School Knowledge*, London, Methuen.

Whitty, G. (1997) 'School autonomy and parental choice: consumer rights versus citizen rights in education policy in Britain', in Bridges, D. (ed.) *Education, Autonomy and Democratic Citizenship in a Changing World*, London, Routledge.

Whitty, G., Power, S. and Halpin, D. (1998) *Devolution and Choice in Education: The school, the state and the market*, Buckingham, Open University Press.

Wilkinson, R. (1996) *Unhealthy Societies: The afflictions of inequality*, London, Routledge.

Wilkinson, R. (1997) *Unfair Shares: The effects of widening income differences on the welfare of the young*, London, Barnardos.

Wilmott, P. and Hutchinson, R. (1992) *Urban Trends 1*, London, Policy Studies Institute.

11 LEAS: The Problem or the Solution?

Anne Sofer

Against the trend in other European countries, the English education system has become highly centralized, while at the same time individual schools have been vested with considerable management autonomy.

Under Conservative governments in the 1980s and early 1990s these changes were carried out in ways which were detrimental to the interests of vulnerable children, though the damage was mitigated to a degree by local education authority action. The new Labour government appears to intend to centralize further, but to use centralized structures to improve the lot of vulnerable groups. Local education authorities are increasingly cast primarily in an agency role. The risks of this strategy are pointed out, together with possible future structural changes.

The Central–Local Debate

Practically every country in the developed world has an education system where there is an 'intermediary' layer, with some sort of locally elected connection, between central government and the individual school. Their powers and responsibilities differ, and it would be difficult to arrange them neatly along an axis from 'centralized' to 'decentralized' – partly because systems can be centralized in one respect (e.g. organizational structure) but decentralized in another (e.g. pedagogy), and partly because there is constant change and movement.

In general the movement is in the direction of decentralization, with more powers shifting to the level of local government. NCH Action for Children has compiled a compendium of information about how the various arrangements that affect children's lives are ordered in the countries of Europe (Ruxton, 1996). This records that in many European countries – France, Greece, Spain and Sweden – decentralization programmes have been under way.

Only in England and Wales has there been a sharp movement in the opposite direction. Twenty-five years ago Maurice Kogan described a system where Secretaries of State 'did not take much to the notion that [they] managed the educational system' and Chief Education Officers 'did not feel themselves to be part of a large scale planning system, whether indicative or imperative … rather … agents of change for their own people within a system of gently suggested guidelines rather than strong national prescription' (Kogan, 1973, pp. 30, 33). Today, by contrast, central government and its quangos appear to have an iron grip and national prescription is the rule.

The issue is not, however, that straightforward. In some ways the English system is more radically decentralized than any other country's – but to the level of the school rather than the local education authority. Foreign visitors are amazed at the managerial autonomy – over premises, budgets, staffing and, increasingly, admissions – that individual schools have.

Two factors in particular have encouraged this trend, which predates the formal introduction of local management of schools in 1990, but has been greatly accelerated by that legislation. One is the association in this country of prestige with independence from the state – a legacy of our social history and class-based institutions. The other is the significance increasingly attributed to strong school leadership as a key determinant of successful education outcomes.

On the other hand, the risks of school autonomy, taken to the extreme, are generally acknowledged. One is the failure of accountability to the wider community. What happens to those children who cannot fit in, or cannot be adequately catered for, within the existing schools as they wish to run themselves? Another is a vacuum of responsibility when schools fail to thrive. Most commentators still see the need for LEAs to take responsibility at least for these two issues. This opinion is by no means unanimous, however, with organizations like the Social Market Foundation and prominent individuals like her Majesty's Chief Inspector for England adopting a critical position on the LEA's record. The question increasingly being asked is whether vulnerable children and vulnerable schools do indeed need an elected intermediary layer of government to support them, or whether there are ways in which central government on the one hand and self-governing schools on the other could meet *all* their needs.

In a recent piece of research into funding mechanisms and levels in different European countries, commissioned by the NUT, the authors were equivocal about the relationship between local control and equal opportunities. Their conclusion was:

> … Countries may face a trade-off in terms of the benefits of devolution (e.g. greater accountability and flexibility) and equity objectives. Given the commitment of most teacher associations and governments to equity in provision as well as the growing popularity of devolution in the education sector, there is a need to consider the potential contradictions between these two objectives and to identify potential mechanisms for safeguarding equity within a devolved system.
>
> (Atkins and Lankester, 1997, p. 36)

The interesting point here is the assumption that central government is more likely to have a levelling up than a levelling down influence if it retains some control of provisions made locally – that vulnerable children are safer in central hands. Has this in fact been our experience?

A Historical Perspective

Historically, the School Boards, forerunners of the Local Education Authorities, were defenders and advocates of the 'vulnerable child' almost by definition. Their mission was to reach those children who were not being educated at all and get them into school. Stuart Maclure's history of London Education describes the energy with which the London School Board set up teams of 'Visitors' who, in the latter decades of the nineteenth century, scoured every corner of the capital to identify the need. One described the state of children in the slums of Bethnal Green:

> The children's lives were a constant round of endless drudgery – they never played as children play, they never seemed even to think; they were prematurely old, and victims of an awful cruelty. They worked at matchbox making many hours, and at other times assisted their parents in disposing of their wares in the streets. The mortality among the young children was appalling.
>
> (Maclure, 1990, pp. 37–38)

The subsequent history tells of the establishment of the care committees, the school meals service, the school medical service, and the special schools. Similar developments were taking place in other major cities. In this context, it is hard to see the local education authority as anything other than a major agent of transformation in the life chances of millions of vulnerable children.

A more detailed look at how these changes were actually effected reveals something of the dynamics of the system. In almost all cases pressure for change and improvement came from individual officers, members or professional workers in the system drawing attention to children's needs, and using the processes of the local authority, as well sometimes as a national campaigning body, to try to get action. Many authorities (e.g. London, Manchester and Bradford) got a name for themselves as progressive and innovative, and their practices were then emulated elsewhere.

Often the pressure for change encountered obstacles. These could be legal (local educational authorities were circumscribed in their powers), financial (the rate payer interest was always lively), or bureaucratic and to do with disputed boundaries with other authorities. In all these cases, the campaigners for change and improvement would take the issue up at national level – either to widen the local authority's powers, or to make certain duties binding, or to rule on demarcation disputes. The issues became hot topics at local and national elections, sometimes helped by public 'scandals' (for instance the revelation that one third of volunteers for the war in South Africa were physically unfit). Eventually government legislated and the local authorities' powers and responsibilities (and sometimes resources) were appropriately adjusted. What began as a pioneering initiative in one authority became national policy and was spread nationally through legislation.

It is interesting to reflect on how this same dynamic lies behind many of the arrangements we have for vulnerable children today. It is mirrored in the Children Act, in the administration of Section 11 of the Commonwealth Immigration Act[1], in provision for Travellers, in the Code of Practice for children with special educational needs, and in many of the programmes funded under the Department for Education and Employment's Standards Fund. The original idea for reform and/or extra provision comes from LEAs, from local and professional interests, and from national advocacy bodies; some LEAs introduce innovations; pressure builds up for these to be extended nationally; legislation then sets standards and expectations, within which there is a degree of local discretion, and central government monitors the results using best practice among the local education authorities as a spur to improvement.

This is the way we have been used to things working in this country until recently. Defenders of the role that local education authorities have played would also point to the structural reforms which they have fought for and implemented over the years – comprehensivization, tertiary colleges, the GCSE, nursery education – as all being essentially inclusive, aimed at pulling in and up the more vulnerable children and schools.

The contrary historical interpretation is that local education authorities have been themselves to blame for the slow pace of improvement in standards. Their tolerance of failing schools and the 'long tail' of underachievement has been the underlying cause both of our national educational underperformance and of the unacceptably high numbers of socially excluded young people.

In reality local education authorities have been part of a national culture which, until relatively recently, thought it both humane and appropriate to confine the pursuit of academic excellence to a minority and which assumed that the majority would enter the world of work unqualified at the age of 16. These attitudes have shifted faster inside the education establishment than outside it, but it is probably true to say that local education authorities tended to think more in terms of structure and resources as ways to redress educational disadvantage than management and quality-control solutions. In that they reflected the mind set of the times.

The Record of Central Government: 1979–1997

A 'Great Debate' about standards in education had been initiated by a Labour Prime Minister, Lord Callaghan, well before the landmark election of 1979, and the sense that all was not well with the system intensified under the new

Conservative government. It did not however specifically focus on the role of local education authorities to begin with and the most significant education legislation of the first Thatcher term, the 1981 Education Act, setting out the legal framework for the assessment and provision for children with special educational needs (SEN), was developed in the conventional collaborative way.

The relationship between central government and local government generally, however, deteriorated sharply during the early 1980s, on the one hand because of the imposition of spending controls and, on the other, because of the political stance adopted by the left-wing Labour administrations which gained power in a swathe of urban authorities. An aggressive 'equality agenda' was promoted, not – as before – in terms of structural and institutional change, but in ways that appeared to be intruding into the curriculum. The right-wing tabloid press' exploitation of 'race spies in the classroom' and books for five year olds promoting homosexual lifestyles produced a climate in which local education authorities were seen as politically dangerous.

This made it possible under the second Thatcher Government for a distinctive new approach to educational policy-making to emerge. This was characterized by strong central direction, imposition without consent, and what seemed at the time impossibly short deadlines. Its features were a radical devolution of powers from local education authorities to schools; closely prescribed national curriculum and national testing, with published results by school and local education authority; the elevation of parental choice as a political priority and a means of raising standards; and the opportunity for schools to 'opt out' of local education authority control and organize their own affairs, including admissions.

This is not the place for a complete analysis of the effects of the Education Reform Act of 1988 and subsequent legislation. Suffice it to say that they were profound and continuing, and that they coincided with, if not actually created, a significant surge in standards and participation at all levels. For the country as a whole, history may judge them to have had a positive effect. For vulnerable children, however, there has been considerable damage, which is summarized below.

The introduction of formula funding for schools, with 75 per cent of the funding being based on a per capita calculation, made it more difficult for authorities to give extra weighting for factors of special difficulty. In some LEAs this meant, on the introduction of local management of schools, a shifting of resources from disadvantaged to advantaged schools.

In addition, the increased ability of popular schools to choose pupils has led to greater polarization between middle-class and working-class schools and decreased likelihood that vulnerable children will find places in the 'better' schools (Woods et al., 1998). This has led to a concentration of deprivation in certain schools, leading to the spiral of decline noted by the Audit Commission:

Many such schools enter financial, social or educational spirals of decline – or a combination of all three. But, under LMS, the effect of formula funding can leave such schools in a position where they neither close nor recover but wither on the vine ... Until such schools close or recover, their pupils suffer an unacceptably low quality of education.

(Audit Commission, 1996a, p. 18)

The competitive mentality encouraged by league tables and open enrolment has also led to an escalation of exclusions. Permanent exclusions in England more than quadrupled between 1991 and 1996 (from 2,910 to 12,476 in secondary schools, and from 378 to 1,608 in primary schools). Research has indicated that groups disproportionately represented among those excluded are boys of Afro-Caribbean origin, children with special educational needs and children looked after by the local authority (Hayden, 1997; DfEE, 1997a; OFSTED, 1996a; see also Chapters 2, 6 and 12).

The limitations imposed by Government on the amount allowed to be spent on central services by LEAs, combined with sustained press criticism of the amounts still being retained, have caused a progressive reduction in preventative services for children in need or in trouble and squeezed resources available for the growing numbers of excluded children. Resources for means-tested discretionary grants (for instance for school uniforms and school journeys) were also affected.

The national curriculum, particularly in the earlier stages of its introduction, has been widely judged to have led to an inappropriate education for some vulnerable children and given schools and LEAs less scope for responding to their needs (Pearce and Hillman, 1998; see also Chapters 7, 8 and 10).

Central resources to support ethnic minority pupils were cut by 25 per cent in 1994, only months after a new programme was put in place (see also Chapter 2).

Finally, the national policy trend towards deregulation hit education in two places where the most vulnerable were the most at risk – school space standards and nutrition standards for school meals.

These are the specifically educational changes. They happened within a wider social and fiscal policy which greatly increased inequality and resulted in larger numbers of vulnerable children, concentrated in particular geographical areas. A stark illustration of the trend is a comparison of the figures for free school meals entitlement in inner London in 1966 (when education priority areas were first considered) and in 1996. Then the highest proportion in an individual school was 29.5 per cent (Maclure, 1990). Thirty two years later the average for inner London local education authority schools is 48 per cent (London Research Centre, 1998).

The Local Education Authority Record 1979–1997

What did the local education authorities do to mitigate these trends and to protect the position of vulnerable children? Apart from drawing attention to the dangers, in a chorus of protest that was increasingly dismissed as the whinging of the education establishment, they put their money where their collective mouth was. Spending on education by local authorities has been consistently higher than the centrally calculated assessment of the need to spend (the SSA). Over the last three years this additional resource has amounted to some £1.7 billion (Local Authorities General Fund Revenue Returns for 1996–7, 1997–8, and 1998–9).

Within these figures the amount spent on special educational needs has hugely increased and is now calculated to stand at some £2.5 billion nation-ally (DfEE, 1997b). This has not been entirely a matter of deliberate policy. It has also been caused by increased demand, itself partly a result of increased poverty and stress, partly the result of the 1981 legislation which gave stronger entitlements to children with special educational needs (without providing additional resources) and partly (ironically) the result of cuts in the preventa-tive services mentioned above which gave rise to an increase in children with formal 'statements', perceived by schools and parents as the only way to get additional support.

Spending by local education authorities on ethnic minority children has also increased in part to make good the shortfall caused by central cuts. In 1997–1998, for instance, they topped up the Home Office-approved programme by £17 million (personal communication, 1998).

Most local education authorities have weighted their LMS schemes so as to give additional resources, within the proportion allowed by government, to schools with high proportions of children entitled to free school meals, or other indicators of greater vulnerability.

Thus it is probably fair to say that in terms of the distribution of resources, LEAs taken as a group have done more for many of the categories of vulner-able children than did central government during this period. They have also invested in systems of monitoring on which much of the nationally available information about the performance of different groups of children is based. The collection and analysis of these statistics was not encouraged by the Conservative government – certainly not in the early years.

That is on the positive side. Against it can be quoted evidence from the Audit Commission, in their reports on the implementation of the Special Educational Needs legislation, on planning for provision for under-5s and the control of school places, that local education authorities have not always managed these changes, and their resources generally, in such a way as to deliver maximum benefit to groups of vulnerable children (Audit Commission, 1992, 1996a, 1996b). OFSTED reports on support for ethnic minority children and on the Education Social Work Service (OFSTED, 1995, 1996b) make similar points. These reports generally, however, draw attention to innovation and good practice as well as weakness. They have been welcomed and generally acted on as local authorities adapted to a more rigorous climate of external assessment and comparative data.

A more serious charge is that on almost any issue where collaboration between the local education authority and another agency is required, particularly where there are arguments about costs and liabilities, local government generally has failed to address needs adequately. The current much quoted example is the education of children looked after by the local authority, subject of central advice and criticism from the Department of Health and OFSTED throughout the 1990s (Department of Health and OFSTED, 1995). (See also Chapter 5.)

The difficulties of multidisciplinary working appear to be highly resistant to solution, though local authorities, at the corporate level, are increasingly experimenting with structural changes aimed at breaking down departmental barriers – with varying degrees of success. Here, as in other areas where local government is acknowledging its own need for improvement, the obstacles to change are not all of its own making. 'Wasted Youth', a comprehensive report on socially excluded young people in the 14–19 age group, listed the inhibiting factors to effective service delivery across departmental boundaries as follows:

- rigidities in organizational structures;
- deep-set professional ideologies;
- insufficient corporate drive;
- resource constraints hampering operational capacity;
- uncertainties and discontinuities resulting from the need to bid competitively for funds;
- legislative requirements restricting flexibility and innovation in the deployment of budgets;
- inadequate funding incentives for collaboration.

(Pearce and Hillman, 1998, p. 84)

Of these, the last four refer to the context provided by central Government. The authors of this survey also point out that local government departments and agencies each follow bureaucratic procedures laid down for them by different Departments of State. An individual child in trouble or need may be subject to a whole array of separate cycles of assessments, plans and reviews which may actually aggravate his or her state of alienation.

The New Labour Government

Thus, in May 1997 the new Labour government faced a situation with the following features:

- The situation for vulnerable children had deteriorated as a result of the previous government's economic, social and educational policies.
- Local government had fought something of a rearguard action to support differential funding for 'deprived' schools, services for children with special educational needs and services for ethnic minority children.
- In general the education provided for excluded children and children in care was poor, and local government and other local agencies were not acting sufficiently corporately to bring about real improvement – a lack of corporateness reflected in central government.
- Local government was increasingly aware of the need to respond to the rigours of external assessment and published league tables. A new more performance-orientated culture was being established. Nonetheless significant voices across the political spectrum were expressing doubt about the continued need for LEAs in anything other than a residual capacity.

The new government's thinking on all these issues has become increasingly clear. Any lingering hopes there may have been that local education authorities would be restored to their previous eminence and security have been quickly dashed. They have been set to work within a newly defined role with equal rapidity.

It is clear that New Labour does not want to present itself as an egalitarian force. Those changes introduced by the Conservatives which allowed popular schools to recruit more favoured social intakes will effectively not be interfered with (despite the withdrawal of grant maintained status as such). Indeed the extension of the specialist schools initiative is likely to exacerbate this trend. 'Standards not Structures' is the slogan to justify this strategy. Thus the clustering of vulnerable children in vulnerable schools will continue, though Education Action Zones are being set up as a means of improving these schools. The LEA role in respect of raising standards is being acknowledged and codified, though more as an agent of central government than as a democratic body legitimately holding its schools accountable on behalf of its local electorate.

The issues of truancy and exclusion and teenage alienation have moved sharply up the agenda and became the first subjects to be addressed by the new Social Exclusion Unit, itself created to bring about more 'joined up thinking' between Departments of State at the national level. Again the solutions proposed – goals and targets and higher minimal standards of provision – give the local education authority a clear, prescribed and exposed position (Social Exclusion Unit, 1998).

The LEA has been told forcefully that it is not going to be the 'monopoly provider' of schools. It never has been, of course, but encouragement of outside organizations (particularly business) to bid to run Education Action Zones reveals a Government impatient for new solutions, and new sources of both ideas and money.

The priority given to the league tables will also continue, and in particular the key indicator of GCSE 5+ A*–C grades. Media attention and parental interest will therefore continue to attach to the performance of the more favoured half of the population, although, for the first time, in the summer of 1998 newspapers picked up the worrying increase in failure at the bottom. These figures had been published in previous years but drew little comment. Possibly the new government's emphasis on social exclusion has something to do with this change of emphasis.

The government will however attempt to make the publication of these performance indicators fairer by including 'value added' data as well. It is introducing a whole new range of performance measures and targets, including in particular, literacy and numeracy targets to be reached by 80 per cent and 75 per cent respectively of 11 year olds, and targets for children looked after by the local education authority. LEAs will be held accountable for the reaching of these targets, again as agents of central government, within a centrally prescribed strategy and programme. They will only be allowed to hold back the resources to fund their work on school improvement after agreeing an Education Development Plan in detail with the Department of Education and Employment (DfEE), a document that is to be written to a tight pro forma.

The Education Development Plan must contain a mandatory annexe on children with special educational needs. An early Green Paper (DfEE, 1997b) on this issue emphasized the priority the new Government would place on inclusion, and on preventative strategies rather than legalistic processes.

Responsibility for the education of ethnic minority children has also been transferred to the DfEE, and is considered alongside other initiatives for raising standards in the newly christened 'Standards Fund'. Undertakings have been given as to future financing, but a higher proportion of resources are to be devolved directly to schools.

LEAs have been given responsibility for co-ordinating educational (and some other) provision for under-5s, with a promise of additional funding. The Department for Education and is Employment, rather than the Department of Health, is taking the lead in this policy area, stressing the need for early intervention to prevent later educational failure.

In short there has been a plethora of initiatives aimed at various categories of vulnerable children, and LEAs are to have a central (but not exclusive) role in administering them – provided they carry out these duties exactly as required.

They are to be inspected by OFSTED, an organization they perceive to be hostile to them, rather than the more methodologically experienced and neutral Audit Commission. They can expect to be 'named and shamed' – and replaced – if they do not live up to government targets and goals.

In general LEAs have been extraordinarily compliant about this new definition of their role. Among the many explanations for this phenomenon are:

political sympathy and support for the government from Labour councils (the majority); relief that they are at least being given a role, and one which after years of ambiguity is relatively clearly defined; and a well-managed process of consultation on the detail of most of the documentation. The stage looks set for a period of radical, and co-ordinated, improvement – overall, and specifically in relation to vulnerable children.

There are, however, some serious risks and weaknesses. First, there is the issue of the quality, competence and motivation of the people who are to deliver all this. Teachers and local education authority personnel, particularly those working in difficult and inner city areas, currently feel at constant risk of exposure and public humiliation, in addition to the admitted difficulties of the job itself. It has always been more difficult to recruit staff in inner city areas (particularly London) and recruitment at all levels is a major problem. The impact on the most vulnerable children is likely to be disproportionately high unless some way is found of attracting high calibre and committed staff.

Second, can the managerialist solution – targets, goals, performance management – which the government inherited from the Conservatives, really deliver for vulnerable children? This is a question on two levels. First, have the right targets been chosen? They do not, as has been pointed out by a number of commentators, give priority to the lowest attainers (Robinson, 1997; Pearce and Hillman, 1998). However the Audit Commission (1998) has suggested a set of possible LEA performance indicators that would focus attention upon the extent of pupil underachievement on specified educational measures.

At a deeper level questions have been raised as to whether too much weight altogether is being put on this general strategy for bringing about improvement. An impression is sometimes given by the 'can-do' enthusiasts at the centre that all problems can be dealt with by (somebody else) managing things better. A number of serious critics are asking if government has not lost sight of the relationship between children's difficulties in school and wider patterns of socio-economic disadvantage and inequality to which it needs to address itself through economic and fiscal policy (Dyson, 1997; Robinson, 1997). (See also Chapter 10.)

Third, the government's 'standards not structures' mantra is preventing a proper discussion taking place of what changes need to be made in the way we organize education – particularly secondary education. The damaging effects on the life chances of disadvantaged children of the highly selective and stratified local school systems that persist in many parts of the country have become a taboo subject (they are elucidated in telling statistics collected from across the country by Newsam (1998). (See also Chapters 2 and 10.)

Finally there is the issue of the democratic deficit. Not only is our country unique in moving from a decentralized to a centralized system, but it is also increasingly governed by appointed bodies, even at the local level. School planning and pupil admissions systems – key issues in relation to equity and therefore often hugely controversial – are now to be decided by government appointed 'adjudicators', under the Schools Standards and Framework Act 1998. The absence of an accountable elected local body is likely to lead to growing frustration.

What Future for Local Democracy in Education?

The reduction in the powers of local education authorities under the Conservatives was part of a wider shift of power to the centre in relation to all local authority functions, accompanied by a reversal of the balance in tax-raising muscle: local government raised two thirds of its spending in 1979, as opposed to only one third now. A government White Paper billed as 'the most radical and comprehensive package of local government reforms for generations' actually does nothing to halt this process. The reforms relate primarily to the internal functioning of local government, favouring changes which concentrate executive authority in fewer hands and reduce the power of committees to that of scrutiny (DETR, 1998). In the longer term this might affect several of the issues discussed in this chapter. For instance, it could weaken the muscle of the local education lobby but on the other hand strengthen the hand of the chief executive/mayor to 'knock heads together' on multi-disciplinary matters. It could give more clout to any locally elected mayor who wanted to confront the government, but on the other hand make local education authorities generally easier for the DfEE to deal with.

In the short term, however, it is likely that the central–local relationship and the role of local education authorities will continue in its current, albeit inherently unstable, form for some years to come. After all, in addition to the seismic changes in the education landscape described above, there has also been a massive, and still ongoing, local government reorganization taking place, and some organizational stability is called for.

But there are at least two possible other scenarios. One is that the voices calling for a further reduction in the local education authority role, and for a national funding agency for schools, get louder. An orchestrated campaign of criticism of 'weak' LEAs and a change of ministers could herald the introduction of more quangos to take over the LEA's role in school funding and school improvement. By then an increased number of Education Action Zones will be under quasi-independent management supervised by the Department in any case. The 'residual' duties relating to vulnerable children, special educational needs and the education welfare service, could then presumably be combined with Social Services responsibilities to make new local authority Children's Departments.

The second possibility, which could be combined with some elements of the first, would be the transfer of some of the DfEE's and central quangos' powers to a new layer of regional government – where responsibilities for training, further education and even possibly higher education would also be placed.

When and if any such reorganizations are mooted, it is essential that those who care about vulnerable children and their education should enter the argument. They should try to ensure that any system introduced is flexible enough to allow for local innovation and response to need; that it gives positive incentives to multi-disciplinary working; and that it strengthens the organizational connection between schools and services for vulnerable children. And most important of all, they should also use such an occasion as an opportunity to open up again the deep structural issues that underlie the inequities in the current system.

Note

1   This Act has now been superseded by the Ethnic Minority Pupil Achievement Grant. See Chapter 2, pp. 29–30.

References

Atkins, J. and Lankester, O. (1997) 'Trends in the funding of schools across Europe', *Education Review* 11, 1, pp. 26–36.

Audit Commission (1992) *Getting in on the Act. Provision for pupils with special educational needs: The national picture*, London, Audit Commission.

Audit Commission (1996a) *Trading Places: The supply and allocation of school places*, London, Audit Commission.

Audit Commission (1996b) *Counting to Five: Education of children under five*, London, Audit Commission.

Audit Commission (1998) *Changing Partners: A discussion paper on the role of the Local Education Authority*, London, Audit Commission.

Department for Education and Employment (DfEE) (1997a) *Permanent exclusions from schools in England 1995/6*, Departmental Press Release, October 1997.

Department for Education and Employment (DfEE) (1997b) *Excellence For All Children: Meeting special educational needs (Green Paper)*, London, The Stationery Office.

Department of the Environment, Transport and the Regions (DETR) (1998) *Modern Local Government: In touch with the people*, London, The Stationery Office.

Department of Health and OFSTED (1995) *The Education of Children Who Are Looked After by Local Authorities, (Summary)*, London, OFSTED.

Dyson, A. (1997) 'Social and educational disadvantage: reconnecting special needs education', *British Journal of Special Education* 24, 4, pp. 152–158.

Hayden, C. (1997) *Children Excluded from Primary School: Debates, evidence, responses*, Buckingham, Open University Press.

Kogan, M. (1973) *County Hall: The role of the Chief Education Officer*, London, Penguin.

London Research Centre (1998) *Education in London: The key facts*, London, London Research Centre.

Maclure, S. (1990) *A History of Education in London 1870–1990*, Harmondsworth, Penguin.

Newsam, P. (1998) 'How can we know the dancer from the dance?', *Forum* 40, 1, pp. 4–9.

Office for Standards in Education (OFSTED) (1995) *The Challenge for Education Welfare*, London, OFSTED.

Office for Standards in Education (OFSTED) (1996a) *Exclusions from Secondary Schools*, London, The Stationery Office.

Office for Standards in Education (OFSTED) (1996b) *Raising Achievement for Bilingual Pupils*, London, OFSTED.

Pearce, N. and Hillman, J. (1998) 'Wasted youth: raising achievement and tackling social exclusion', London, Institute for Public Policy Research (IPPR).

Personal communication (1998) Telephone conversation with a senior Home Office official.

Robinson, P. (1997) *Literacy, Numeracy and Economic Performance,* London, Centre for Economic Performance, London School of Economics.

Ruxton, S. (1996) *Children in Europe*, London, NCH Action for Children.

Social Exclusion Unit (1998) *Truancy and School Exclusion*, London, The Stationery Office.

Woods, P., Bagley, Y.C. and Glatter, R. (1998) *School Choice and Competition: Markets in the public interest?*, London, Routledge.

12 Combating Unequal Access to Education: The Work of a Local Education Authority Educational Psychology Service

Irvine S. Gersch, with Terry Cope, Graham Pratt, Gill Sassienie, Shungu Hilda M'gadzah, Satwinder Saraon, Michael Sutoris and David Townley

This chapter will outline the work of one educational psychology service in attempting to combat educational disadvantages. We describe the mission and aims of the service and discuss the concept of disadvantage and access to education. We then present an overview of the Educational Psychology Service, to indicate how resources are allocated and then describe some direct work with children and families. We shall then consider our work with schools as organizations and work with other agencies before speculating about some possibilities for the future.

Introduction

The London Borough of Waltham Forest, located in East London, covers the areas of Leyton, Leytonstone, Walthamstow and Chingford. The mission statement of the Service is as follows:

It is the mission of the London Borough of Waltham Forest Educational Psychology Service to provide a service which applies psychological understanding and skills to promote the education, development and well-being of children and young people, particularly those experiencing significant difficulty and disadvantage, by working with children and young people themselves, their families, teachers and other professionals, and also by contributing to organizational and policy development.

A study conducted by one of the authors (Pratt, 1991) showed that wanting to 'make a difference' was one of the common values held throughout the Service and the mission statement expresses also the long-held conviction that to stand any chance at all of reducing inequality and combating disadvantage in a practical way it is necessary for psychologists to operate and contribute at several levels: individual, family, classroom environment (including teachers and peers), whole school and LEA levels.

Such an approach to combating disadvantage means that, as well as their involvement in assessment and programme planning for individual children with special needs, psychologists are involved in working with teacher colleagues on school organizational development in response to pupil needs in such areas as behaviour, bullying and school attendance. To a practising educational psychologist the concept of disadvantage has both strengths and weaknesses. On the positive side it is a term that can lead to action.

For example, Natriello et al. (1990, p. 13) defined the educationally disadvantaged as 'students who are not succeeding due to insufficient experiences in at least one of the three domains of school, family and community' (see Chapter 1, p. 2), which immediately suggests a framework for interventions, programmes and empirical research. However, on the negative side, the term 'disadvantage' can be interpreted as a deficit model that locates the causes of problems experienced by individual students 'in the heads' of the students themselves. Such an approach can be contrasted with that of Rutter et al. (1979) and the subsequent school effectiveness movement, that stress the importance of the school as an organization which has the power to influence the success or failure of both individual and whole groups of students.

The various definitions of disadvantage have been discussed in Chapter 1 and will not be further detailed here. In that chapter a helpful operational definition, underpinning some of the thinking within the Service, is offered by Walraven (1997). This definition refers to children 'at risk' (who may be considered as disadvantaged) who are in danger of failing at school, in their social life, or in making a successful transition to work. Educational, social and vocational failure are predicted by a range of factors, including poverty, ethnic status, family circumstances, language, type of school, geography and community.

In practice, educational psychologists have to separate the ongoing individual casework side of their work (with its emphasis on assessment and programmes of support and intervention for the individual student) from action research and policy development projects. This is because educational psychologists are working within severe time constraints, and there is a duty to complete statutory assessments within relatively short periods of time. For both practical and ethical reasons it is, in practice, very difficult to use the needs and problems of individual students to act as a lever for systemic change – although there are links, for example, the adoption of the Student Report (Gersch and Holgate, 1991), a structured questionnaire used to obtain student views of their problem, in LEA procedures for statutory assessments of students needs under the 1996 Education Act.

The examples of the work of the Service which follow in this chapter will therefore illustrate these two strands and cover such diverse activities as working with individual children with language delay, assessment and interventions for students with behaviour and learning difficulties, involvement in local authority resource allocation through a school based audit, working with schools to reduce exclusions and bullying, and responding to central government initiatives and requirements.

At the time of writing (in early 1998) the whole national framework of education is undergoing review. The publication of the government White Paper *Excellence in Schools* (DfEE, 1997a) set targets for the entire national education system until 2002.

This was followed by the (consultative) Green Paper *Excellence for all Children* DfEE, 1997b) which dealt specifically with special education. The emphasis of both documents is on combating disadvantage, inclusion of all children, standards rather than structure, support for children rather than bureaucracy and the benefits of early intervention with agreed policies and frameworks when problems with children's educational development do occur. The need for significant progress in meeting the needs of children with emotional and behaviour difficulties (EBD) merited a whole chapter in the Green Paper and is regarded as a key indicator for the future.

LEAs, of which educational psychology services are a part, will be the subject of inspection by the Office for Standards in Education (OFSTED). Perhaps most importantly for educational psychology services, the Green Paper acknowledges and accepts the view that a large amount of educational psychologists' time has become tied up in statutory (i.e. LEA based) assessment of children at the expense of earlier more preventative work in schools. Reducing the number of statutory assessments and changing the balance to enable educational psychologists to work at the school based stages of the Code of Practice (DfE, 1994a) which operates as the equivalent of a highway code for special needs, is strongly advocated in the Green Paper, but it is acknowledged that this may require significant changes in both the Code of Practice and also the training and supply of educational psychologists.

The government's legislative plans for education (DfEE, 1997a) have also confirmed that LEAs will be required to work with schools, social services departments and voluntary and private sector providers to draw up Early Years Development Plans which will co-ordinate work in this sector for the first time. LEAs will have to draw up Behaviour Support Plans by January 1999 to co-ordinate educational support and provision in the area of behaviour management. The current range of activities by the Educational Psychology Service described in this chapter are a foundation for meeting these new demands. The 1996 Education Act and its precursors have served to shift the balance of educational psychology work away from school based early intervention to combat disadvantage, and towards more individual statutory assessment of students with the most severe needs. Given that educational psychologists have limited time available they have had to give the highest priority to those cases which are being assessed by the LEA under the 1996 Act.

Overview of the Educational Psychology Service

Background Information and Setting

This chapter is based upon the experience of one London Borough Educational Psychology Service, namely Waltham Forest. It comprises just under 100 schools, a population of 30,000 children and is set in the North East of London. One part of the borough borders the county of Essex whilst another is only a few miles from the inner city in the East End of London. There are three distinct areas of the borough, Chingford, Walthamstow and Leyton/Leytonstone.

The population of the borough is made up of a number of ethnic groups, including black and Asian families, so an important challenge for the Service is to serve the whole of this community. In many parts of the borough there are levels of poverty, unemployment and social disadvantage which are well above the national average. Equal opportunities forms one of the basic tenets of the Educational Psychology Service (EPS). This is the conviction that all children, young people and families in the community of Waltham Forest have equal rights to access the services of an educational psychologist. To further this belief, the service has made every endeavour to recruit members of ethnic minority groups on the team, with some success, and we now have two educational psychologists from ethnic minority backgrounds.

The Service is organized into three geographical teams, each with approximately four full-time equivalent educational psychologists led by a senior educational psychologist. In all, there are currently the equivalent of twelve full-time educational psychologists. These include the Principal Educational Psychologist, a job shared Deputy Principal Educational Psychologist post, two Senior Educational Psychologists, one of whom is a tutor on the initial training course for educational psychologists at the University of East London, and main grade educational psychologists, three of whom are senior practitioners.

An educational psychologist with special responsibility for pre-school work attends a weekly referral meeting at a local multi-disciplinary Children's Centre. Her work also involves meetings with parents and observing and assessing children, advising parents about educational issues and carrying out statutory assessments.

A senior educational psychologist supervises the Portage team based at the Children's Centre. The Portage service is a scheme designed to help the families of children under the age of 5 years with special educational needs, to develop new and useful skills. The Portage team members visit homes, check on the child's progress and devise suitable programmes for parents to apply with their children. The senior educational psychologist leads regular meetings in which the home visitors raise concerns and issues regarding the families they visit. The senior educational psychologist also carries out initial visits to all referred families and organizes training.

The Statutory Assessment Framework

Educational psychologists carry out statutory assessment of children's special educational needs under the 1996 Education Act in line with the *Code of Practice on the Identification and Assessment of Special Educational Needs* (DfE, 1994a). The Code specifies a staged approach to assessment, and outlines the steps schools and LEAs need to take. Educational psychologists may work at stages 1 and 2 of the Code of Practice (the earliest stages) in schools, on a consultation basis, in order to prevent further difficulties. However, they are more likely to be involved directly when difficulties become more serious. Stage 3 usually requires direct assessment of the child. Stage 4 involves the psychologist giving advice to the LEA regarding the child's needs, requirements and provision, based upon a comprehensive and direct assessment of the child's progress, strengths, difficulties, attitudes, response to provision, family circumstances and needs. Educational psychologists typically will have interviewed the child, observed her or him in class, carried out some tests and met with parents, teachers and other relevant professionals. This assessment may lead to the LEA deciding to produce a Statement of Special Educational Need (SEN), which is a formal document which identifies the child's needs and states the provision required. Stage 5 work is for children who already have a Statement of their special educational needs, and typically involves educational psychologists attending annual reviews.

Many of the children included in this assessment process could also be viewed as experiencing social disadvantage. Educational psychologists, in their work, are very conscious of this, and aim to ensure that meetings, letters and contacts are as parent friendly as possible. Some examples are given in the next section of this chapter. The LEA has also decided to issue some key letters to parents about the SEN process via the headteacher of the school, rather than a more anonymous LEA officer – again in order to make the procedure more accessible to parents. Further, where some children have to travel to specialist provision and this may cause difficulty to their parents, transportation is made available to children, for example, to attend the language group run by the EPS.

Other Services Provided

Services provided within the framework of the EPS service involve other professional workers working with educational psychologists. For example a team of around 120 special needs assistants work in mainstream schools and nurseries to support children with SEN. They are recruited and allocated to schools by the EPS under the direction of a senior educational psychologist, who also delivers their training needs. These assistants work with such children either individually or in groups, helping classroom teachers to implement the children's individual education plans with the aim of enabling them, as far as possible, to remain in their mainstream school environment.

A large number of the children receiving this support may also experience social disadvantage and the recruitment, induction and training of the assistants by the educational psychologists aim to ensure that they are aware of the totality of the child's environment and community.

In addition there are five different language groups operating at the EPS centre for children of primary age who are experiencing difficulties in the development of their language skills, and a pre-school language development group. Children attend the groups with a specialist speech therapist and a special needs assistant in order to receive tailor made programmes of support. The majority of the children are able, on leaving the programme, to continue in their mainstream schools. The EPS also manages provision for excluded pupils, either those aged 11–15 years who are permanently excluded from school, or those in Year 11 who do not wish to return to school but who would accept a preparation for a career, independence and citizenship.

The Service has also pioneered the 'Student Report' which was referred to in the *Code of Practice on the Identification and Assessment of Special Educational Needs* (DfE, 1994a). Publications on involving children and student reports have been published, both nationally and internationally (see, for example, Gersch and Gersch, 1995; Gersch et al., 1996). The aim has been to increase the active involvement of children in assessment, and to stress the importance of listening to children.

Some four years ago, in response to a number of parent appeals to the SEN Tribunal, a local Conciliation Service was set up by the Educational Psychology Service and co-ordinated by the Principal Educational Psychologist. This involves a parental interview, often a 'second opinion' and collection of new data. Since its conception some 30 cases have been resolved, and all but one case settled without the need for a formal hearing. For parents of children with SEN, particularly those from disadvantaged backgrounds, such a service aims to ensure that their views are heard and taken into account, and to support families for whom the bureaucratic maze can be impossibly daunting.

The School Visit Formula

In Waltham Forest, as in all boroughs, there are limited resources to be allocated as fairly as possible. One of these resources is the allocation of educational psychologists' time in schools. All the educational psychologists in the teams, apart from the Principal, visit schools regularly. A school visit takes approximately three hours. In order to counteract educational disadvantage the aim is to allocate the number of psychologists' visits to schools according to the needs of the schools and particularly the special educational needs of the children in each school. In allocating school visits in Waltham Forest a formula is used in which the following variables are taken into account:

- whether the school is primary or secondary (primary schools have more visits per capita);
- the number of pupils on the school roll;
- the number of pupils who have a statement of special educational needs;
- the number of pupils who have special educational needs but who do not have statements; and
- the severity of need of those pupils who have special educational needs but who do not need a statement.

The Audit

Allocation of financial resources to schools to support children with special educational needs who do not need a statement is organized via an audit. The audit lists the number of children with special educational needs in each school and these are graded according to level of need. Roughly speaking the criteria used to grade the level of special educational needs correspond to stage One, Two and Three of the Code of Practice although there are anomalies.

The finance allocated to schools via the audit is not, however, attached to individual children, as is the finance from statements, but is for the schools to use as they judge fit to support all children with special educational needs who do not need a statement. This is to ensure that schools can use the funding resource flexibly.

The methods used to determine the allocation of school visit time and resources result in those schools serving disadvantaged areas tending to receive the highest priority, in terms of funding and visits by Educational Psychology Service staff (but see Chapter 11).

Working with Children and Families

Working with Children

A significant proportion of educational psychologists' work is directly with children and young people, usually as part of the assessment of their special educational needs. Most educational psychologists have relatively limited opportunity for direct intervention with children although some counselling and other forms of therapy do take place. Educational psychologists' involvement in interventions with children occurs mainly through other adults, such as teachers and classroom assistants who are in regular direct contact with the children.

The assessment of children's needs involves collecting and triangulating data from a variety of sources, including interviewing adults who know the child well, inspecting and evaluating recorded data about interventions used with the child and their outcomes, observation in settings familiar to the child, as well as the more traditional activities of direct interviewing and testing of the child. This multifaceted approach to assessment is more appropriate for disadvantaged children than a 'one off' individual psychometric assessment as it emphasizes:

- assessment in context;
- assessment of the child's progress over time;
- assessment of the effectiveness of the provision the child is receiving; and
- listening to and taking into account the child's view.

Working with Families

As educational psychologists we would subscribe to the view that parents and carers play a critical role in facilitating children's educational achievement. The effects of social disadvantage on a child's development and education are partly mediated through families.

Some of the ways in which this process may operate are that:

- a family's economic disadvantage may result in a scarcity of books, lack of space to complete homework, and lack of opportunity for experiences outside the immediate home environment;
- socio-economic stresses may result in parents lacking time and energy for facilitating their child's education;
- parents may lack confidence, knowledge of the system, or literacy and communication skills to be effective advocates for their children's needs;
- if parents own educational experiences were largely negative they may find it difficult to engage collaboratively with schools;
- parents may lack sufficient knowledge of their children's educational or other needs to be able to meet them, or ensure that they are met; and
- schools and educational professionals may fail to engage some families in a collaborative way, for instance because of stereotyped attributions regarding the parents knowledge of or interest in their children.

It should be emphasized that these factors may be operating in families from all socio-economic groups, but a combination of them is more likely to occur in the most disadvantaged families. Educational psychologists' involvement with children always takes place with parental knowledge and consent. In the vast majority of cases educational psychologists meet families on one or more occasions. As far as possible this takes place in a setting which is both convenient and comfortable for the family (including at home where appropriate).

While educational psychologists cannot resolve the underlying causes of socio-economic disadvantage, we believe they have a part to play by intervening at the level at which the effects of disadvantage are mediated. Some examples of this intervention are:

- facilitating collaboration between schools and families in meeting children's needs by ensuring as far as possible that plans are made at meetings attended by parents;
- facilitating the process of such meetings by enabling the parents' views to be heard, and promoting an agenda of problem-solving, rather than confrontation and recrimination; and
- encouraging schools to take the family's perspective into account, and advocating their views; informing and empowering parents regarding procedures affecting their child; advising parents regarding their children's needs and how they may participate in meeting them; keeping parents fully informed of the progress of their child's assessment, for instance by sending them copies of all reports and documentation.

An example of a situation where an educational psychologist intervened to enhance educational opportunities concerned an 8-year-old girl with communication and behaviour difficulties, who attended a mainstream school. Her mother was looking after the girl and her brother on her own, and facing acute difficulties, including very limited financial resources, social isolation, virtually no opportunities for child-care (because the girl's behaviour was so difficult) and clinical depression. When the school raised concerns with the parent about the girl's behaviour and hygiene, she found it difficult to explain the stresses in her life, and was perceived by school staff as defensive and unhelpful. When the educational psychologist attended the child's review, he was concerned about the lack of communication between school and parent. He arranged to meet the parent at home and gained insight into her situation; he was then able to use this in subsequent meetings and discussions with the school to reframe the school's approach from one focusing on blame, to one where they were able to acknowledge the difficulties, and look for ways of supporting the mother to help her child more effectively.

Working with Schools

Perhaps one of the most underexploited areas in the educational psychologist's repertoire is that of organizational psychology. From a systems perspective, problems exhibited by particular members of an organization are symptomatic of stresses experienced by the organization as a whole. Thus, problems such as disruptive behaviour may be more effectively resolved by intervening at the organizational level than by attempting to intervene directly with the pupils themselves. For example, research conducted by OFSTED indicated that the key variable in accounting for the significant variation found between schools in exclusion rates was the culture and the ethos of the school (OFSTED, 1996).

'Action on Bullying' and 'Action on Exclusion' are two action research projects funded through GEST (Grants for Education Support and Training, now the Standards Fund) and managed by Waltham Forest Educational Psychology Service. The objectives of the initiative were the successful completion of a number of practical school-based projects designed to reduce the incidence of exclusion and bullying in the participating schools and the dissemination of good practice among Waltham Forest schools. In addition, one of the authors is seconded to a multidisciplinary Behaviour Support Project, also funded through the Standards Fund, which works at a whole-school level within the LEA to promote preventive approaches to behaviour management.

Each initiative comprises a policy development component and a practical intervention so that the whole-school level, as well as the level of the individual pupil or the classroom, is addressed.

Using an Action Research Framework

The initiatives were based on an Action Research framework which comprises three elements. First, the clarification phase involves the collection of baseline data and information about alterable factors that contribute to the problem. Second, the intervention phase involves the design and implementation of an intervention to change one or more of these alterable factors. Finally the evaluation phase assesses the effectiveness of the intervention and this may go on to inform future practice and further intervention. In this way action research can become a cyclical process. Project leaders from the participating schools attended training days led by members of the EPS. The content of the training days included policy development, research into exclusion and bullying, action research techniques, problem analysis, strategies, planning interventions, evaluation techniques, project evaluation and report writing.

Action on Bullying

Research into and interest in bullying is comparatively new, indeed the first book published on the subject in the UK, *Bullying in Schools*, edited by Tattum and Lane, did not appear until 1988. Since then there has been a huge upsurge in publications on the topic and numerous overviews of the literature are included amongst these.

The most extensive study of bullying in the UK was conducted in Sheffield in 1990 (Whitney and Smith, 1993; reported in DfE, 1994b). The results showed that bullying is widespread, with no schools found to be without bullying, and it has been suggested that if the findings of the study were replicated throughout the country then up to 450,000 pupils could be victims of regular weekly bullying (Flood, 1994). Whitney and Smith found that children are more likely to experience bullying if they:

- lack close friends in school;
- are shy;
- come from an overprotective family environment;
- belong to a different racial or ethnic group from the majority;
- are different in some obvious respect from the majority;
- have special educational needs; and
- have poor social skills in interacting with others.

Both girls and boys bully, although boys are more frequently involved, mainly acting singly whereas girls tend to bully in groups. The most common form of bullying for both genders is name calling, but girls are more likely to be victims of indirect forms of bullying such as social isolation while boys are more likely to be victims of physical aggression or threats of violence. However, as when dealing with any aspect of behaviour, it would be a mistake to regard bullying as being entirely a function of the characteristics or predisposition of the individual who bullies. The actual occurrence of bullying depends ultimately on the extent to which the school environment facilitates or inhibits bullying behaviour. Stephenson and Smith (1987), for example, found that staff in schools where there was a low incidence of bullying were more likely to disapprove openly of bullying and to emphasize preventive approaches to tackling it than staff in schools where there is a high incidence of bullying.

Outcomes

Several of the schools involved in the Action on Bullying initiative produced a number of creative interventions which were demonstrated to be effective in tackling bullying:

- mixed-age Circle Time activities helped to increase older pupils' sense of responsibility for supporting younger, more vulnerable pupils;
- reorganization of playground activities resulted in a substantial reduction in the number of key stage one children for whom playtime was an unhappy experience;
- raising awareness about bullying was a successful strategy in increasing pupil confidence in reporting incidents of bullying; and
- empowering bystanders to act resulted in a substantial reduction in the reported incidence of bullying.

Action on Exclusion

In recent years the numbers of pupils who have been permanently excluded from school have increased dramatically, rising from 2,910 in 1990–1991 (DfE, 1992) to 11,181 in 1993–1994 (DfE, 1995) and continue to increase, rising to 13,581 in 1995–1996 (Parsons, 1996). In fact, this increase may be less dramatic than these figures suggest: information about permanent exclusions has been collected systematically through Form 7 referrals only since 1994–1995. The reliability of the data to this date is now being called into question, with the implication that earlier figures may underestimate considerably the incidence of permanent exclusion. (See Chapter 6 for a fuller discussion of school exclusion.)

At least 80 per cent of all exclusions, permanent and fixed-term, occur in secondary school and about four times more boys than girls are excluded (OFSTED, 1996). In the OFSTED survey black Caribbean pupils represented 3 per cent of the school population but 23 per cent of exclusions, while in the National Exclusion Reporting System (NERS) data for 1992, 12.5 per cent of those excluded had statements of special educational needs. Nationwide over 100,000 pupils may be out of school on fixed-term exclusions at any one time.

OFSTED conducted a survey of 16 LEAs in 1995–1996 to find out whether, and if so why, some schools are more effective in managing pupils' behaviour so as to avoid exclusions (OFSTED, 1996). They found that schools which exclude few pupils tend to be better at:

- implementing an effective behaviour policy;
- applying suitable rewards and sanctions;
- monitoring exclusions;
- providing pastoral support; and
- tailoring their curriculum to meet individual need.

OFSTED also found that exclusion is associated with, but not determined by:

- low levels of basic skills, particularly literacy;
- limited aspirations and opportunities;
- families under financial or emotional stress;
- poor relationships with peers, parents or teachers; and
- peer pressure to behave in ways likely to result in conflict with authority.

Outcomes

Through their action research projects schools showed that they can support pupils with behaviour difficulties successfully and reduce their vulnerability to exclusion. The success with which this can be achieved, however, depends, amongst other things, on there being in place a comprehensive behaviour policy that is implemented consistently and that includes preventive and educative responses to behaviour difficulties. A number of the participating schools concluded that the small-scale achievements of the project could be extended if they were to be built into whole-school systems and procedures.

The main findings of the Action on Exclusion initiatives were that:

- Schools can achieve significant reductions in exclusion rates through strategic action.
- Opportunities for pupils with behaviour difficulties to talk about their experiences and to analyse their own behaviour enabled them to assume a greater responsibility for their actions and to think about alternative ways to deal with difficult situations.
- Peer group support can be effective in enabling pupils with behaviour difficulties to reduce the incidence of disruptive behaviour in lesson time.
- Pupils with higher educational attainments may be more successful in overcoming their behaviour difficulties.
- The use of special needs assistants as 'buddies' for pupils with behaviour difficulties can be effective in improving self-esteem and reducing the risk of exclusion.
- The use of adult mentors for previously excluded pupils can be effective in avoiding further exclusion and in reducing the number of incidents in which these pupils became involved.

As indicated earlier, given the fact that children from disadvantaged backgrounds are represented in groups of children experiencing exclusion and bullying, the benefits resulting from the projects will be particularly relevant to such children and their families, although this was not an explicit aim of these initiatives.

In addition to specific school-based action projects of the type just described the educational psychologists in the service have worked with schools which were designated as requiring special measures following OFSTED inspections. In one school, for example, they were involved in helping a school to set up a programme of behavioural intervention and staff support which was instrumental in enabling the school to come out of special measures.

Working With Other Agencies

Educational psychologists in Waltham Forest work with various other agencies in attempting to combat educational disadvantage. For example they liaise with social workers to support the education of children who are disadvantaged by their home situations, particularly those who are in the care of the local authority. There is copious evidence to show that such children have a much greater than average likelihood of educational difficulties (see Chapter 5); educational psychologists allocate significant amounts of time to negotiating arrangements in such cases, which typically require particularly detailed and sensitive management.

Educational psychologists also liaise with educational visitors who are trained teachers working with pre-school children and their families, (particularly in areas of greatest social need), helping them to prepare for the expectations of school life. They also work with speech therapists, doctors, psychiatrists, nurses and other health care specialists in a variety of settings, including the Child and Family Consultation Service.

Working in Partnership with the Multicultural Support Service – One Joint Initiative

The EPS and the Authority's Multicultural Support Service have been working together to produce ways of helping schools to assess the needs of refugee children. It is estimated that there are approximately 46,000 refugee children in British schools (Refugee Council, 1997), with around 5,000 refugee families living in the borough of Waltham Forest (Waltham Forest Refugee Advice Centre, Annual Report for 1995–1996). In school these children experience a number of difficulties which can include social isolation, difficulties in accessing the curriculum and in coming to terms with a different culture, language and religion, and meeting different expectations and roles. In addition they may encounter racism.

The two services have collaborated to produce ways of helping schools to assess the needs of their refugee children in the light of such concerns about issues such as the fact that, in many schools, such children were targeted for additional support *only* if they were exhibiting inappropriate behaviour and causing disruption within the classroom.

Other issues included the number of such children considered by schools to require extra time and exposure to the school system and also to English as a second language. There was also felt to be a need for proper induction and admission procedures and for formal assessment of the children's educational needs, as well as the need for a more consistent method of collecting information at an early stage to ensure that schools and other agencies could work in a co-ordinated way.

It was agreed that an interview schedule which elicited information about the child's background and early experiences would be helpful for schools in order to identify refugee children with Special Educational Needs. This form would also help in triggering referral to other appropriate agencies. Such a schedule was designed and piloted in three secondary and two primary schools. These schools, which were involved in the early consultation, stressed that the document was helpful in identifying and supporting vulnerable children and that it could be integrated into their school induction packages. A guidance booklet for interviews is now being produced and the schedule is currently being piloted by the refugee support teacher on newly arrived families.

In addition to this project educational psychologists work closely with specialist teachers dealing with refugee children and families at an individual casework level. Also, the authority has a large number of Afro-Caribbean pupils, a disproportionate number of whom (especially boys) are excluded from schools, as in many other LEAs (see Chapters 2 and 6). Waltham Forest employs a team of teachers, in its African-Caribbean Attainment Project, to promote the cultural and educational development of these pupils, and one of the senior educational psychologists liaises closely with this team. This psychologist has also commissioned and undertaken research for the University of East London on supporting the achievements of Afro-Caribbean boys and the mentoring of such pupils. Service training days in the EPS include opportunities for presentation by members of the community from different ethnic cultural groups. This continued training and time for reflection is highly valued by members of the service.

Looking to the Future

A Constraint Analysis

In 1998, one of the authors of this chapter was a trainee educational psychologist, and as part of a trainee project, examined some of the factors constraining the work of educational psychologists, particularly with regard to equal opportunities. Having interviewed some colleagues and examined documentation, she concluded that several factors seemed to serve to hold the service back from meeting some of its aims. Such factors included:

- a lack of time;
- the need for more specific guidance for staff;
- the need for more knowledge; and
- the need to provide training for all members of the team, including clerical staff, as well as educational psychologists.

It was suggested that there was scope for increased training opportunities, casework monitoring and revisiting practice guidelines regularly. It is acknowledged by the Service that all such practices require ongoing review and updating, and there are opportunities, both at staff meetings and planning events, for such reviews to take place.

As the previous section has indicated, the work and future of educational psychology services is closely tied to that of the local education authorities in which they are based. Local education authorities have themselves been described as needing to modernize to fit in with the Government's standards agenda and needing to prove their own effectiveness in improving education (TES, 1998). Some outlines of the changes and developments that educational psychology services will have to make do seem to be emerging. Educational psychologists will have to not only prove themselves to be well-managed and trained but also to be effective in adding value at or above the costs of their own upkeep and maintenance.

First, the knowledge base that educational psychologists apply may need to be more obviously based on a clearly articulated and soundly structured framework that can be demonstrated to produce results and also have the capacity to be refined and improved in response to psychological knowledge and research. Second, if they are to apply this knowledge educational psychologists may need to negotiate a different balance in favour of their role as applied psychologists compared with their role as local government officers involved in resource allocation or, what has been named more directly, 'Street Level Bureaucrats' (Laffin, 1986). Third, educational psychologists must be on the lookout for new patterns of disadvantage that emerge, e.g. the disadvantage of those without skills in information and communications technology. Fourth, if early intervention to overcome disadvantage is to be successful they will need to work not only with children, parents and teachers but even more closely with their colleagues in other front line services such as health and social services departments.

The authors of this chapter believe strongly that LEA-based educational psychology services are in a good position to respond to these challenges and the Waltham Forest Educational Psychology Service is currently working with its colleagues in local government to respond to central government initiatives and also with its colleagues in professional bodies and university training departments to set the frameworks in place for developments in training and research.

As indicated in the mission statement, the Educational Psychology Service aims to help children from *all* backgrounds; however, given the high correlation between children with SEN and those from disadvantaged backgrounds, it is not surprising that a significant proportion of time of the Educational Psychology Service is directed towards such children and their families. For the future, we feel this should continue to be an important part of the role of an Educational Psychology Service.

Authors' Note

The contents of this chapter are the responsibility of the authors alone and do not necessarily represent the views of the employing LEAs.

Contributors

Dr Irvine S. Gersch is Principal Educational Psychologist, Mrs Terry Cope and David Townley are Deputy Principal Educational Psychologists, Michael Sutoris is Senior Educational Psychologist, Shungu Hilda M'gadzah is Senior Educational Psychologist (and Associate Tutor at The University of East London), Satwinder Saraon is Educational Psychologist and Gill Sassienie is Educational Psychologist in the London Borough of Waltham Forest. Graham Pratt is Principal Educational Psychologist in Southend-on-Sea, Essex.

Acknowledgement

The authors would like to acknowledge the help of Natacha De Lantivy, Educational Psychologist in Training and now Educational Psychologist for the London Borough of Brent.

References

Department for Education (DfE) (1992) *Exclusions: A discussion paper*, November 1992, London, DfEE.

Department for Education (DfE) (1994a) *Code of Practice on the Identification and Assessment of Special Educational Needs*, London, Central Office of Information.

Department for Education (DfE) (1994b) *Bullying – Don't Suffer in Silence: An anti-bullying pack for schools*, London, HMSO.

Department for Education (DfE) (1995) *Final Report on National Survey of Local Education Authorities: Policies and procedures for the identification of, and provision for children who are out of school by reason of exclusion or otherwise*, Commissioned by the DfE and conducted by C. Parsons and Colleagues at Canterbury Christchurch College, London, HMSO.

Department for Education and Employment (DfEE) (1997a) *Excellence in Schools* (White Paper), London, The Stationery Office.

Department for Education and Employment (DfEE) (1997b) *Excellence for All Children: Meeting Special Educational Needs*, London, The Stationery Office.

Flood, S. (1994) 'Bullying – cause, effect and prevention', *Young Minds Newsletter* 17, pp. 11–12.

Gersch, I.S. and Gersch, B. (1995) 'Supporting advocacy and self-advocacy: the role of allied professions', in Garner, P. and Sandow, S. (eds) *Advocacy, Self-Advocacy and Special Needs*, London, David Fulton.

Gersch, I.S. and Holgate, A. (1991) *Student Report*, London Borough of Waltham Forest.

Gersch, I.S. with Pratt, G., Nolan, A. and Hooper, S. (1996) 'Listening to children: the educational context', in Upton, G., *The Voice of the Child: A handbook for professionals*, London, David Fulton.

Laffin, M. (1986) *Professionalism & Policy*, Aldershot, Avesbury Press.

Natriello, G., McDill, E.L. and Pallas, A. M. (1990) *Schooling Disadvantaged Children: Racing against catastrophe*, New York, Teachers College Press.

Office for Standards in Education (OFSTED) (1996) *Exclusions for Secondary Schools 1995/6*, London, The Stationery Office.

Parsons, C. (1996) *Final Report on Follow Up Survey of Permanent Exclusions from Schools in England,* Canterbury Christ Church College.

Pratt, G. (1991) *The Organisational Culture of a Local Authority Educational Psychology Service at a Time of Change in the British Educational System*, submitted September 1991 as the Management Project Component of the MSc (Educational Management) Course, University of East London.

Refugee Council (1997) Refugee Children in School (unpublished statistics), cited in Rutter, J. (1998) *Refugee Education: Mapping the Field*, Stoke-on Trent, Trentham Books.

Rutter, J. (1998) *Refugee Education: Mapping the Field*, Stoke-on Trent, Trentham Books.

Rutter, M., Maugham, B., Mortimore, P. and Ouston, J. (1979) *Fifteen Thousand Hours: Secondary schools and their effect on children*, London, Open Books.

Stephenson, P. and Smith, D. (1987) 'Anatomy of a playground bully', *Education* 18 September, pp. 236–237.

Tattum, D. and Lane, D. (1988) *Bullying in Schools*, Stoke-on-Trent, Trentham Books.

Times Educational Supplement (TES) (1998) 18 December, p. 4.

Walraven, G. (1997) 'Introduction to Part One', in Day, C., Deen, D. van and Walraven, G. (eds) *Children and Youth at Risk and Urban Education: Research, policy and practice*, Leuven-Apeldoorn, EERA and Garant.

Waltham Forest Refugee Advice Centre (1997) *Annual Report for 1995–96*, London, Waltham Forest Refugee Advice Centre.

Whitney, I. and Smith, P.K. (1993) 'A survey of the nature and extent of bullying in junior, middle and secondary schools', *Educational Research* 35, pp. 3–25.

13 Co-ordinated Services for Disadvantaged Children: An International Perspective

Peter Evans

This chapter provides a brief economic rationale for the need to improve education systems for all children, including the disadvantaged, whose full involvement in work and society is crucial for the future stability of the economies of developed countries. Those 'at risk' form a substantial group whose needs are unmet and for whom special provision must be made if they are to succeed at school. But this support must go beyond the school system and involve social and emotional development recognizing that successful growth is dependent on concern for the whole child, the family and the community in which they all live.

Public services, as traditionally organized, are finding it increasingly difficult to meet the real needs of disadvantaged children and families and are searching for a new *modus operandi* through increased co-ordination intended to improve the quality and relevance of the services available. Many countries are supplementing this approach through community involvement, especially of the voluntary sector in the development of a new civil society. The chapter discusses examples of this approach drawn from the pre-school stage where prevention is emphasized and the school age and transition to work periods. Countries highlighted are Australia, Canada, Finland, Germany and Holland.

Background

There is one issue which remains a key concern for all countries, and which has implications for the successful education and early experiences of children and youth. It is that the world's globalized economy demands its citizens become better educated if they wish to participate in the labour market and avoid the possibility of social exclusion associated with poverty and the denial of rights. In response to globalization, in many countries of the world, educational systems are undergoing reforms which seek to improve their effectiveness and the standards obtained by the children whom they serve. In addition, concerns about equity of provision are raised which include the move to the full inclusion of children with disabilities into mainstream schools.

A further and very forceful pressure for change comes from the emergence of the so called 'knowledge economy' which is set to replace the current industrialized economies of many countries in the next millennium. Here, knowledge and learning are becoming the indispensable assets, not only to the individual but also to the company and are replacing manual skills in importance. Knowledge and an openness to lifelong learning give enterprises flexibility and afford a greater opportunity to adapt to changing market opportunities. Thus, the knowledge economy stresses, in particular, the importance of high level literacy and numeracy skills along with problem solving skills, and the ability to work flexibly and in teams.

For many governments, the response to these trends and pressures has been to decentralize decision-making and planning, since this is viewed as a way to reduce central government costs, to promote local flexibility and increase allocational efficiency (Klugman, 1997). In addition a now widely held and preferred model of service delivery is based on the recognition that client need can be better met through more responsive local service structures that can involve the community in its entirety, and that this is more important than agency bureaucratization (OECD, 1996).

While this model is certainly desirable, the need to maintain an effective link between national policy-making and local delivery is strengthened by globalization and by international agreements which can impact on individual citizens or groups. This chapter will describe some examples of local services delivered in the context of national policy frameworks intended for disadvantaged students and families. But before turning to these developments, two other important factors are pressing for reforms to be made. They are changing demographics and the growing emphasis on human rights – including children's rights.

Demographic Factors

It is now well known that the balance between the old and the young is changing. The birth rate in most developed countries has now fallen below the replacement rate (Halsey, 1993) which means that our populations are decreasing in size and are only likely to be maintained through immigration. This fact, allied to the increasing numbers of retired citizens, means that all people of working age need to be working and contributing to the economy simply to maintain the tax base to support our current standards of living and to maintain retirement pensions. Having a student population who are not learning the skills necessary for survival in the new labour market is simply not acceptable. Not only do they not contribute to the tax base but in many countries, they also draw long-term benefits from it. Furthermore, the poverty which almost inevitably ensues is associated with a decline in mental and physical health adding yet more strain to public health and social services (Whelan and Whelan, 1995).

Human Rights

Democracies do not stand still and the protection of human rights is emerging as yet another powerful force on education systems. The ratification of the Convention on the Rights of the Child by the UN in 1989 (UN, 1989) is a considerable step forward but there remain growing concerns for issues of equity in education especially with regard to gender, ethnic minority status and regional disparities. (See Chapters 2 and 3 for a discussion of the first two of these issues). Furthermore, the right for disabled students to be educated in mainstream schools, alongside their peers, is an ever-growing policy objective (OECD, 1997).

Taken together these factors indicate the need for substantial reform in the ways in which all children and families are supported and educated and it is perhaps not surprising that in this environment research work that stresses prevention has resonated with policy-makers. It presents the dream scenario. Fewer child and family problems, lower costs, higher standards and labour market compatibility. At least these are some of the aspirations.

The remainder of this chapter will introduce the reader to some of the ways in which various countries are developing community-based services for disadvantaged children and youth.

Children who are failing in school, and who are disadvantaged are a great cause for concern in all developed countries, although comparative prevalence estimates are not easy to obtain. The proportion of children said to be at risk of school failure varies between about 15 and 30 per cent (OECD, 1995a) and this estimate is generally understood not to include children with disabilities whose prevalence estimates also vary substantially between approximately 1 and 10 per cent of the school age population (OECD, 1995b). These figures must be interpreted with caution since they are not based on any true scientific classification procedure but reflect instead a complex interaction of epidemiological factors, educational policy and practice (OECD, 1995a).

Nevertheless, these figures reveal the extent to which the current normative conceptualization of education systems, including schools and other support services, are maladapted to the needs of their present clientele and how far they require substantial additional support if all needs are to be met. In the past failure has been tolerated since the labour market was able to absorb those students with little interest in 'school learning' and with lower academic attainments. However, this attitude is now unacceptable, and the failure of these students can no longer be viewed as the necessary by-product of an inefficient industrial process, but as a challenge to be met by the system which must play a much greater part in helping to produce citizens who are fully included and able to take full part in society.

One approach to this problem has been the recognition that the successful development of children is highly dependent on the family contexts. Services need to address the needs of the whole child and the family and social structure in which they are raised. Co-ordinating services and marshalling community support is seen as one way forward and the next section provides country examples of how this is working for pre-school aged children, school aged children and young people making the transition to work.

Country Examples: Co-ordinating Services for Disadvantaged Children and Families

The examples given here are drawn from case studies described in full in OECD (1996, 1998). Involving communities and co-ordinating services to support disadvantaged children and families has roots which can be traced back at least to the turn of the century (e.g. Webb and Webb, 1963). The key idea of 'partnership' can be identified in a number of different countries in their approaches to policy about care. In Germany for example, the current philosophy of social care is based on earlier determined principles of an obligation to work and subsidiarity – whereby help and care are first seen as the responsibility of the family, relatives and the neighbourhood, then of voluntary and statutory agencies and finally of national organizations. More recent developments have stressed service co-operation and co-ordination in planning preventive services for children and youth which meet their needs across the age range. In the Netherlands, co-operation between education, primary health care, youth welfare work, manpower services, justice, the police and social services has been stressed in an effort to develop a preventive youth care policy and the link between education and labour market entry has recently been given especial emphasis (Rauwenhoff Committee, 1990).

Pre-School Programmes

While, pre-school programmes feature strongly in some developed countries, there nevertheless remains a lack of general provision for children in this age range. Perhaps it is partly because the statutory responsibility for children of this age cuts across many government departments or ministries, that this period provides interesting examples of the widest collaboration to develop support for families and children. Two examples will be described more fully from New Brunswick in Canada and Holland in Europe.

Canada (New Brunswick) – Healthy Children and Families Ready to Learn

The province of New Brunswick is on the eastern seaboard of Canada bordering on Nova Scotia, Quebec and the US State of Maine. Community based support services for families and children have been under development there since the mid to late 1980s. Services for young children and their families are developed in the context of the early childhood initiatives (ECI). The ECI bring together the collaborative efforts of the public health and medical services division and the family and community services division of the Government of New Brunswick. They have been developed within a general framework of service integration throughout the Province which was stimulated by the recognition that parents, teachers and administrators need better access to support from other professions to help to improve all children's level of education. The ECI are planned to bring young children to school who are as healthy and ready as possible to achieve their potential. There are seven major components.

These provide:

(a) enhanced pre-natal screening and intervention in order to increase healthy pregnancy outcomes;
(b) improved post-natal screening and intervention in order to enhance factors and conditions known to foster healthy growth and development;
(c) the re-targeting of pre-school clinics to 5.5 years of age in order to support the healthy growth and development of pre-school children;
(d) home-based early intervention services aimed at improving childhood outcomes and enhancing family self-sufficiency;
(e) integrated day care services with goals to achieve full participation of the high priority child in developmentally appropriate child care services, and improved childhood outcomes among high priority children;
(f) social work prevention services whose goal is the prevention of the abuse and neglect of children, through the strengthened parenting competencies of high priority parents; and
(g) home economics services whose goal is to have priority families develop skills in the areas of resource management and family development with the intention of stimulating greater self-reliance.

The services are co-ordinated across the entire province via a single entry point system through the public health nurse. Regional public health co-ordinators register priority families, conduct an assessment and refer the families to a range of existing government and community based services including the school districts. At 3.5 years a student health profile form is completed on each child and is passed on to the school before entry into kindergarten.

Holland – Providing Home-Based Support to Strengthen Pre-School Provision

In Holland, welfare and health care policies were decentralized some years ago and, in recent years, there has been a move to decentralize aspects of education policy with the goal of creating a more coherent response to the problems of deprivation. Within this general policy framework which covers all children and youth, pre-school aged children have not been excluded.

Home-based support is an important element of pre-school provision for disadvantaged families and for those with disabled children. In Holland a project called MOVE, developed in Emmen, is a good example of how this can work. The development of community-based services that will sustain themselves is complex and the determinants need to be right as the following example shows.

Emmen is situated in the northeast of Holland. It is a community of some 54,000 people, with the greatest industrial concentration in the north of Holland and an unemployment rate in 1994 of 15.5 per cent, about twice the national average. Holland has used the principle of the educational priority area (EPA) in order to target funds to disadvantaged families mainly through primary schools. Because of its background Emmen has been engaged for over 20 years in national projects intended to help it overcome its traditionally low level of education. For example at the end of the 1980s Emmen participated in an experiment on integrated municipal youth policy which encouraged the development of neighbourhood networks for youth care services. One outcome of this work was the identification of high numbers of delayed children of pre-school age and the need for preventive services which would expand the possibilities for toddlers and the involvement of parents.

The EPA in Emmen comprises a network of services for children at risk especially of primary school age as well as developed pre-school playgroups. The latter cater for some 9 per cent of the 0–4 age group, which while being indicative, almost certainly underestimates the size of the at risk group, which in primary schools covers those with low socio-economic status, accounting for about 25 per cent of the population.

Perhaps as a result of this long-term engagement with services for the disadvantaged, Emmen also has available a large number of services for children and families, which are publicly advertised on posters, and which parents can use to help obtain advice or support etc. From these posters it is clear that more than eleven institutions deal with the pre-school period and that in many cases more than one institution covers the same area. For example seven different bodies deal with 'nourishment' and 'support with upbringing'.

It was in the context of this on-going collaboration at the community level and following further attempts to co-ordinate or integrate services concerned with compensatory policy, under the general rubric of a Foundation for Educational Priority, that project MOVE was born in Emmen. MOVE was the implementation plan that followed a working party report which formulated the following policy goals intended to make services supply more attuned to customer demand. The central objective, the realization of an integrated set of measures, offering optimal chances of development for children aged 0 to 6 carried three sub-objectives:

(a) stimulating and improving the developmental possibilities for young children by offering family-oriented activities;

(b) backing up and strengthening appropriate child-rearing methods and neighbourhood services; and

(c) preventing and/or decreasing problems in the development and up-bringing of young children.

MOVE also responded to the need to co-ordinate the growing number of programmes that were being offered for 0–6 year olds. These were seen as:

(a) being fragmented and lacking continuity;

(b) often operating in isolation and not co-ordinated with other programmes to benefit the recipients;

(c) too linked to the possibility of external funding sources;

(d) not fully thought through;

(e) driven by particular civil servants or institutions; and

(f) providing a dislocation between supply and demand, whereby the supply was either determined independently of client need, or with no evident means to get the service to the client, or where the methods used to identify clients were viewed as stigmatizing and for this reason self-defeating.

The project's name MOVE was deliberately chosen to reflect both the Dutch abbreviation of the project and the English verb 'to move' – indicating the intended movement towards integration of services in other communities. It is recognized that the problems caused by educational deprivation call for a broad range of solutions. To increase their chances of success, children and their parents need to be positively encouraged and supported through co-operation between education and welfare including health care, help services, welfare work and child care. This co-operation must result in a clear and well-tuned supply of facilities for parents and children. On the one hand family-oriented programmes are needed and, on the other, an accessible infrastructure of services, which calls on parents to play an active role in the stimulation and guidance of the development of their children.

The project plan was devised to support the ongoing work based on the objectives of education priority policy, i.e. to improve educational opportuni-ties for the disadvantaged. Particular goals were to have by 1997:

(a) 75 per cent of children in the priority programmes participating in the pre-school programme;

(b) all pre-school playgroups and schools affiliated to the priority programme collecting information on the course of development of priority children; and

(c) 75 per cent of priority parents with a child between 3 and 12 years partici-pating annually in events which help them make an active contribution to the learning and development of their children.

The main innovative element in MOVE is the figure of the 'go-between' mother. She may well be a member of the cultural or ethnic community to which the family belongs and works on building up a relationship with the family in the home and links their demands to the existing supply. In other words, an investment in relations and trust is the basis for change which forms around meeting family needs. The go-between mother develops made-to-measure approaches in linking supply and demand. For example by:

(a) specific approaches to link the family with the facility;
(b) activities to stimulate the development of young children;
(c) made-to-measure activities to support the child's upbringing; and
(d) methods to signal problems and develop preventive strategies.

Introducing a new approach such as MOVE requires a co-ordinated effort across many levels of the system which, in the example cited, was certainly helped by earlier national policy and the involvement of Emmen in the practice emanating from it. Furthermore, needed additional funding was secured through collaboration between the management and field level workers and a local foundation provided support in developing the methodology and training of staff. The team leader was a key appointment and, after training, carried out preliminary developmental work on the implementation of the project by making contacts locally and assembling a basic package of facilities. The management team supports the go-between mothers in identifying appropriate services and in their work with the families.

School-Aged Children

The examples described above which concentrate on pre-school children have focused on co-ordinating services in the context of community support with parental involvement being given a priority in promoting preventive approaches. As children become older parental involvement in the education of their children, remains imperative, but can change form.

The examples to be featured in looking at community support during the school age period, come from Finland and Australia. They reflect responses to very different problems in urban and rural environments. In Finland the issue is supporting families and especially co-ordinating social services and health. In Australia, an approach to involving Aboriginal communities is reviewed.

Finland has been in the throws of rapid economic change and has been experiencing uncharacteristically high levels of unemployment following the collapse of the Soviet Union. The country has looked to involving communities more fully in finding solutions to help children in difficulties.

Finland – Decentralization and the Local Co-ordination of School-Based and Day Care Services

In Finland, there has been a strong tradition of social welfare for many years and education, health and social services are free although taxation is high. The recent downturn in the economy has led to a reconsideration of the structure and function of some of these 'top-down' services along with a search for greater economies.

Services organized in this way are inevitably highly regulated, and following the recognition that a rationalization was required, laws and policies were adopted to help to make the services more responsive to local needs. Especially significant in these changes was the adoption of a policy of Local Population Responsibility (LPR). According to this principle, a multi-professional team of social welfare and health professionals is given responsibility for a small geographically defined area containing 2,000 to 4,000 people. The aim is to improve the co-ordination, functioning and accessibility of services to better meet the needs of service users. Important focuses of this policy are family-centred approaches, community care and prevention.

Along with this policy came changes in the law which adjusted the nature of the funding process, allowed for flexibility in the place of provision and facilitated the sharing of client information. Taken together these reforms gave substantially increased freedoms to municipalities to spend monies and organize services with more versatility and more relevance to meet local demands. Mäkelä, et al. (1993) argue that LPR holds possibilities for fostering creative local experiments involving multi-professional and non-hierarchical teams, provided that inherent difficulties between status and pay for the professionals involved and their practice ethics can be overcome.

In the town of Jyväskylä there is an elementary school and day care centre which is unusual in Finland since it provides day care services and elementary school for children aged between 1 and 8 on the same site. It serves a new residential area with a socio-economically mixed population with a number of families with serious problems. The main purpose of the combined provision is to integrate the educational content of the day care programme with the school curriculum. It is also expected that children with problems will be identified earlier and that transition between the two facilities will be easier than if they are separate. In addition, school-aged children will be able to benefit from on-site after-school care which will be a great deal more convenient for parents. Joint training was provided for staff before the facility was opened in order to familiarize them with each other's working practices and perspectives.

Considerable emphasis is placed on collaboration with parents and the community. They are seen as equal partners and staff get to know them and to ascertain their personal interests and their goals for their children. They are invited to annual assessments of the children and the facility is open for community use outside of school times. It also provides other community services beyond its basic day care educational functions. These include a day care worker for parents of sick children, a nurse and a local social worker to help families through crises, and a meal service for elderly residents. The centre also collaborates with local churches on various projects and the local library to provide children with books.

South Australia – Services for the Children of Indigenous Peoples Embedded in a State-Wide Strategy

Aboriginals and Torres Strait Islanders have a disadvantaged position in Australia. Reports indicate that their mean income is less than two-thirds that of the national figure. Retention rates in school are one-third that of other students; unemployment rates are 2.6 times that of other Australians; life expectancy at birth for females is 20 years less; and they are 15 times more likely to find themselves in prison.

The Australian government has over the past few years made considerable progress in implementing policies of social justice for all Australians with particular concerns for the plight of the indigenous peoples. Reconciliation, or the bringing together of indigenous and non-indigenous peoples became formal government policy in 1991 following the creation of a Council of Reconciliation.

The Murat Bay District Council in the South Australian community of Ceduna has received national recognition for its work with the Aboriginal community. A local economic plan, jointly negotiated, has been drawn up to address efficient and effective service delivery networks within the local council boundaries to meet the needs of all community residents. This plan essentially co-ordinates the budgets of a number of different responsible agencies to avoid overlap and waste. The Aboriginal community was not easily engaged in this development and the council needed to take considerable initiative to reach out to engage them.

In addition, the council benefited from the South Australian Attorney General's crime prevention initiative. Through discussion with residents five areas were identified that needed to be addressed to fight crime: youth; domestic violence; alcohol and drug abuse; education and skills development to combat unemployment; and community development. Eighteen different programme needs emerged (see Collins and Miller, 1992):

(a) a homework centre away from the school environment to support children who lack the necessary supports at home;

(b) a school breakfast programme;
(c) a local women's shelter/hostel/accommodation centre and crisis inter-
     vention services for domestic violence and child abuse;
(d) a detoxification/rehabilitation centre;
(e) literacy programmes for youth and adults;
(f) a mediation service;
(g) more police aides to assist with communication with specific groups;
(h) support services for victims of crime;
(i) more cross-cultural information, interaction and integration;
(j) more involvement of the elderly and youth to alleviate fears about each
     other;
(k) family support systems related to child-rearing;
(l) more adequate parental supervision of children;
(m) easily accessible information on parental rights and responsibilities;
(n) housing facilities for homeless youth;
(o) more employment opportunities for the entire population;
(p) availability of and access to leisure facilities for those under the age of 18;
(q) transportation to cater for the needs of youth; and
(r) more adequate street lighting and public telephones in the Housing Trust
     area.

To begin the task of implementing these reforms, committees were set up
for each of the five areas. Their function was to determine priority areas for
funding, to give advice about implementation, to evaluate the results, and to
submit progress reports to the District Council.

The education sector is also particularly responsive to the needs of
Aboriginal children. An Aboriginal pre-kindergarten has the goal of helping
to socialize Aboriginal children in an environment which is sensitive to their
culture, helps them with Aboriginal language and prepares them for regular
kindergarten. In the kindergarten, Aboriginal health services are provided as
well as dentistry. Since many of the children are transients, whose basic needs
have not been met adequately, the staff co-ordinate with the local child care
and family day care centres.

As in other countries these developments in Ceduna operate within the
context of a more general strategy for the development of community-based
services in South Australia, where a strategy for co-ordinating services for
school children with social and behavioural problems has been outlined by
Stratmann (1988) and which incorporates the following:

(a) Agreement to be reached at the chief executive level as to the range and
     extent of services to be provided by each agency at the local level.
(b) Inter-agency networks (school response teams) relating to specific clusters
     of schools be formally identified and effectively maintained.

(c) To facilitate inter-agency co-ordination, clusters of schools be identified which are as compatible as possible with the Health and Welfare Sector boundaries, and with the clusters of schools being identified as a base for Superintendents within the Education Department.

(d) Multi-disciplinary, district-based student-support teams be established in the Education Department. It was suggested that initially these teams would be made up from existing personnel in the Education Department from project teams and support services, guidance officers, social workers, attendance officers, etc. They would offer services to students referred from the same cluster of schools referred to above. The team managers would have a major role in the maintenance of the inter-agency networks as well as being the points of contact for school based personnel and accepting responsibility for case management plans for individuals.

(e) Specific programmes enhancing teacher skills in behaviour management to be developed.

(f) At least one form of withdrawal facility or programme be available in each Education Department area, on the basis that it is used also as a vehicle for staff development and as a catalyst for change within the referring schools.

(g) More joint welfare and education intensive personal supervision for some students be provided through the Department for Community Welfare Intensive Adolescent Supervision Programme, in close co-operation with Education Department personnel.

(h) Expansion of specialist Child and Adolescent Mental Health Services and Department for Community Welfare personnel, deployed specifically to support school children with social and behavioural problems.

(i) The co-location of community health, education and welfare services be formally adopted as policy in the Department for Community Welfare, Education Department and Health Commission, and every effort be made to identify school premises which could be made available for co-locating services on a permanent or visiting basis. This would provide a service base for clusters of schools and, where possible, might provide the site for a withdrawal facility.

Transition to Work

The process of transition to work begins at an early age. For many disadvantaged students additional support can be needed from the last years of the primary school right through to the end of upper secondary education. In Canada the Eastwood school in Waterloo Ontario (OECD, 1998) provides a good example. There students from as young as 10 years can receive extra help in helping them to begin to learn the skills necessary for work. More generally the programme focuses on using a wide range of community groups to provide authentic work experience for students and to support them socially. Changing family circumstances have left too many children bereft of supportive grandparents or benevolent aunts, uncles and siblings and in this approach community resources are marshalled to compensate for the lack of these supports.

But city administrations can also play a key role in helping to co-ordinate efforts to help youth at risk engage effectively with work and training. Over the last decade the city of Duisburg in Germany has put vocational training for disadvantaged youth at the top of its list of priorities. Demographic change in the age structure of the population, economic recession, and the decline of the coal and steel industry, on which Duisburg's early prosperity was based, have widened the gap between the demand for vocational training and the supply of apprenticeship positions, leaving many young people unoccupied.

To combat the problem of youth unemployment, the city has created three special committees: the youth unemployment committee, the vocational help group for young people and a co-ordinating committee (to integrate efforts and advise the youth unemployment committee). They have attempted to build a network of services in Duisburg to meet the multi-faceted needs of its most disadvantaged and poorly qualified young people.

One of the principal agencies in the network is Duisberg's youth office. This is the city's umbrella organization for all youth services, and has links with representatives from public, private and political bodies with whom it plans services. Two of its closest partners are the employment office and the Duisburg branch of the RAA (the Regional Centre for Foreign Children and Youth). The employment office co-operates with many other stakeholders in the network through both formal and informal agreements. While its closest partner is the youth office, it also liaises extensively with free associations which run programmes to facilitate the transition to work. The RAA in Duisburg has extended its role beyond its normal one – namely addressing the problems of foreign youth – to deal with the city's youth unemployment. It plays a significant part in building bridges between educational social and employment services. Its social educators and teachers are important providers of vocational counselling, and have found a special niche in dealing with youth at risk of dropping out of school early, and unemployed youth who have been out of school for several months. The RAA meets regularly with other stakeholders in the network for service planning and case management, and also to maintain a shared database. One of its closest partners is the vocational counselling service, although at times the relationship is considered rather too close since their work can overlap.

Typical of the schools visited by the RAA's staff is the Bertholdt Brecht Vocational School in Duisburg. This school provides the kind of dual training, including vocational education and apprenticeship experience, for which Germany is famous. However, more unusually, it also provides full-time vocational education for those who cannot obtain an apprenticeship, and a general or academic education for those who might wish to go to university. The school works closely with the youth office, the youth unemployment committee and local companies. For disadvantaged youth who are unable to cope in a normal vocational institution, Duisburg also has a vocational training centre. Youth attending the centre spend some of the time in a normal vocational school and in job placements, but also receive special training in social skills. In addition to vocational teachers, the centre also employs social educators who can address both the educational and social welfare needs of students, and are specially selected for their interpersonal and communication abilities. Key partners of the centre are local vocational schools, companies, and the employment office which makes every effort to find its students work.

Cohesion amongst the partners in Duisburg's youth services network has been promoted by the huge need for support amongst under-qualified young people, and by the sharing of a common goal – to ensure that all young people make a successful transition to work. The traditional reluctance of school teachers to co-operate with social welfare agencies has been overcome by employing other teachers to perform social work functions.

The outcomes of Duisburg's efforts to integrate its youth services are reflected in a comprehensive annual report on education and employment by the statistics office which tracks students destinations after leaving school. All agencies involved in the network co-operate in producing the office's database. Statistics show that the number of children dropping out of school in Duisburg has declined. Duisburg has also proved itself successful in reducing youth unemployment.

Concluding Comment

These examples of community based services developed to meet the needs of families and students of all ages in a wide range of very different and difficult circumstances reveal how effective such an approach can be. The cases speak for themselves in the levels of complexity and variety that are involved in developing services that respond to the needs of people. They are different in that they have developed in a context of more general reforms to service provision which have involved their own forms of central and local government in decision-making and over a very substantial period of time, but they are similar since educational success is a common goal around which a wide range of services are united in supporting families and children. Given this evidence it is not surprising that centrally administered 'delivered' services have difficulty in addressing the true needs of the families and children involved.

Overall Discussion

If countries, are to continue to grow and prosper in the next millennium then all will have to respond rapidly to the economic and social developments which are taking place throughout the world and this means substantial changes in the way education, health and social services operate. This chapter has given examples of how communities can become part of these reforms essentially through the implementation of a services integration agenda which puts the needs of families and children at the heart of planning and involves the whole community, including as well, business, churches and the voluntary sector in a constructive elaboration of common social and educational goals in the creation of the new civic society.

Providing community based services requires substantial co-ordination and co-operation between a diverse range of actors across a vertical structure running from the community, and the practicalities of implementation, through to government which usually sets the legal framework and has responsibility for justifying the use of the taxpayers' money which, in turn, supports the developments on the ground. At this level it is important not to forget that community based services will need to have, strong support from central government with changes in the law being made as and when necessary, which may have to cover issues relating to the sharing of budgets across departmental boundaries, the training of professionals and allowing for information on clients to be shared across professional groupings. This last issue is of some concern to civil rights groups.

Creating these changes is neither easy to initiate nor to sustain. They need a great deal of determination and forward vision. The fact they are happening all over the world is important in convincing countries' administrators that other ways can be better and providing international perspectives is very important in this regard. No magic formulae are being proposed since the implementation details are too varied from country to country. What is clear though is that reforms are necessary and the community based services solution is one of the few on offer which is consistent with our democratic future.

References

Collins, R. and Miller, V. (1992) *Draft Two Year Crime Prevention Plan for Ceduna, Together Against Crime*, Ceduna, South Australia, District Council of Murat Bay.

Halsey, A.H. (1993) 'Changes in the family', in Pugh, G. (ed.) *30 Years of Change for Children*, London, UK, National Children's Bureau.

Klugman, J. (1997) 'Decentralisation: a survey from a child welfare perspective', *Innocenti Occasional Papers*, Economic and Social Policy Series, EPS 61, Florence, UNICEF.

Mäkelä, M., Winter-Heikkila, M., Astrom, M. and Rokka, S. (1993) 'Local population responsibility – old wine in new barrels?', *Journal of the National Research and Development Centre for Welfare and Health* 11–13.

Organization for Economic Co-operation and Development (OECD) (1995a) *Our Children at Risk*, Paris, OECD.

Organization for Economic Co-operation and Development (OECD) (1995b) *Integrating Students with Special Needs into Mainstream Schools*, Paris, OECD.

Organization for Economic Co-operation and Development (OECD) (1996) *Successful Services for Our Children and Families At Risk*, Paris, OECD.

Organization for Economic Co-operation and Development (OECD) (1997) *Implementing Inclusive Education*, Paris, OECD.

Organization for Economic Co-operation and Development (OECD) (1998) *Co-ordinating Services for Children and Youth At Risk – a world view*, Paris, OECD.

Rauwenhoff Committee (1990) *Education–Labour Market: Towards an effective pathway*, The Hague, Alphen aan den Rijn.

Stratmann, P. (1988) *Interagency Responses to School Children with Social and Behavioural Problems*, Adelaide, Australia, Department of Premier and Cabinet.

United Nations (1989) *Convention on the Rights of the Child*, New York, UN.

Webb, S. and Webb, B. (1963) *English Poor Law Policy*, London, Frank Cass.

Whelan, B.J. and Whelan C.T. (1995) 'In what sense is poverty multidimensional?', in Room, G. (ed.) *Beyond the Threshold*, Bristol, Policy Press.

14 The Social, Economic and Political Climate in the United States and the Education of People of Colour

Carl A. Grant and LaVonne J. Williams

This chapter discusses the social, economic, political and educational conditions of African Americans, other people of colour, and the poor in the United States of America over thirty years. Using the 1968 Report of the National Advisory Commission on Civil Disorder as the baseline, this chapter compares and contrasts housing, health and medical attention, crime and police practices, unemployment and underemployment, income and poverty; political representation; and de facto segregation in schools, overcrowding in classrooms, poor quality of instruction and facilities between 1968 and 1998 for African Americans, other people of colour, poor people and mainstream European Americans. Also, several education and social programmes designed and implemented to help African Americans, other people of colour, and the poor are presented. The chapter concludes by arguing that much work remains to be done in order for the social, economic and political climate in the United States to be of such a condition that it fosters an equal and equitable education for students outside the dominant culture.

Introduction

Since the early days of the United States there have been social, political, economic and educational inequities directed towards people of colour. In this chapter, we will use the 1968 *Report of the National Advisory Commission on Civil Disorders*, – commonly referred to as the Kerner Report in honour of the Chairperson of the Commission – as the standard to examine and compare and contrast the present social, political, economic and educational conditions for people of colour and poor people in the United States. The Kerner Report was commissioned by President Lyndon B. Johnson in 1968 after race riots in over twenty urban areas (e.g. Atlanta, Cincinnati, Detroit, Newark). We decided to use areas addressed in the report as a framework for writing this chapter. For each of the following decades (1978, 1988 and 1998) areas covered in the Kerner Report are examined to update the state of the nation. Thirty years later the 1998 update was released: *The Millennium Breach.*

Richer, Poorer, and Racially Apart: A Thirty Year Update of the National Advisory Commission on Civil Disorders (Eisenhower Foundation and Corporation for What Works, 1998)

The Kerner Report identified three levels of intensity, which included twelve areas of grievances that were extremely problematic to citizens of colour and involved issues of equity, equality and full democratic participation. We have organized this chapter using the grievance structure of the Kerner Report: *social* (housing, health/medical attention, crime and police practices), *economic* (unemployment/underemployment, income and poverty), *political* (political representation) and *educational* (de facto segregation, overcrowding, poor quality of instruction and facilities). Following our comparison of these grievances – then and now – we will describe several educational and social programmes that are implemented to improve the education for poor children and children of colour. Most of these programmes are appropriate – with modifications – for other countries.

Social Conditions

The Kerner Report had one basic conclusion: 'Our nation is moving towards two societies, one black, one white – separate and unequal' (p. 1). African Americans (identified as 'Negroes' in the original report) and other minorities were being deprived of fair and equal life opportunities as well as full democracy. Social inequities were seen in the areas of housing, medical attention and police protection.

Housing

The Kerner Report concluded that African Americans and other people of colour were living in dilapidated, old, overcrowded, substandard and segregated housing. Forty per cent of the African American population living at or below the poverty line were forced to live in central city housing where many of the riots took place, while most European Americans lived in well-cared for neighbourhoods that were separated from non-whites.

Since the 1980s and 1990s, urban planners and politicians have recognized that the large multiple occupancy urban dwellings (e.g. Cabrinia Green, Chicago; Pruitt Igoe, St Louis) are not suitable for family life (e.g. because of crime and poor property management). In several cities these massive structures are being torn down, and being replaced with small housing units. However, in some cases, people of colour who move into smaller units face different problems. Parenti argues that:

> Private housing developments built with federal assistance are often rented to low-income people for a year or two in order to qualify for

federal funds, then renovated or sold to other private owners who, not held to the original contract, evict the tenants and turn the units into high price rental property or condominiums.

(1988, p. 109)

Also, some African Americans and other people of colour are moving to smaller geographical areas, cities of 50,000 or less, where the housing is better and the crime rate is low. Additionally, the 1980s and 1990s have seen a major growth in the African American middle class, including many middle-class African Americans buying homes in the suburbs. In the 1990s, 32 per cent of all African Americans living in the metropolitan areas moved to the suburbs. However, in contrast to the move to the suburbs, an increasing number of affluent African Americans are buying homes in all-black middle- and upper-class neighbourhoods, where they do not experience the everyday racism that sometimes occurs in integrated neighbourhoods. In spite of housing options, 57 per cent of African Americans still reside in the inner city (US Bureau of the Census, in Mabunda, 1997, pp. 527, 529). Furthermore, the thirty year update of the Kerner Report, *The Millennium Breach. Richer, Poorer, and Racially Apart* (Eisenhower Foundation and Corporation for What Works, 1998), reports: 'America's neighborhoods and schools are resegregating along racial lines' (pp. iii, 6).

Health/Medical Attention

For residents of the inner city, poverty means deficient diets, inadequate shelter and clothing, lack of medical care, and often an unawareness of health needs. African Americans and other people of colour are often the uninsured poor and in need of financial assistance in meeting medical expenses. The Kerner Report claims that non-whites in the lowest income group spent less than 50 per cent as much as whites in the lowest income group on health and medical attention, and non-whites in the highest income group spent 73.4 per cent of what whites in the highest income group spent (p. 271). Reasons for the differences in spending between whites and non-whites are several: non-whites usually have a lower income, higher rent, more family members, pay a higher cost for food and consumer goods, and have less conveniently located health services.

In the 1990s hospitals and medical services are more conveniently found in the inner cities. Nevertheless, in the 1990s, pre- and post-natal care is not accessible to many poor pregnant women living in the inner city, and child immunizations are lower than in many poorer nations. For example, the lack of immunization of children of colour between 19–35 months is at more than one-third of that population, with 38 per cent of black children and 41 per cent of other children of colour not adequately immunized (Children's Defense Fund, 1995, p. 32). Also, in the mid-1990s, as a result of inadequate funding of the Women, Infant and Children (WIC) federal programme which provides food supplements and medical and other services for low-income infants, children and pregnant and nursing women, fewer than half of those eligible were served. Furthermore, a new threat to poor children is AIDS, and African American children constitute more than half of all the AIDS cases reported in children under thirteen (National Urban League, 1995). The Center for Disease Control estimated that by 1997, over 10,000 children in the USA would be affected by AIDS, with most of them poor (Center for Disease Control and Prevention, 1997).

The key to improved health status for poor children and children of colour is financial. Good health care in the USA, that includes preventive care, is very expensive and few people can afford good health care unless they have medical insurance. Millions of low-income working and/or unemployed families are not covered by private or public health insurance. A report by the Children's Defense Fund (1995) claims that, in 1993, nearly one out of seven children – more than 9.4 million children nationally – as well as an estimated 500,000 or more pregnant women were uninsured. The decline in employers providing health coverage for children is not because of a drop in employment, but, instead, because fewer employers are offering or subsidizing health insurance plans with coverage for dependants, and also because some employers are hiring only part-time workers in order not to have to pay the health benefits they would have to pay to full-time workers (Children's Defense Fund, 1995, pp. 27, 28).

Crime and Police Protection

The Kerner Report describes how crime in the inner city made life for people living on or below the poverty line different to the life of most middle-class white Americans living outside of the inner city. The crime rates of index crime (e.g. homicide, rape, robbery, burglary, grand larceny and auto theft) were three times higher than the crime rate in suburban areas; the highest amount of crime occurred in the low-income, older neighbourhoods encircling the downtown areas of larger cities. Although these crimes were committed by a small percentage of the inner-city residents, the majority of the inner-city residents faced a far greater chance of being victimized than the residents living in higher-income areas. The Kerner Report states: 'for non-whites, the probability of suffering from any index crime (other than larceny) is 78 per cent higher than for whites' (National Advisory Commission on Civil Disorders, 1968, p. 268). In addition to this potential victimization, inner city residents felt a sense of insecurity because of a lack of adequate and fair police protection. The Kerner Report also notes:

> When calls for help are registered, it is all too frequent that police
> respond too slowly or not at all … When they do come, [they] arrive

with many more men and cars than necessary … brandishing guns and adding to the confusion.

(p. 308)

Also, the Kerner Report quotes David Harley of *The New York Times Daily News*, who discusses another way the police do not protect African American inner-city residents, which is by ignoring crimes committed between residents:

> To put it simply, for decades little if any law enforcement has prevailed among Negroes in America, particularly those in the ghettos. If a black man kills a black man, the law is generally enforced at its minimum. Violence of every type is rampant in the ghetto.
>
> (Kerner Report, p. 308)

For the poor, little has changed in 1998. The National Urban League (1995) argues: 'We are confronted daily with news stories of crisis: from police violence [e.g. Rodney King] to gang violence, to domestic violence, children are often the innocent victims guilty only of living in the wrong place at the wrong time' (p. 10).

Over the last two decades black on black violence is one of the major sources of crime and one of the major sources of the demoralization and despair within the African American community. For example, over 80 per cent of the deaths of African American youth are caused by gunshots, and in 1987, homicides accounted for 42 per cent of deaths among African American male youth. Also, a young African American male is six times more likely to be murdered than a young African American female, nine times more likely than a white young male, and 26 times more likely than a white young female (Isaacs, 1992, p. 5).

The rising violence among African Americans, according to many in the black community, has reached epidemic proportions. However, when the problem of violence among African Americans is addressed by mainstream society, the focus is not on prevention (e.g. education, after school programmes and good jobs) and public health, but instead it is on remediating the problem by using the criminal justice system and additional police to 'control' the problem, or by keeping it in the African American community. The role of the criminal justice system as a controlling agency is learned very early in the life of low-income school children. Shust (1986) argues:

> It's strange how the schoolyard fight and shoplifting cases in the middle-class neighborhoods rarely result in the youngsters' being charged. The police call the kids' parents to pick them up, and they send them home with a warning to stay out of trouble. But when the same incidents

happen in the less affluent neighborhoods, children are arrested and charged and brought to court.

(quoted in Parenti, 1988, p. 127)

This double standard is known and resented by poor young people of colour, and leads to their being afraid and/or having a lack of respect for the police; and it serves to promote a cynicism about institutional authority which often lasts for a lifetime.

Economic Conditions

Unemployment and Underemployment

The Kerner Report found that widespread unemployment and underemployment were the most persistent and serious grievances in areas where people of colour and the poor lived, and the Report claimed that they are inextricably linked to the problem of civil disorder (Kerner Report, p. 24). At that time Daniel Moynihan stated:

> The principal measure of progress toward equality will be that of employment. It is the primary source of individual or group identity. In America what you do is what you are: to do nothing is to be nothing; to do little is to be little … [f]or the Negro American it is already, and will continue to be, the master problem … It is the measure of Negroes' competence, and also of the competence of American society … Employment not only controls the present … but … is creating the future as well.
>
> (National Advisory Commission on Civil Disorders, 1968, p. 252)

The Kerner Report further noted that the 1967 African American unemployment rate was more than double that of whites. Additionally, to compound this unemployment problem, the report noted that many professions and vocations have a history of keeping people of colour out or hiring very few of them. Employment available to the African American and urban poor was low-status and unpleasant; the wages were substandard; achieving job tenure was doubtful; there were few or no opportunities for meaningful advancement; and, in most cases, people of colour were the last hired and the first fired. For example, the report notes that while 6 per cent of white males were non-farm labourers, 20 per cent of the males of colour were non-farm labourers; and while only 6 per cent of the white males were service workers, 16 per cent of non-white males were service workers (p. 254).

In the 1990s the unemployment and underemployment situation for African Americans and other marginalized people still remains a major problem. Data from the US Bureau of the Census shows that, in 1990, the unemployment rates for blacks were two-and-a-half times as great as those for whites (Mabunda, 1997, p. 541). Discrimination in the job market is the cause of much of the variance in unemployment rates between blacks and whites. Although middle- and upper-middle-class blacks have received increased occupational and economic opportunities, when taking into account the total black population, they fall behind whites in every measure of socioeconomic standing, including higher levels of unemployment. Also, blacks are in dispro-portionately more blue-collar jobs. For example, data from the United States Census revealed that, in 1991, 18 per cent of all employed blacks held managerial and professional positions, compared to 31 per cent of whites. Additionally, data on employment of labourers and other related positions reveals that 22 per cent of blacks work as labourers compared to 13.2 per cent of whites (Mabunda, 1997, pp. 541, 542).

Income

In 1968, the median black income was only 58 per cent of the median white income, and 20 per cent of all blacks were making no significant economic gains despite the general prosperity of the time (Kerner Report, 1968, pp. 251, 252). In 1991 there was only a minimal (1 per cent) improvement in the median income gap between blacks and whites. Now the black median income is 59 per cent that of whites (Mabunda, 1997, pp. 542, 553). Also, blacks' and Hispanics' personal and family income continues to be unequal to that for whites. In 1995, the median income was $35,766 for whites, $22,393 for blacks, and $22,860 for Hispanics. However, incomes under $10,000 were more disparate, with 10.6 per cent of the white population, 24 per cent of the black population, and 19.9 per cent of the Hispanic population in this lowest income level (US Bureau of the Census, 1997, p. 465). Also, the 1997 income data shows how race is the major player at three different levels of income analysis. Income categories between $10,000–$24,999 had racial distributions of 24.3 per cent of whites, 30.3 per cent of blacks and 33.7 per cent of Hispanics. Incomes categories between $25,000 and $49,999 had racial distri-butions of 31.7 per cent for whites versus 28.2 per cent for blacks and 28.7 per cent for Hispanics. Incomes over $50,000 had the racial distributions of 33.8 per cent for whites, 17.4 per cent for blacks and 17.7 per cent for Hispanics (US Bureau of the Census, 1997, p. 465).

   The middle-level income category shows the closest distribution among the three races, with a difference of only around 3 per cent (31.7 per cent against 28.2 and 28.7 per cent), which is consistent with the increasing numbers of blacks and Hispanics who are achieving middle socio-economic status because of increased levels of education and other employment oppor-tunities. However, access to the third level is difficult to obtain because of the glass ceiling, and vestiges of institutional racism and everyday racism.

Furthermore, the *Millennium Breach Report* (Eisenhower Foundation and Corporation for What Works, 1998) states that:

> From 1977 to 1988, the income of the richest 1 per cent in America increased by 120 per cent and the incomes of the poorest fifth in America decreased by 10 per cent during a time of supply-side tax breaks for the rich and against the poor.
>
> (p. iii)

Kevin Phillips (quoted in the *Millennium Breach*, p. iii) argued this meant that 'the rich got richer and the poor got poorer'. Also, the *Millenium Breach* notes, ' ... the working-class got poorer. The middle-class stayed about the same in absolute terms, so it, too, lost ground relative to the rich' (p. iii).

Poverty

The Kerner Report declared that the chronic unemployment in the central city was the fundamental cause for the persistent poverty. Poverty was defined as extending beyond absolute deprivation to being a relative deprivation – inequality – 'because it encompassed social and political exclusion as well as economic inequality' (p. 258). According to the Kerner Report (1968), '11.9 per cent of the total white population, and 40.6 per cent of the non-white population lived within the poverty range' (p. 258).

By 1990 the poverty rate had improved somewhat for non-white and whites, down about 9 per cent so that 31.9 per cent of African Americans were living at or below the poverty line. Also, 1990 census data reports that the highest rate of poverty (56.1 per cent) is in single female households with children, and the second highest rate (48.1 per cent) is in single female households without children (Mabunda, 1997, p. 546). The impact of unemployment, underemployment and low wage income upon the family is easily seen in the adverse consequences in the well-being of children. In 1995, the percentage of children living in poverty ($15,569 for a family of four in 1995) was 20 per cent (US Department of Health and Human Services, 1997, p. 48). The number of children raised in extreme poverty (with incomes below 50 per cent of the poverty line) was 60 per cent higher in 1995 than it was in 1975. Additionally, in 1989, the poverty rate was 12.1 per cent for white children, 16.7 per cent for Asian American children, 31.8 per cent for Hispanic children, 38.3 per cent for Native American children and 39.5 per cent (more than three times the rate of poverty for whites) for black children (US Department of Health and Human Services, 1997, p. 49). Furthermore, the *Millennium Breach Report* notes that, 'Today, the child poverty rate in the United States is 4 times the average of Western European countries' (p. iii).

Political Climate

Political Representation of People of Colour

In 1968 the residents of the inner city believed, as the Kerner Report noted, that the local government was not responding to their needs and grievances and they were excluded from the processes of government. In 1970, there was a total number of only 1,469 black officials elected to the federal, state, city and county government and serving on education boards. For example, there were nine black congressmen in the House of Representatives and one black senator.

In 1993 the total number of black elected officials was 7,984. Of that number, 561 were members of the US and state legislatures; 4,819 were elected officials to city and county offices, 126 were elected to law enforcement positions, and 264 were elected to positions in education. In that same year, the total number of elected Hispanic officials was 5,170. Of that number, 182 were elected as state executives and legislators, 2,023 were elected as county and municipal officials, 651 were officials in judicial and law enforcement, and 2,412 were elected to education and school boards (US Bureau of the Census, 1997, p. 286). Although there is an increase in the political representation for people of colour between 1960 and 1990, people of colour are still locked out of much of the political system. For example, if we look at local elected officials in 1992, it is noted that there is an inequitable distribution of officials according to race: a total of 405,905 whites; 11,542 blacks; 5,859 Hispanics; 514 Asian Americans and Pacific Islanders, and 1,800 Indigenous People. Also, the increasing number of men of colour as big-city mayors presents a false picture of political representation. Since 1971 there have been only two African American US Senators; and the number of other senators of colour has fluctuated between two and four. Between 1971 and 1998 the combined number of African American congresspersons (the combined total from the House of Representatives and the Senate) increased from 12 to 39 but still constituted only 9 per cent of the House of Representatives, a significant under-representation of the 12 per cent of US Americans who are black. Four per cent of the House of Representatives in Congress in 1993 were Hispanic – Hispanic representation had grown over the decade but the 9 per cent of US Americans who are Hispanic are still under-represented. There are two Asian American senators, six Asian American members of the House, and only one Native American senator in Congress.

Presently, there are several barriers to full representation and participation in the political process: first, voter registration is a tedious process, especially for low income citizens; second, district gerrymandering, – the dividing of a geographical area into voting districts to give unfair advantage to one party in an election – often has black voters spread out over several districts or confined to one or a few districts, thereby containing their influence; and third, white attitudes towards black candidates, which may be considered the most challenging barrier to overcome. For example, when Jesse Jackson ran for the presidential nomination of the United States in 1988, he made an excellent showing. Jackson's showing surprised many astute political observers, especially and including news reporters who continued to ask, 'What does Jessie want?' Since these reporters, and many other white Americans, had a difficult time imagining Jessie Jackson, an African American man, as President of the United States, they also had a difficult time believing he wanted to be president (Ploski and Williams, 1989).

Inadequate Education

The Kerner Report found that the educational system was a serious source of grievance, with complaints centred upon the dominance of de facto segregation, the poor quality of instruction and facilities, and deficiencies in the curriculum.

De Facto Segregation

The Kerner Commission reported, in its study of 75 major central cities, that nearly '90 per cent of all African American students attended schools which had an African American majority … and that 83 per cent of all white students attended schools with 90–100 per cent white enrolments' (National Advisory Commission on Civil Disorders, 1968, p. 426).

The same de facto segregation still exists. For example, in 1990, due to demographic changes and 'white flight' to the suburbs, major cities such as Washington DC, Atlanta, Detroit, Baltimore, Memphis and New Orleans had African American majorities and five of the largest cities in the USA were more than 50 per cent African American. Also, two-thirds of all African American students and three-quarters of all Hispanic students attend segregated school (Children's Defense Fund, 1995). Also, today, racial segregation in school, which was identified as a major problem in the Kerner Report (1968), is still a reality, especially for language-minority students. Orfield (1986) argues that the majority of Hispanic students attend schools that serve minority populations.

Overcrowding in Schools, Poor Quality of Instruction and Facilities

A major problem in 1968 that affected the quality of education African Americans received was classroom overcrowding. Overcrowded classrooms lead to shortages of educational materials and resources. In 1964, for example, over 40 per cent of the African American elementary schools in Chicago had shortages of supplies and textbooks, and had class enrolments of over 35 students, whereas only 12 per cent of the primarily white elementary schools faced a similar deficit in learning materials and an overcrowding situation (Kerner Report, 1968).

Jonathon Kozol (1991), in *Savage Inequalities*, illuminates the existence of similar problems today. Kozol presents a picture of educational inequality which includes high class enrolments of 37 students and a lack of textbooks. Also, Kozol observes that schools are understaffed and that, in some cases, there is a ratio of 930 students to one counsellor. Additionally, he describes the students' learning conditions as uninspiring, with libraries that are windowless, claustrophobic and without reference books and encyclopaedias. Feldman (1992) claims that in some large cities, such as New York, one some-times hears of classrooms with enrolments of 47 students and teachers holding classes in hallways and closets. Additionally, in a number of classrooms there is no, or a lack of, science equipment. Furthermore, as a teacher in Baltimore stated:

> We consider ourselves lucky at the elementary level if we have specialists for art, music and physical education. And, although the problems of weapons, violence and gangs have migrated down to the elementary level, we consider it a luxury to have a school nurse, guidance counsellor or security officer in a Baltimore school
>
> (Feldman, 1992, p. 17)

The Kerner Report stated that the quality of teaching was poor in urban schools. In the 1990s many would argue the same, also noting that teachers in the urban schools often have less classroom experience and professional skills than elsewhere. Olson and Jerald (1998) states:

> [N]ewly hired teachers in the urban schools are more likely than their counterparts in suburban and rural districts to have no teaching license or an emergency or temporary one. Teachers in high-poverty secondary schools, whether urban or rural, are the least prepared and the most likely to lack even a minor in the subjects they teach. Such schools tend to have a larger share of new, inexperienced teachers.
>
> (p. 16)

Another problem plaguing urban schools is the shortage of teachers of colour. A survey conducted by New Teacher Incorporated found that 92 per cent of the largest urban districts reported an immediate need for teachers of colour (Olson and Jerald, 1998). Closely connected to this dilemma is the problem that although many prospective teachers of colour are interested in working in urban areas, only 20 per cent of undergraduates in teacher education are teacher candidates of colour (Olson and Jerald, 1998, p. 16).

Conditions such as inexperienced teachers, a shortage of teachers of colour, larger classes and a lower tax base to support education, make it exceedingly difficult for students in the inner city to receive a quality education. The *Millennium Breach Report* (Eisenhower Foundation and Corporation for What Works, 1998) states: 'In urban public schools in poor neighborhoods, more than two-thirds of children fail to reach even the "basic" level on the national tests' (pp. iii, 7).

Deficiencies in the Curricula

In 1968 schools offered curricula that were written from a dominant Eurocentric perspective and often used stereotypes to represent people of colour. Native Americans were portrayed as noble savages as they helped white settlers, or as ruthless savages who massacred white people, especially helpless white women and children; Mexican Americans were mainly discussed in relationship to struggles with the United States over Southwestern territory; Asian Americans (predominantly of Chinese ancestry) were featured as peaceful and industrious helpers in constructing the Continental Railroad and often shown in their homeland attire as they worked in Californian mines; and African Americans were portrayed as enslaved people longing for their freedom or free people struggling for more civil rights. During the 1960s, African Americans and other people of colour began to demand authentic, accurate and greater representation in the school curricula. Teachers and parents in many states (e.g. Michigan) organized committees to demand that textbook publishers publish accurate, honest and fair accounts of the roles of different ethnic groups in United States history.

Presently many educators are arguing for a culturally responsive curriculum and pedagogy (Banks, 1994; Gay, 1995; Grant and Sleeter, 1997; Ladson–Billing, 1994). Nevertheless, the multicultural perspective that is presently in textbooks has not caught up with the perspective suggested by these scholars. In an analysis of 47 grade 1–8 textbooks (with copyright dates between 1980–8), Sleeter and Grant (1991) report:

> Whites consistently dominate textbooks, although their margin of dominance varies widely. Whites receive the most attention, are shown in the widest variety of roles, and dominate the story line and lists of accomplishments. Blacks are the next most included group. However, the books show blacks in a more limited range of roles than whites, and give only a sketchy account of black history and little sense of contemporary black life. Asian Americans and Hispanic Americans appear mainly as figures on the landscape with virtually no history or contemporary ethnic experience, and no sense of the ethnic diversity within each group is represented. Native Americans appear mainly as historical figures, although there are a few contemporary stories in reading books.
>
> (p. 97)

Sleeter and Grant (1991) also observed that there is very little interaction among the different groups of colour (e.g. Latinos and Asian Americans), and most interaction is between an ethnic group of colour and whites (e.g. Asian Americans and European Americans). Sleeter and Grant (1991) state:

> Furthermore, very little interaction among different groups of colour is shown. For example, black cowboys were in the West with Native Americans, Chinese Americans, Japanese Americans, and Filipino Americans. These groups are only shown interacting with whites. In addition, the books contain very little about contemporary race relations or issues for which these groups are currently struggling. They convey an image of harmonious blending of different colours of people, dominated by white people, and suggest that everyone is happy with current arrangements.
>
> (p. 97)

The Kerner Report cited several reasons why urban students achieve poorly in comparison to whites. First, since the vast majority of urban public schools were segregated, urban students were deprived of exposure to more educationally advantaged children, therefore administrators, teachers, parents and the students themselves thought the urban schools to be inferior, which affected both teaching and learning. Second, there was a lack of adequate services to deal effectively with the health, emotional and mental needs that often occur with impoverished children, which made teaching more challenging and reinforced teachers' negative attitudes. The third reason was high student turnover.

Today, many African Americans strongly argue against the *need* for African American students and other students of colour to sit next to a white student in order to learn. Instead, these African Americans argue that it is the poor quality of teaching, the lack of a culturally responsive curriculum and pedagogy, the refusal to use students' native language and/or provide a language maintenance programme, run down school facilities and societal neglect and marginalization that are the major reasons that African Americans and other students of colour are not achieving their potential.

Promising Educational Programmes, Models and Practices

In the USA, educational programmes for marginalized and poor children fall within several categories: early childhood intervention, early literacy intervention, schools restructuring, population specific schools and programmes, parent–school partnerships, and teaching practices.

Carl A. Grant and LaVonne J. Williams

Early Childhood Education that Develops Student Readiness

Head Start

Operation Head Start, a federal intervention programme to improve opportunities for pre-school children from low-income families, began in 1965. The goal of Head Start is to improve health, social and emotional development, relationships with family, sense of self-worth and cognitive and linguistic skills (Dalta, 1970, p. 3).

Since its conception Head Start has been the subject of harsh criticism. One argument is that it is based on a deficit model of learning theory which argues that students of colour come to school with several deficiencies (e.g. a lack of academic readiness, a mismatch between home and school culture) that are located in the student or the student's family. The focus of Head Start is getting the child ready for school rather than getting schools ready to serve diverse children. A second argument against Head Start is that it is underfunded and serves only a portion of the nation's poor. In 1995, only 35 per cent of the children eligible for Head Start were accepted into the programme. A third argument is that students accepted into a Head Start programme are often segregated according to class and race (Swadener, 1995, p. 70).

However, Head Start, with some adjustments (e.g. making pre-school educational experience more culturally and linguistically congruent to those of the children), presently continues to survive the arguments made against it, and is considered one of the nation's most responsive and effective programmes helping pre-school children from low-income homes. The *Millennium Breach Report* (Eisenhower Foundation and Corporation for What Works, 1998, p. iv.) notes that every $1.00 spent on pre-school yields $4.75 in benefits later on (see also Chapter 8).

Early Literacy Intervention

Reading Recovery

Reading Recovery is an intensive one-on-one tutoring programme developed in New Zealand by Marie Clay in 1979. In this programme, first-grade students experiencing difficulty learning to read spend a half hour each day with a well-trained specialist reading books and participating in writing activities. Two important assumptions of the Reading Recovery programme are, first, that students having difficulty learning to read can be taught to read in 12–16 weeks, and second, having attained a set of reading skills, these students should be able to make reading progress for several years without further remedial reading assistance. The results of the programme, according to Slavin et al. (1994), who reviewed several research studies on Reading Recovery, are that 'the effort [results] of Reading Recovery are impressive at the end of the implementation year, and they maintain [the achievement gains] for at least two years' (p. 156).

Read to Succeed

The Read to Succeed programme is a one-to-one tutoring programme for students in grades one through five. The programme has three goals: to improve reading abilities of children with severe reading difficulties; to create a model for improvement that could be duplicated in other schools; and to create a model for preparing undergraduate and graduate education majors to assist children with reading difficulties. The programme uses a language experience approach, children's books, content area reading, and phonics taught through spelling and writing. Tutors meet with students for at least one hour after school each week for activities which include reading a book for enjoyment, writing a story and learning weekly spelling words.

The first results of the programme published in 1986 indicated that all three goals of the programme were being met (Bader, 1986). A more recent evaluation of this programme at eleven sites also indicates that it continues to have positive results. At all eleven sites the majority of the students (71 per cent or more) in the programme are reading at or above grade level. Bader (1998) states:

> some second grade children began on the pre-primer level and were reading at the 1.5 level at the end of the year and third grade children reading at the 1.0 level were reading at the 2.5 level at the end of the year.
>
> (p. 2)

School Restructuring

Small Schools that Engage Each Child

One approach to helping urban students is enroling them in small schools. Schools with low enrolments provide more nurturing and productive teacher–student relationships, a safer and more secure emotional climate, and instructional flexibility that responds to students' specific learning styles. Schools with smaller enrolments are being implemented in several cities. The 21 New Visions Schools in New York City are an example of these low-enrolment schools that engage each student. They have shown higher attendance and lower drop-out rates than other public schools within the city and the students' academic achievement levels are above average (Annie E. Casey Foundation, 1997, p. 7).

The James Comer School Development Program

The James Comer School Development Program, started in 1968, replaces traditional school management and organization with a school governance and management team which integrates the social service programmes within the school and intensifies parental participation in all aspects of school. The School Planning and Management team, comprising of the principal, teachers, teacher aides and parents, collaborates to establish the school's tone, attitudes and values. The use of the Comer model is designed to build a strong bridge between the school and home, and to enhance parental and community support of and commitment to education. The Comer model has successfully turned many schools in urban areas around (Ramierez-Smith, 1995).

The Coalition of Essential Schools

A programme developed by Theodore Sizer in 1984 is a school restructuring design that helps high schools. The programme provides broad directions but allows local educators to construct the specific curricula and instructional methods suited to the needs of their school, community and students. An assumption of this programme is that good schools are unique and they must reflect their community and have the support of teachers, students and families. This means that the decision-making is done by the superintendent, principals, teachers, parents and influential community members, from the bottom up, not from the top down.

Population-Specific Schools and Programmes

African American-Centred Education

Afrocentric education places the African American student at the centre of the education programme (e.g. curriculum and instruction). Asante (1980) argues that Afrocentricity is a 'transforming agent' for the restoration of the Afrocentric worldview, '... [it is] a personal transformation process that enables an individual to transcend a consciousness born out of Otherness and realize Afrocentricity' (p. 12). For African American men, Afrocentric programmes have shown promising results in advancing self- and community respect, a sense of belonging and being of value to humankind. One example is the Louis Armstrong Manhood Development Program in New Orleans, which is designed to nurture and care and to provide an environment that is welcoming, respectful and comfortable to young people, along with structured opportunities for sustained relationships with others. It also provides opportunities and training for young people to contribute to their community and family. Central to this programme is getting African American boys enroled when they are young. Also, educators at the school argue that the programme must be comprehensive in scope and content in order to overcome any outside negative influences which the students may confront.

Marva Collins School

The Marva Collins school in Chicago has gained a national reputation for successfully educating African American children. Marva Collins believes that children with high esteem live up to what is expected of them. The Collins programme demands high expectations of each and every student. At the beginning of the school year students, families and teachers write a mission statement. Students also write aims, goals and objectives of desired accomplishments to be achieved within a certain period of time for themselves, the school, or the family. Students are taught that they have a responsibility for their lives, including the choices that they make, and that they alone are the determining factor in attaining the goals that they set for themselves. The curriculum at the Collins' school includes phonics-based reading instruction, literature based on all cultures of the world (such as Aesop's Fables and Greek mythology), and maths which utilizes manipulative, fact drills and skills. The learning environment is dynamic and highly-structured with a great deal of teacher–pupil interaction. Classrooms have no more than twenty students.

Bilingual and ESL Programmes

Due to the significant numbers of children that are immigrants or refugees to the USA, bilingual and ESL (English as a Second Language) classes are critical to the educational success of these students. Although there are many different types of programmes for language minority students, the most effective programme is the two-way developmental bilingual programme. An example of this would have language majority and language minority students working together as peer teachers, and with teacher instruction in both majority and minority languages. A study by Thomas and Collier (1997) found that only by using quality, long-term (5–6 years) enrichment bilingual programmes (e.g. two-way bilingual education and late-exit developmental bilingual education) will students have the cognitive and academic development needed to be academically successful in English as they reach the high school years.

Parent–School Partnerships

Families and Schools Together

Families and Schools Together (FAST) is a two-year programme that began in 1988 and is presently operating in twenty six states. The programme is an early-intervention/prevention, school-based, collaborative, multifamily-support programme developed for elementary students identified by teachers as having behaviour problems such as school failure, substance abuse, teenage pregnancy, violence and delinquency. FAST is an eight-week programme that utilizes parent–professional partnership to engage low-income and isolated families into the programme. This programme (FAST) integrates concepts and practices of community organizing with clinical techniques proven effective that are based on family therapy and play therapy. The process and outcome evaluation indicate that students show statistically significant improvements in anxiety/withdrawal, conduct disorder and attention span. Child functioning gains are maintained in the two year follow-up study. Social gains are observed within families as well – FAST parents become more involved at school, maintain friendships with other parents met in the programme, gain employment after being on welfare or return to school, and become more involved in the home and community than prior programme involvement (McDonald et al., 1997).

Teaching Practices

Culturally Responsive Teaching

Growing numbers of research studies are showing that students whose teachers use a culturally responsive pedagogical style that matches that of their learning style show achievement gains (Au and Jordan, 1981; Valdez, 1996; King, 1995). Culturally responsive African American teachers, for example, are observed to do the following: (1) perceive themselves as advocates for their students and parental surrogates; (2) employ a teaching style filled with the linguistic patterns within the black community, which includes call and response, high emotional involvement, gestures and body movements, frequent spontaneous and lively discussions, and many forms of repetition; (3) use the students' historical and everyday cultural experiences to relate new concepts to prior knowledge; (4) develop a strong and warm personal relationship with students both inside and outside of the classroom, perhaps by teasing and joking with students in a dialect and/or slang; and (5) teach using authority and push students to achieve as they limit the amount of classroom disruptions and run the class in ways that contribute to students' achievement.

Conclusion

After evaluating many of the strategies that are intended for poor students of colour or poor white students, Stringfield (1994) concludes that special programmes having the greatest gains for urban poor students have the following characteristics: (1) focused attention on issues of initial and long-term implementation; (2) institutionalized reform – such reform, for example, could include a rethinking of the school curriculum and instruction in order to promote equity for all students, greater involvement of the students parents and the local community, and a change in how the school is organized and administrated; (3) focused efforts on early grades (before a pattern of failure set in); (4) the encouragement of whole school restructuring rather than pull-out programmes; (5) bilingual or ESL classes implemented for language minority students; and (6) programmes were externally designed, such as the Comer's School Development Program, rather than locally developed. It should be noted that Stringfield's latest strategy (1994) supports the Comer model, more so than the Coalition of Essential Schools model (see page 240), nevertheless both models are reported to produce good results.

Finally, the social, economic, political and educational conditions for people of colour and poor people are in some ways better and in some ways worse than they were in 1968. They are better because there is a growing population of middle-class people of colour, and institutional discrimination and racism is not as publicly overt as it once was. They are worse because there are still large numbers of poor people who are trapped in poverty because of poor schooling and a lack of employment opportunities, or menial employment opportunities, that do not allow them to move up to the middle class. Also, racism and many of the other 'isms', hide behind code words such as 'at-risk', 'English only' and 'colour blind'. Although cloaked in code words in order to be hidden or at least not recognized, racism and other 'isms' are live and active in US society.

The words that President Johnson said to the nation on 27 July 1968, when establishing the Kerner Commission, still ring true today:

> The only genuine, long-range solution for what has happened lies in an attack mounted at every level – upon the conditions that breed despair and violence. All of us know what those conditions are: ignorance, discrimination, slums, poverty, disease, not enough jobs. We should attack these conditions – not because we are fired by conscience. We should attack them because there is simply no other way to achieve a decent and orderly society in America ...
>
> (National Advisory Commission on Civil Disorders, p. xv)

Also needed, however, is the leadership and the will of the people of the Unites States to turn these words into action.

References

Annie E. Casey Foundation (1997) *Kids Count Data Book: State profiles of child well-being*, Baltimore, MA, Annie E. Casey Foundation.

Asante, M.K. (1980) *Afrocentricity*, Buffalo, NY, Amulefi.

Au, K. and Jordan, C. (1981) 'Teaching Reading to Hawaiian Children: Finding a culturally appropriate solution', in Trueba, H.T., Guthrie, G. and Au, K. (eds) *Culture in the Bilingual Classroom: Studies in classroom ethnography*, pp. 139–152, Rowley, MA, Newberry House.

Bader, L. (1986) 'Improving reading through university and public school cooperation', *Journal of Children and Youth* 7, 2, pp. 37–43.

Bader, L. (1998) *The Reading People: A report to the Candace B. Thoman Foundation*, p. 1–2.

Banks, J. (1994) *Multiethnic Education: Theory and practice*, 3rd edn, Boston, MA, Allyn & Bacon.

Center for Disease Control and Prevention (1997) *HIV/AIDS Surveillance Report*, Atlanta, GA, Author.

Children's Defense Fund (1995) *The State of America's Children Yearbook*, Washington, DC, Children's Defense Fund.

Clay, M. (1979) *The Early Detection of Reading Difficulties: a Diagnostic Survey with Recovery Procedures*, 2nd edition, London, Heinemann Educational.

Collins, C.M. and Choen, D. (eds) (1993) *The African American*, New York, Viking Studio Books.

Dalta, L.E. (1970) 'Head Start's influence on community change', *Children* 17, p. 193.

Eisenhower Foundation and Corporation for What Works (1998) *The Millennium Breach: Richer, Poorer and Racially Apart. A thirty year update of the National Advisory Commission on Civil Disorders*, Washington, DC, Author.

Feldman, S. (1992) 'Children in crisis: the tragedy of under-funded schools and the students they serve', in *American Educator. The Professional Journal of the American Federation of Teachers* 16, p. 8–17, Washington, DC, American Federation of Teachers.

Gay, G. (1995) 'Bridging multicultural theory and practice', in *Multicultural Education, the Magazine of the National Association for Multicultural Education* 3, pp. 4–9, San Francisco, Caddo Gap Press.

Grant, C. A. and Sleeter, C. E. (1997) *Turning on Learning: Five approaches for multicultural teaching plans for race, class, gender and disability*, 2nd edn, Upper Saddle River, NJ, Prentice Hall.

Grubb, N. and Lazerson, M. (1988) *Broken Promises: How Americans fail their children*, Chicago, IL, University of Chicago Press.

Isaacs, M.R. (1992) *Violence: The impact of community violence on African American children and families*, Arlington, VA, National Center for Education in Maternal and Child Health.

Kerner Report – see National Advisory Commission on Civil Disorders (1968).

King, J. (1995) 'Culture-centered knowledge: Black studies, curriculum transformation, and social action', in Banks, J.A. and McGee Banks, C.A. (eds) *Handbook of Research on Multicultural Education*, New York, NY, Macmillan.

Kozol, J. (1991) *Savage Inequalities: Children in America's schools*, New York, Crown.

Ladson–Billing, G. (1994) *The Dreamkeepers: Successful teachers of African American children*, San Francisco, CA, Jossey-Bass.

Mabunda, L.M. (ed.) (1997) *The African American Almanac*, Detroit, MI, Gale Research Inc.

McDonald, L., Billingham, S., Conrad, P., Morgan, A., Payton, N. and Payton, E. (1997) 'Families and school together (FAST): integrating community development with clinical strategies', *Families in Society: The journal of contemporary human services*, pp. 140–155.

National Advisory Commission on Civil Disorders (1968) *Report of the National Advisory Commission on Civil Disorders* (Kerner Report), New York, Bantam Books.

National Urban League (1995) *The State of Black America 1995*, New York, National Urban League.

Olson, L. and Jerald, G. (1998) 'The teaching challenge', *Education Week* 27, 17, p. 16.

Orfield, G. (1986) 'Hispanic education: challenges, research, and policies', *American Journal of Education* 95, pp. 1–25.

Parenti, M. (1988) *Democracy for the Few*, 5th edn, New York, St Martin's Press.

Ploski, H. A. and Williams, J. (eds) (1989) *The Negro Almanac: A reference work on the African American,* 5th edn, Detroit, Gale Research Incorporated.

Ramirez-Smith, C. (1995) 'Stopping the cycle of failure: the Comer model', *Educational Leadership* 52, pp. 14–15.

Shust, D. (1986) 'They call it "Juvenile justice" ', in Parenti, M. (1988) *Democracy for the Few*, 5th edn, New York, St Martin's Press.

Slavin, R. E., Karweit, N. and Wasik, B. (eds) (1994) *Preventing Early School Failure: Research, policy and practice*, Needham Heights, MA, Allyn & Bacon.

Sleeter, C.E. and Grant, C.A. (1991) 'Race, class, gender, and disability in current textbooks', in Apple, M. and Christian-Smith, L. (eds) *The Politics of the Textbook*, New York, Routledge.

Stringfield, S. (1994) *Urban and Suburban/rural Special Strategies for Educating Disadvantaged Children: Findings and policy implications*, Washington, DC, US Department of Education.

Swadener, B. (1995) 'Stratification in early childhood policy and programs in the United States: historical and contemporary manifestations', *Educational Policy* 9, 4, pp. 404–425.

Thomas, W. and Collier, V. (1997) *A National Study of School Effectiveness for Language-Minority Students' Long-Term Academic Achievement*, Washington, DC, National Clearinghouse for Bilingual Education.

US Bureau of the Census (1997) *Statistical Abstract of the United States: 1997*, 117th edn, Washington, DC, U.S. Department of Commerce.

US Department of Health and Human Services, Office of the Assistant Secretary for Planning and Evaluation (1997) *Trends in the Well-Being of America's Children and Youth*, Washington, DC, Child Trends, Inc.

Valdez, G. (1996) *Con Respecto: Bridging the Distances Between Diverse Families and Schools*, New York, NY, Teachers College Press.

15 Support for Lifelong Learning

John MacBeath

This chapter considers some of the limitations in current thinking about 'lifelong learning' and the divide between school education and education beyond school. It argues that, in a context of educational disadvantage, lifelong learning has to be conceptualized and realized in a cradle-to-grave sense.

The argument is illustrated with reference to early years and early education and developed in the context of one specific initiative – 'study support' which exemplifies how a bridge can be built between in-school learning and independent, self-directed, learning.

The Learning Age?

The Learning Age is the title of the Government Green Paper (DfEE, 1998a). The real reason for its demotion from White to Green may never be truly known, but it stands accused of being too soft, too wishful, too New Age. It has none of the hard edge of *Excellence in Schools* (DfEE, 1997), a truly 'White' Paper with parameters and structures, a clear sense of time and place, a set of solid foundations on which to build for the future. Of themselves these two documents and their relative statuses provide a metaphor for school education and lifelong learning.

The great hope for school education, spanning half a century and more, was that it would be the avenue through which opportunities would be opened up and background rendered irrelevant. For some it did indeed provide that avenue, sometimes spectacularly so. At a system-wide level, however, it has not fulfilled that dream. Indeed, we can see as children move through the system, a widening of the gap between the highest and the lowest achieving. School cannot compensate for society, said Basil Bernstein in 1970, and on the cusp of the new millennium we know that he was right.

In 1966 James Coleman et al. produced a landmark study, *Equality of Educational Opportunity*. It came to the same conclusion as had Basil Bernstein, arguing that if we want to change things we have to deal with what happens outside school as well as with what happens inside. Considerable energy, many research studies and much political rhetoric have been spent in trying to prove otherwise but the brave, the visionary and those who care recognize that it is time to break the mould.

The mould to be broken is not simply the one which attempts to contain education within prescribed times, designated buildings, time boundaries and sequential age-related curricula, but the one which limits lifelong learning to those agencies (further education, training agencies and employers, for example) that take up the running only once school is out.

Where and when does lifelong learning start? To be meaningful it must be six months or more before birth, in that crucial plastic period when the unborn child is manufacturing its intelligence and thrives on the richest possible learning environment. Vital opportunities for intellectual and emotional growth follow in the days, weeks and years up to school age, during which time the capacity and the desire to be a lifetime learner are seeded and nurtured. In the following decades from five to twenty-five the opportunities of those early years bear fruit. The foremost educational priority must therefore be with the early years. Not an anxious push to ensure that all children can master reading by a particular age but that the groundbed of emotional intelligence, well-being, security and trust are laid so that children will feel safe enough to learn and, when they fail, to risk again. This will probably require a much more radical set of approaches than is currently on offer. New community schools in Scotland, full-service schools and Education Action Zones might be the locus for the development of more ground-breaking family-centred initiatives. In Chapter 8 of this volume Kathy Sylva took up the argument on education in the early years.

There is a chicken within the egg of this argument of course. The future well being of that rising generation is in the hands of those currently in full-time formal education. If we view education as an investment in the future as well as for personal consumption, the gilt-edged investment is in helping children and young people to mature into adults, stable and self-fulfilled enough to be role models and educators for the next generation.

That may be a goal too far for politicians and policy-makers whose measures of success rarely exceed the length of their own political lifespan. There is, however, much support for such a far-sighted view in the literature, the rhetoric and the hard research. It comes in the OECDs *Learning Beyond Schooling* (1995), UNESCO's *Learning: The treasure within* (1995), the European Commission's *Teaching and Learning: Towards the learning society* (1996), the Government Green Paper *The Learning Age* (DfEE, 1998a) and from employers, the European Round Table of Industrialists document *Education for Europeans: Towards the learning society* (1994). In their document the European employers say this:

> in nearly all European countries there is an ever-widening gap between the education that people need for today's complex world and the education they receive. Too many disillusioned young people drop out of

educational systems through failure or rebellion, and work through with only minimal skills.

(European Round Table of Industrialists, 1994, p. 6)

The document refers to the chain of learning, with the five key links:

- pre-school education
- basic school education
- general and vocational education
- higher education
- adult education.

It is in the links of this chain that social exclusion starts, or more accurately, is recreated from generation to generation. Failure and rebellion are closely intertwined. From the viewpoint of the anxious, vulnerable young person struggling to establish a sense of self, every failure at school is seen as another assault, another confirmation of low self-worth, another piece of evidence that school learning is difficult, threatening, irrelevant.

Diener and Dweck (1978) identified two kinds of responses to a difficult task. One was to meet the challenge and to rise above the occasion. The other was to turn inwards to blame oneself. The 'helpless response' was to measure personal worth and intelligence against the task and to settle for the explanation that you just weren't clever enough. Allied to this self-deprecating attitude was to blame the task. The task itself was 'stupid', or 'boring', a choice of words which mirrors back to the learner his or her own self-concept.

'Learned helplessness' is a term now in common currency (Martin, 1997). It describes people who have found that being passive rather than active makes for an easier life, that there are comforts in being a victim rather than a victor. This is, however, rarely a conscious choice. Its roots may be found in early childhood where a cry brought food and comfort and the baby learned that the environment would accommodate itself to her immediate needs. Being acted on by your environment, as opposed to acting on it, leads to accepting what it tells you about yourself and what you are as a person. The child with an already simmering low self-esteem is a ready candidate for a school structure and system which authenticates and certificates that view of her place in the world.

Helplessness can be learned in school and in some cases it may be consciously taught. 'I will tell you what to do'; 'I will tell you when to move'; and 'I will tell you what to think' are hopefully more redolent of a bygone age, but they are still often implicit messages rather than crudely explicit. The messages are often simply absorbed bit by bit, slowly and inexorably over time through the structures, rules and norms of the school day.

After the Second World War there was disquiet about the ease with which so many German people had, during the Hitler era, been so willing to relinquish their own personal authority and judgement, and to be so helplessly led. Research by an American team (Adorno et al., 1950) identified what they called an 'authoritarian personality' – people who not only treated their perceived inferiors in an authoritarian manner but also deferred to those perceived to be in authority above them. A later study by Stanley Milgram (1974) found a relationship between the authoritarian personality and need for order and structure from others:

> those who score high on the scale that measures fascistic tendencies crave organisation and order above all; those with modest scores on this scale, are comfortable with, or even look for, a degree of chaos, inconsistency and contradictory minutiae.

> (Milgram, p. 7–76)

Learned dependence can kill. There is interesting physiological evidence (Martin, 1997), now for phenomena such as voodoo death – people who die as a result of a spell cast on them by the witch doctor. Their strong belief in the authority of the magic man is enough to inhibit brain and body and produce the most fatal of self-fulfilling prophecies. Chances of a premature death or a long life are closely correlated to power and influence and to social networks. People with circles of friends or relatives on average live longer than social isolates. Having positions of power and influence, as against being controlled by others, is also an indicator of longevity.

Social exclusion is, in the words of the National Working Party on Social Exclusion, structural, dynamic and multidimensional. It grows and matures in the context of systemic unemployment, industrial change, breakdown in traditional family structures, social fragmentation and reductions in public spending. Social exclusion is dynamic because it develops its own impetus and is eventually driven by a powerful in-built accelerator. It is multidimensional because physical conditions, health, work, power, opportunity, ability, character, learning and self-efficacy are all interlocking pieces of the same jigsaw.

Education, Education, Education

The three educations of the Labour Government are not of themselves enough to remake history, economics and global competition but they may, with imagination and commitment, provide in-roads for the marginalized and disenfranchised.

One starting point is a concerted push on standards of achievement, steadily pushing up the numbers who achieve A to C passes at GSCE. Many schools are able to demonstrate significant success, a 50 per cent or more increase, from 50 to 75 per cent or 20 to 30 per cent. The alternative route of General Vocational Qualifications (GVQs) swells the numbers. There are, however, inherent dangers here too. Although further and higher education and employers look for certification and often use it as a first stage screening device, they place the highest premium on personal qualities and social attributes. Universities have traditionally used school examination achievement as a proxy for the capacity to meet the demands of a university education. They have little or no interest in the content of subjects achieved at secondary school since most university courses start anew and if, as in the case of a foreign language, they assume a substantial prior knowledge, they also recognize that a keen student will catch up on classmates within a year or so. What they look for, at least what many faculties look for, are people with the capacity to learn, to be creative, inquiring, enthusiastic, critical, open-minded, proactive and self-motivated.

These are the same kinds of qualities sought by employers. A University of Sheffield analysis of 10,000 newspaper advertisements for graduates carried out in 1989 came up with the following top ten skills or qualities:[1]

1   oral communication
2   teamwork
3   enthusiasm
4   motivation
5   initiative
6   leadership
7   commitment
8   interpersonal skills
9   organizational ability
10 foreign language competence.

A major British multinational company uses a points weighting in recruiting new staff, with top credits going to recruits who have been an organizer or president of a school club, editor of school, university or community newspaper, or have had involvement or leadership in a local political party. Points (on a five point scale) are also awarded to positions such as:

- chair of a Rag Week
- chair/leader Young Farmers
- chair of a school council
- school captain or prefect
- manager of the school tuck shop
- stage manager or producer
- organizer of charity drive
- scout/brownie/guide leader
- dance or large function organizer
- holiday tour leader
- organizer of a dance, jumble sale, fête
- officer in the training corps

- Duke of Edinburgh Gold Award
- responsible role in the family business
- leading involvement in Young Enterprise.

All of these are examples of where the skills from the Sheffield 'Top Ten' find expression and a fertile training ground. There would be few in education who would take issue with such a set of qualities. They underwrite the curriculum of the nursery and infant school, and researchers such as Daniel Goleman (1996) have provided vivid and powerful accounts of leadership, initiative, teamwork, organizational ability and interpersonal skills in the work and play of the nursery and primary schools. They find evidence that some of those playful skills are powerful predictors of success in later life; they illustrate the importance of early years teachers in cultivating and nurturing those precious and precocious skills.

The question we have to ask of schools is – to what extent do the structures of curriculum, examinations, pupils groupings, age cohorts, teacher–learner relationships and the physical environment of classrooms help teachers to sustain that growth over time? How far does the vertical design of school experience from five to sixteen promote those two most cherished aims of curricular architects – coherence and progression?

One of the most insightful critics of curricular design is Harvard's David Perkins. He argues that many of the most essential skills tend to fall into the luxury class. He refers to the 'luxury of understanding' (Perkins, 1998). Very often the school cannot afford the time, or the energy to turn knowledge into understanding nor the opportunity to help teachers acquire the expertise which teaching for understanding presupposes.

As understanding is squeezed out by an overburdened and remorseless curriculum so too are other things that make human beings into social and moral beings. We might add to the list of luxuries the luxury of personal development, the luxury of moral discourse, the civilizing luxury of the aesthetic arts. The more we treat these as luxuries the more threadbare becomes the quality of experience we provide for children and young people. It is not that the Government fails to recognize the importance of citizenship. It has set up a Commission to investigate the place of citizenship, under the chairmanship of Sir Bernard Crick, but where does it find a place in an already overstretched curriculum? A citizenship hour? Such a curriculum insert approach would guarantee its failure as citizenship is not easily taught but is learned through the structures and cultures of the school itself and through the relationship of these to the family, community and society at large.

Without serious attention to the arts and to the lived lessons of citizenship school life is reduced to its bare necessities life and becomes an anxious obstacle race through the key stages at seven, eleven, fourteen. This age/stage related curriculum, which puts its faith in a number of dubious assumptions about child development, generates its own problems. In Britain it is 'a problem' if children are not reading by seven, but not so in some other countries where children learn to read later but no less successfully. Countries that fared badly in the international concourse on literacy scores – Denmark or Iceland, for example, have extremely high adult literacy rates and, the real litmus test, adults who turn to books as a source of pleasure and enlightenment. Considering what many of the adult population in Britain actually read, if they ever do read, we might pause to wonder about all the pressure and anxiety expended. Reading is more an attitude than a technique and the same is true of so much of learning – technique without feeling, knowledge without insight, certification without meaning.

There is a growing danger that in schools' competitive pursuit of examination certification, understanding, insight and meaning are bypassed and that exam passes are, mistakenly, treated as rising standards. Of course we fail young people if we do not give them the best possible chance to achieve examination success. However, we fail them more fundamentally if we push, cajole and spoon feed them so that they pass their exams but fail miserably as lifelong learners.

Peter Hannon (1993) offers an interesting comparison between the home and the school learning environments.

Home	School
spontaneous	planned
flexible	timetabled
shaped by interest	shaped by curriculum
vertical age group	horizontal age group
close informal relationships	distant formal relationships
multiple roles	pupil role
accounts for much variation	accounts for little variation
in achievement	in achievement

How well, we must ask, does one context prepare children to thrive in the other? How well does the home environment prepare children to succeed in school? How well does the school environment help children to learn at home when they are left to their own resources?

The research evidence points in one direction. That is, when we understand how the transitions between organizational cultures of home, school and work operate we have the key to lifelong learning. When we know what strategies will bridge those transitions most effectively we will be able to make a substantial and significant difference.

Study Support – A Vehicle for Lifelong Learning

One promising development that has helped to achieve both of those purposes – to enhance our understanding and provide concrete strategies is study support. From the humble origins of the homework club study support has rapidly matured into a movement of immense significance. It is immensely significant because it provides the intermediate link between learning in, and learning out, of school.

Its purpose is defined by the Department for Education and Employment as:

> to raise achievement by motivating young people to become more effective learners through activities which enrich the curriculum and improve core skills. These activities take place on a voluntary basis out-of-school hours.
>
> (DfEE, 1998a)

In that document the DfEE illustrates in words and pictures a range of activities such as:

- homework clubs
- space and support for coursework and exam revision
- help with key skills, including literacy and numeracy and ICT
- creative ventures (music, drama, dance, film)
- mentoring by adults or other pupils
- learning about learning (thinking skills, accelerated learning)
- community service (crime prevention initiatives, environmental clubs)

The common link is re-engaging young people with education, raising self-esteem and motivation, rehearsing and reinforcing skills, introducing new skills, broadening the base of achievement.

Howard Gardner (1983) defines the successful student as:

> he/she knows how to use opportunities for learning which are distributed throughout his or her environment. This includes not only books and libraries, media and electronic information, but the learning resources of people – teachers, friends, family, mentors and employers.
>
> (p. 19)

This provides the strongest rationale for study support. It is what schools, further and higher education are there to do but fail to do successfully for all, or even most young people because teachers lack the time, the resources or the pedagogical know-how.

At the core of the best study support initiatives is a belief that success can be for all, intelligence can be acquired, students can learn how to motivate themselves, how to plan, how to organize and how to use the most up-to-date techniques of accelerated learning. But there is also a commitment to the belief that successful students are also interdependent learners, sharing and collaborating with one another.

The extended school day and schools-after-schools are receiving increasing attention internationally but they are not being systematically evaluated, and often rest on unquestioned assumptions. The extended school day, which offers simply more of the same, or more of what has already failed to work for some young people, might prove to be counterproductive. On the other hand, a shorter school day with more opportunity for study support, mentoring, coaching and community projects may prove to be more effective. We do not yet know the answers to these questions but there are some clear pointers to hand.

Research into study support (MacBeath, 1991, 1992) found that its voluntary nature, the informal context, the easy-going relationships between students and teachers and the student-led agenda were all factors in attracting young people. They also helped to sustain their interest and motivation. For disenfranchised young people, at risk, in some cases truanting during the school day, study support offered a lifeline.

There were benefits for teachers too. Freed from the pressure of the classroom, teachers said that they were able to stand back, to watch young people at work, and to reflect on how effectively they were learning. Teachers spoke about study support as a laboratory, or an incubator, as a place where you try something out, plant the seeds of an idea, and watch it develop. As a testing ground for new approaches to learning and teaching study support is seen as having an immense potential.

Under this broad (and unfortunately named) umbrella of 'study support' is a growing alliance of initiatives, Easter and summer schools, study centres in football clubs, and new-style 'universities' – the Tower Hamlets Summer University, Birmingham's Children's University and University of the First Age. Children and young people enter on a voluntary basis, sometimes with a shove from parents or peers, but they then quite typically volunteer to stay on for a further week. In their evaluations of the experience there are common persistent themes – learning can be fun. Learning can be stimulating and fulfilling, and something you actually choose to do in your summer holidays.

Much of the attraction of summer schools and study support generally is, of course, their sociability. But then that is the best aspect of school and, as we have already seen in studies of longevity, is essentially what is human about human beings. Learning is an intensely social activity and it is in relationships between people that ideas are born, memories are shaped and intelligence is created. The physicist David Bohm said this:

> Thought is largely a collective phenomenon … As with electrons we must look on thought as a systemic phenomenon arising from how we interact and discourse with one another.
>
> (Bohm, 1983, p. 199)

The potential benefits of study support are not just for individual teachers and pupils, nor even only for school improvement, but for wider policy-making at national, and even international level. Thanks to study support we know a great deal more about learning. We have seen the difficult transition for many teachers in moving from a teaching to a learning perspective. Helping children learn is, in some respects, a much harder task than teaching.

We found in our work with study support centres that teachers, by their own admission, were often not very practised or confident in helping young people to think for themselves, to allow them to solve problems their own way, or to talk their way to personal meaning. The pressures to stay in control and get through the syllabus didn't leave time to develop ideas, engage in debate and to take side excursions into interesting speculative territory. Ironically this was very much a characteristic of 'progressive' primary schools who now find themselves caught up in the same single-minded pursuit of accreditation as their secondary colleagues.

Some schools taught techniques such as brainstorming, concept mapping, skimming, scanning, key words/key ideas, but then found it puzzling that these techniques weren't used by young people. Teachers were perplexed as to how to help students integrate such practices into their own learning styles and study habits. In Entwhistle's (1987) epistemology, young people need to be both strategic and deep learners. That is, they need to have at their finger-tips a range of tricks and techniques for passing examinations (strategic) and at the same time a conceptual facility with ideas, and a meta-cognition (deep) which guides them as to when to use one, the other, or both.

In a number of schools, study support offered a strong and direct challenge to mainstream practice and caused teachers to take a longer harder look at how they taught and what they expected of young people after the teaching was over. Some teachers reported a genuine problem with study support students. They had become more demanding, more impatient with poor teaching, more creatively dissatisfied. For some teachers this was exciting. For many it was an extra unneeded headache (MacBeath, 1992).

Where Now?

Since the beginning of the 1990s there has been a massive expansion of study support and it is a feature of thousands of schools, libraries and community centres nationwide. The growth of study support has been, in part, because it was seen to work. In large part it has grown because it had the impetus from visionary people such as Molly Lowell in the Prince's Trust. In 1998 alone the

Trust raised the profile of study support to new heights. They published a National Code of Practice (Prince's Trust, 1997) with a foreword by the Prime Minister. This was followed this year with a series of handbooks illustrating exemplary practice and success stories from across the country (Prince's Trust, 1998). The Trust produced a CD-ROM to accompany these and held workshops and conferences in most major British cities. They set in train a three year evaluation project (Myers and MacBeath, 1998) which now holds data on over 10,000 young people and the 54 schools which they attend. Through the Trust, and together with the Teacher Training Agency, Keele University and Christchurch College in Canterbury are piloting teacher professional development programmes for study support.

The Trust's initiatives along with those of Education Extra and Kids Club Network were instrumental in persuading the Government to make a very significant investment in study support. Through the New Opportunities Fund £300 million will be spent over the next year to support study centres nationwide, including the establishment of centres in Premiership Football Clubs. Those clubs who have taken the lead, among them Newcastle United and Sheffield Wednesday, have already demonstrated the immense attraction and powerful potential of learning sites based in unusual and compelling venues such as the players lounge at St James's Park.

The policy implications are far-reaching. Schools cannot provide the whole of education, and education should not be seen as synonymous with school. We have over-invested and outplayed the school effect. We have concentrated too single-mindedly on the 'nine to three' school at the expense of a wider understanding of learning. We still know too little about home learning and homework is still conceived too narrowly. Study support has demonstrated ways of going beyond the physical confines of the school as well beyond the boundaries of the imagination. The 14-hour school, with openings for breakfast clubs and access to resources in the early morning and twilight and evening sessions until 9 or 10 o'clock, already exist. The widening clientele of study support to encompass adults in a range of roles points to a more diverse and flexible future for schools as community learning centres.

There is significant work to be done in training teachers in the range of skills needed in informal and voluntary learning, including collaborative work with volunteers and tutors, the co-ordination and management of centres and the integration of school-based and out-of-hours learning. However much schools improve their pedagogy, there will continue to be a growing need to focus on how young people learn outside school. Ivan Illich's (1971) 'convivial networks' for learning are becoming a reality in the 1990s in the shape of the Internet and other instant information systems. They will offer as yet unimaginable opportunities for learning exchange which will inevitably increase the power of those who master the medium, and further open the gap between them and the disenfranchised. Study support with an emphasis on learning and information skills will come to play an even more significant role in that future, but its form will depend on how prescient teachers, researchers and other policy visionaries are. Without that vision schools may suddenly be overtaken by the future. We look forward to a new Learning Age White Paper with a bold vision and practical strategies for lifelong learning and learning for life.

Note

1 For further information contact Dr Jenny Wellington, The University of Sheffield.

References

Adorno, T.W.E., Frenkel-Brunswick, L.D. and Sanford, R.N. (1950) *The Authoritarian Personality*, New York, Harper.

Bernstein, B. (1970) 'Education cannot compensate for society', *New Society*, 387, pp. 344–347.

Bohm, D. (1983) *Wholeness and the Implicate Order*, New York, Ark Paperbacks.

Coleman, J.S., Campbell, E.Q., Hobson, C.J., McPartland, J., Mood, A.M., Wienfeld, F.D. and York., R.L. (1966) *Equality of Educational Opportunity*, Washington, DC, Office of Education.

Department for Education and Employment (DfEE) (1997) *Excellence in Schools*, London, DfEE.

Department for Education and Employment (DfEE) (1998a) *The Learning Age*, London, DfEE.

Department for Education and Employment (DfEE) (1998b) *Extending Opportunity: A national framework for study support*, London, DfEE.

Diener, C. and Dweck, C. (1978) 'An analysis of learned helplessness: the processing of success', *Journal of Personality and Social Psychology* 39, pp. 940–952.

Entwistle, N. (1987) *Understanding Classroom Learning*, London, Hodder & Stoughton.

European Commission (1996) *Teaching and Learning: Towards the learning society*, Brussels, The European Commission.

European Round Table of Industrialists (1994) *Education for Europeans: Towards the learning society*, Brussels, ERT.

Gardner, H. (1983) *Frames of Mind*, New York, Basic Books.

Goleman, D. (1996) *Emotional Intelligence*, London, Bloomsbury.

Hannon, P. (1993) 'Conditions of learning at home and in school', in *Ruling the Margins*, University of North London Institute of Education.

Illich, I. (1971) *Deschooling Society*, New York, Harper & Row.

MacBeath, J. (1991) *Learning for Yourself*, Quality in Education Centre, University of Strathclyde.

MacBeath, J. (1992) *A Place for Success*, London, Prince's Trust.

Martin, P. (1997) *The Sickening Mind*, London, Flamingo.

Milgram, S. (1974) 'Some conditions of obedience and disobedience to authority', *Human Relations* 18, pp. 57–76.

Myers, K. and MacBeath, J. (1998) 'Changing your life through study support: how will we know if it makes a difference?', *Paper Delivered to the American Educational Research Association*, San Diego, April 1998.

Organization for Economic Cooperation and Development (OECD) (1995) *Learning Beyond Schooling*, Paris, OECD.

Perkins, D. (1998) 'Learning for understanding', *Paper given at West Lothian/Quality in Education Seminar*, September 1998.

Prince's Trust (1997) *The Code of Practice: Out of School Hours Learning*, Glasgow, Quality in Education Centre, University of Strathclyde.

Prince's Trust (1998) *The Handbook: Study Support*, Glasgow, Quality in Education Centre, University of Strathclyde.

United Nations Educational Scientific and Cultural Organization (UNESCO) (1995) *Learning: The treasure within* (The Delors Report), Paris, UNESCO.

16 Overview

Theo Cox

The Challenge of Disadvantage

What clearly emerges from the contributions to this book, together with the evidence summarized in the Introduction, is that social inequalities related to poverty and class are still widely prevalent throughout Western industrialized countries, not least in the UK, and, as Grant and Williams make clear in Chapter 14, in the USA. These disadvantages are compounded by forms of discrimination relating to gender and ethnicity and also the tendency of some teachers and other professional workers to make stereotypical judgements of pupils on the grounds of their background, behaviour or other characteristics. Within the context of globalized world trade and the growth of the 'knowledge economy', the sharp decline in the demand for unskilled labour, and the collapse of the youth employment market, at least in Europe, young people leaving school with no credible educational qualifications and not able or willing to embark on further education or training are truly disadvantaged.

Mortimore and Whitty (Chapter 10) assert that societies still maintain social divisions and a 'powerful sense of hierarchy' which is resistant to change. Against this background they consider that the drive to improve the effectiveness of schools and thus raise educational standards generally has exaggerated the extent to which schools can challenge these structural inequalities. They argue that the gap between socially advantaged and disadvantaged pupils might increase, rather than diminish, if all schools were brought up to the same level of effectiveness. In their view the problems facing schools with large intakes of disadvantaged children are greater than the standards related policies of the present British Government recognize. Their argument is reinforced by the conclusion of Lucey and Walkerdine (Chapter 3) that social class differences are more salient than gender differences in relation to school achievement and academic motivation. They highlight the contrast between middle-class and working-class parents in respect of their levels of drive, ambition and 'know-how' in respect of their children's education and future, with working-class boys being particularly vulnerable in the context of the demise of traditional manual jobs. The research evidence described by the present writer (Chapter 9) supports the view that attitudes and motivation for academic learning are less committed among lower-class children and adults, particularly white working-class boys, and often further weakened by negative peer group pressures in school. The extent of under-achievement in England is illustrated by the fact, reported in Chapter 10, that half of the relevant age group fail to succeed in GCSE examinations at the levels traditionally expected.

This is not to argue that escape from disadvantage is not possible for, as Halsey points out (TES, 1999a), there has been a growing demographic trend in our society for working-class children and their parents to move upwards in social class terms. Also, an analysis of the occupational status at age 33 of members of the National Child Development Study (NCDS) sample in rela-tion to their earlier background and personal characteristics found that intellectual capacity and tenacity in working towards a given objective were much better predictors of adult occupational status than early social class and related variables (Saunders, 1997). Saunders concluded that the occupational class system in Britain is more meritocratic than had previously been assumed.

However, such mobility appears most likely to occur where the individual's personal resources and circumstances offer significant support for his or her aspirations (see, for example Pilling, 1990, Cox and Jones, 1983, and also Chapters 5 and 6 in this book). Where the quality of a child's education is inferior and other supportive or protective features are weak or lacking then the prospects of lower working-class children and young people are likely to be severely constrained by social disadvantage. The chapters in Part I of this book bring out very clearly how the education and life chances of certain groups of children are seriously threatened by a potent combination of educa-tional and other disadvantages, in particular: children from ethnic minority groups; those looked after in local authority care; poor school attenders; and children presenting emotional and behavioural difficulties in school.

The chapters in Part I also reveal how the operation of market-oriented educational policies, inherited by the present British Government from the previous Conservative administration, appear to have further exacerbated the disadvantages experienced by these vulnerable children. As Tomlinson puts it (Chapter 2) new forms of inequality and new disadvantages are emerging as the educational system tries to lever up educational standards for all. She focuses upon ethnic minority children but other chapters in this section reveal how these consumer-led policies, characterized by competition between schools for enrolment and school performance tables, are also adversely affecting the life chances of other vulnerable groups. The social polarization of school intakes under the pressures of competition is denounced by Tomlinson and by Mortimore and Whitty, and also by Sofer (Chapter 11), who claims that the damaging effects on the life chances of disadvantaged secondary school children by highly selective and stratified school systems has become a taboo subject under the present British Govern-ment's 'standards not structures mantra'. In addition to being more subject to social stratification as a result of these policies these vulnerable children are also more likely than others to be excluded from their schools which are driven by an anxiety to maintain or improve their status in the performance tables (see Chapters 5, 6 and 12).

Combating Educational Disadvantage

The Limits of Educational Solutions

If in our society there are indeed structural inequalities associated with class, gender and ethnicity, as some contributors to this book powerfully argue, then it follows that Governments cannot rely upon educational measures alone to eliminate poverty and the disadvantages often linked with it (see Chapter 1). As Mortimore and Whitty (Chapter 10) put it, policies which tackle poverty and related aspects at their roots are more likely to be successful than purely educational interventions, although dynamic school improvement policies must have a major place in co-ordinated economic, social and educational policies. They argue for a stronger interventionist role for local educational authorities (LEAs), as part of such overarching policies, in order to target resources on schools in socially disadvantaged areas. Similarly Sofer (Chapter 11) questions the adequacy of the present British Government's strategy for bringing about educational improvements for disadvantaged pupils through its managerial approach of target-setting and performance management for LEAs and schools. She asks whether the Government has lost sight of the relationship between children's learning difficulties and wider patterns of social disadvantage and inequality, which need to be addressed through economic and fiscal policies. In the same vein Grant and Williams (Chapter 14), after reviewing the US scene, conclude that much work remains to be done in order for the social, economic and political climate to reach the condition of fostering an equal and equitable education for students outside of the dominant culture. Such a judgement is especially significant given the fact that the national drive to eliminate the 'educational war on poverty' begun by President Johnson has been largely sustained since its inception (see Chapter 1).

Such arguments are not new in the debate on social and educational disadvantage. In their wide ranging analysis of British and American approaches to combating poverty Silver and Silver (1991) observe that the issues and goals which were uppermost during the earlier decades had not been superseded by the changed economic and political frameworks and priorities of the 1970s and 1980s.

> The issues and the targets have not gone away. Many of the activities and dynamics generated still continue. The controversies still simmer. The roles of government, public agencies, private finance and people, in relation to

education and participation in educational processes, while differently contoured, remain to be argued over. The relation between education and other social and economic policies is still subject for debate.

(Silver and Silver, 1991, p. 9)

While the main thrust of the present New Labour Government in Britain appears to be to tackle educational disadvantage through its efforts to raise educational standards in general, through its target setting policies, school and LEA inspections and its National Literacy and Numeracy projects, its establishment of the Social Exclusion Unit (see Chapter 1) represents a clear acknowledgement of the need for them to go beyond purely educational solutions to the problems of disadvantage. Their recognition of the vital need to co-ordinate policies across several key Government departments in this endeavour is commendable. Moreover, in its annual Government report for 1997–1998 (HM Government, 1998), there is an acceptance of the fact that inequality has grown in Britain despite ever higher spending on welfare, with more than one fifth of households having no bread winner, and one in three children living in poverty. Through its Social Exclusion Unit it promises to produce an annual report on poverty in Britain and its success in alleviating it.

It remains to be seen whether the British Government's present policies will tackle educational and social disadvantage and social exclusion at its roots as hoped, and regular independent and self-monitoring of its progress in meeting this goal is clearly essential. The New Policy Institute, a think tank, has recently published a proposed set of key indicators of deprivation and social exclusion for the Government's consideration (TES, 1998a). These include the number of pupils gaining no GCSE Grade C levels or above, a traditional benchmark of 'success', but a report from another think tank, the Institute for Public Policy Research (TES, 1998b), recommends that the Government's educational targets should be based on the proportion of 16-year-olds failing to get at least 20 GCSE points, which is roughly equivalent to 5 D Grades, since this would encourage schools to concentrate more on its weaker pupils.

The setting of clear standards and targets for education (and other areas of public service) seems set to retain a firm place in the British Government's policies to combat social exclusion, but such targets need to take full account of the social and other determinants or influences upon performance in each domain. Even then the standards need to be applied with flexibility and it is encouraging that the Government's earlier policy of 'naming and shaming' of schools officially judged to be failing has now been abandoned under new procedures which allow such schools two years to improve before matters are taken out of their hands (TES, 1998c). In the present volume Carroll (Chapter 4) argues that if the publication of the performance of LEAs in meeting targets for the reduction of truancy rates leads to the Government taking punitive action against those failing to do so, this would be unjust to those LEAs with a high proportion of socially disadvantaged inhabitants. He advocates that such LEAs should, rather, be given more resources to tackle the inherent social problems, including more educational psychologists and education welfare officers. (See Chapter 12 for an account of how educational psychologists are helping schools to combat truancy and social exclusion.)

Government targets and nationally prescribed educational policies should also be fully sensitive to gender and ethnicity issues. Gregory (Chapter 7) raises the question of how equality of opportunity for all pupils can be provided for pupils not familiar with traditional school literacy practices. She stresses the need for teachers to be helped to a greater awareness of the cultural practices which such children experience before school and at home. Such a need has implications for the present Government's national literacy drive and its home–school contracts designed to support children's homework.

Co-ordinated and Community-Based Approaches

In Chapter 13 Evans points out that many governments have responded to the challenge of raising educational standards, especially of at-risk pupils, by decentralizing decision-making and planning as a way to reduce costs, to promote local flexibility, and to increase allocational efficiency. This trend is coupled with a recognition that client need can better be met through responsive local structures that involve the entire community. He emphasizes, however, that it is essential to maintain effective links between national policy-making and local service delivery and his chapter provides several examples from OECD countries of how such locally based solutions are meeting the educational, social and economic needs of at-risk young people and their families. An account of similar, community-based projects targeted on disadvantaged areas in Scotland can be found in Nisbet and Watt (1994). In many of these the former Scottish regional authorities have played a leading role.

As Sofer points out (Chapter 11) the highly centralized educational system in England and Wales, although coupled with the devolution of management powers to schools, contrasts with the decentralizing trend in other European countries described by Evans. Under the British New Labour Government LEAs are increasingly cast in an agency role in which they are to be held strictly accountable for their attainment of centrally prescribed targets, for example, on school standards of literacy and numeracy, school exclusion and truancy rates. At the same time their traditional discretionary power to allocate funds and resources to support schools serving highly disadvantaged areas has been severely eroded. In her judgement this managerial approach, while having some advantages, carries serious risks and weaknesses, especially the loss of local democracy in the planning and decision-making process, for example, with regard to the co-ordination and planning of school admission systems. Like Evans she argues that educational systems should have enough flexibility to allow for local innovation and responsiveness to need, and to encourage multidisciplinary working and strengthen organizational connections between schools and services for vulnerable children and families.

Evans discusses elsewhere the challenges and essential requirements in establishing successful integrated or co-ordinated services for children and families at risk (OECD, 1996) and these also emerge in some of the contributions to the present book. For example Jackson (Chapter 5) considers that the ambitious objectives of the British Government's major new policy initiative aimed at strengthening the local authority's management of the public care system cannot be reached without a profound shift in the attitudes and assumptions of local authority officers and councillors, and Sofer highlights some of the difficulties of multidisciplinary working which have been highly resistant to change on almost any issue where collaboration between LEAs and other agencies is required. Focused inter-professional training and active community involvement will probably be key agents in achieving the required attitude changes.

While the main thrust of the New Labour Government's educational policies is a strongly centralist one, its policy initiatives launched by its Social Exclusion Unit appear to allow considerable scope for the kind of local community empowerment described by Evans. As outlined in Chapter 1 these initiatives include the New Deal for Communities Programme, which forms part of a national strategy for neighbourhood renewal, and the Education Action Zones (EAZs) now being established in selected areas of both urban and rural deprivation. At the time of writing 25 such zones have been chosen in England (there are none planned for Wales) and a new round of applications for a fresh tranche of zones is being publicly invited. The EAZs are obviously a key weapon in the Government's attack upon the roots of social exclusion and their success in meeting their self-determined educational and other objectives will be keenly followed. The thinking and funding underpinning the new EAZs seems to be considerably more ambitious than that which drove the running of the Educational Priority Areas (later renamed Social Priority Areas) following the publication of the Plowden Report (see Chapter 1). Their introduction has been cautiously welcomed by several contributors to the present volume and is certainly in keeping with the policies of targeting resources for the disadvantaged in designated educational priority areas which have been adopted for some time by other European and OECD countries such as Ireland, Holland and France (see Chapter 13, Day et al., 1997, and Kellaghan et al., 1995).

A critical analysis of the first round of EAZ applications was commissioned by the Education Network (described as part of a local authority controlled company) and published in October 1998 (Riley et al., 1998). This was based on a careful study of nearly 60 applications from which the final selection of 25 was made by the Government. Despite the fact that there were no published criteria for judging the applications the authors of the report infer those aspects of the proposals which appear to have been influential in guiding the official response to them. They characterize the first tranche of applications as safe rather than boldly innovative in their vision and approach but attribute this, partly at least, to the short time-scale allowed for the submission of applications and the Government's lack of published evaluation criteria.

On the basis of their scrutiny of both successful and unsuccessful applications the authors of the report draw together recommendations for the development of EAZ policy and practice. Among these are that a more extended process of preparation and consultation in the planning stage of applications would enable ideas to be introduced from voluntary and community groups and other areas of the public sector, who were not well represented in the first tranche. Similarly students and parents were not usually represented directly in the Action Forums making the applications and there was generally little reference to the involvement of young people themselves in the shaping of the initiatives. Zones will need to adopt targets that are quantitative, qualitative and relate directly and clearly to student learning goals. At the same time a multi-agency approach to development and delivery would address the broader policy agenda for tackling social and educational disadvantage.

Implications for government EAZ policy include the need for greater clarity about whether the initiative is about innovation, raising achievement or tackling social disadvantage (or perhaps all of these), and greater clarity about the process and criteria for selection. The authors also query the current concept of an EAZ as a geographical area large enough to encompass clusters of up to 20 schools since this appears to exclude smaller areas of acute need, and they call for a variety of models for future zones. They also recommend systematic and continuing evaluation by government of the policies, practices and outcomes associated with the EAZ projects. In its brief introduction to the EAZ policy (DfEE, 1997) the Government commits itself to a careful evaluation of the success of the zones as their work progresses but details of how this will be done are still awaited.

The final comment of the report's authors is that the EAZ initiative, which they describe as a 'high profile, high stakes' one, holds real opportunities for change but its future potential depends upon the degree to which its focus can be sharpened and linked to a more comprehensive strategy for improvement and to the wider social policy agenda. This conclusion is reinforced by the fact that, by its selective nature, the initiative can only be expected to raise standards and tackle disadvantage in the chosen areas unless there is to be a systematic programme of dissemination and replication of its successful features in the many remaining disadvantaged areas. Since this report was produced the Government has launched a major campaign to attract applications beyond the LEAs. The Education Secretary is quoted as saying that he particularly wanted to see applications from schools partnered with parents, community groups and with business (TES, 1999b).

Educational Approaches

Clearly education lies at the heart of approaches to combat educational disadvantage. However wide-ranging social and economic programmes to alleviate social disadvantage might be, in the final issue their effectiveness will be judged in terms of how much they improve the quality of the education received by disadvantaged pupils and the scope of their further educational opportunities. The British New Labour Government, through its School Standards and Framework Act, has placed a statutory obligation upon LEAs and school governing bodies to promote high standards, and, as described in Chapter 1, has introduced a number of educational policy initiatives in support of this legislation. Its Improving Schools programme advocates a five-stage cycle of target setting, within a self-evaluation framework linked to external inspection.

Several chapters in this book describe government and other initiatives aimed at helping schools to raise their standards of teaching and support for disadvantaged pupils. Chazan (Chapter 6) describes a promising Positive Alternatives to School Exclusion (PASE) project at the University of Cambridge which is designed to help schools to find more acceptable alternatives to exclusion from school, as well as a range of strategies which schools and teachers can use to improve vulnerable pupils' behaviour and adjustment. Carroll (Chapter 4) describes some measures to reduce pupil absenteeism and Gersch et al. (Chapter 12) describe ways in which educational psychologists are actively collaborating with schools and other professional school services in support of vulnerable children, including those most at risk of exclusion. Grant and Williams (Chapter 14) describe a range of promising educational models, programmes and practices currently in operation in US schools, including the Comer Project which integrates social service programmes within schools, intensifies parental participation and aims to enhance parental and community support for education. Mortimore and Whitty (Chapter 10) also highlight a number of educational intervention projects of considerable promise and advocate public support and funding for them in the UK.

MacBeath (Chapter 15) refers to the new community schools in Scotland and full service schools which may provide the possible locus for innovative family-centred initiatives. Certainly locally based initiatives of this kind should significantly boost the school attitudes and learning motivation of hitherto educationally disadvantaged students, although as discussed by the present writer (Chapter 9), a national campaign to raise pupil commitment to learning may well also be necessary. The Government's Study Support Scheme described by MacBeath is a major initiative aimed at linking school, community and work-related learning, which includes a national network of study centres, some located within Premier football clubs. He regards these centres, which aim to re-engage young people with education, and to lift their self-esteem and their motivation to learn, as a lifeline for students disaffected with the traditional school curriculum.

Several contributors to this book call for Government and schools to develop a curriculum and pedagogy which is more sensitive and responsive to the cultural traditions and practices of ethnic and other minority groups. Tomlinson (Chapter 2) comments that the national curriculum, introduced in Britain by the previous, Conservative Government, quite explicitly excluded reference to multicultural and anti-racist initiatives. Gregory (Chapter 7) asserts that, in Britain, there is a general lack of recognition of cultural differences in the learning processes of minority group families, in contrast to the USA. She criticizes, in particular, the English national curriculum in this regard. However Grant and Williams (Chapter 14) make it clear that, even in the USA, there is still much need for educators and schools to be more sensitive to pupils' cultural backgrounds and traditions. Examples of educational initiatives taken within one LEA to support multicultural teaching and learning are presented by Gersch et al. (Chapter 12).

As Mortimore and Whitty (Chapter 10) point out more needs to be done to provide opportunities for learning beyond the years of compulsory education. While welcoming the New Labour Government's lifelong learning initiatives (see Chapter 15), they make several suggestions as to how the Government could help disadvantaged people to extend their education and they refer to important recommendations in the Kennedy Report on further education. In November 1998 the Government announced funding of £725 million to support a massive expansion of further education targeting disabled and disadvantaged people (TES, 1998d). This appears to signal the high priority which the Government places on further education in its drive towards a more inclusive society.

Early Childhood Education

While well co-ordinated and funded school improvement and further education programmes must be central elements in combating educational disadvantage, one could argue that the highest priority of all should be accorded to the prevention of such disadvantage through high quality early education and family support programmes. Sylva (Chapter 8) summarizes the now substantial research evidence that early educational intervention in the lives of children and families in disadvantaged circumstances, especially children from age 3–6 years, can prevent, or at least greatly reduce the risk of their later educational failure and social exclusion. The best long-term benefits of pre-school education are strongly associated with active, play-based curricula which not only provide a sound intellectual and motivational foundation for learning at school and beyond – truly lifelong learning – but also promote children's social commitment and the development of positive, collaborative social relationships. However, Sylva expresses concern about the trend towards more formal, teacher-directed learning in Britain, particularly in infant reception classes (see Sylva, 1997), and strongly recommends a shift in the character of the present national 'Desirable Outcomes' of early education towards a more socially and motivationally oriented curriculum.

Britain's New Labour Government certainly appears to have a strong commitment to the importance of investing in high quality, universal pre-school education for all children whose parents want it. Currently there is provision of places for all four-year-olds in England and Wales to receive such education and the Government has recently announced a target of providing nursery or other pre-school places for two thirds of three-year-olds by the year 2002 (TES, 1998e). It is also funding the large scale Effective Provision of Pre-School Education Project (described by Sylva in Chapter 8) which is designed to evaluate the most effective curricula and forms of educational provision for young children in England and Wales, including the socially disadvantaged. It has also recently launched its Sure Start Scheme, which is a cross-departmental (Education and Health) initiative targeted on children under 4 years of age and their families in areas of social disadvantage (Sure Start Unit, 1998). Over the next three years the programme will support the development of 250 local projects providing co-ordinated core services in designated centres which are designed to meet local needs effectively, taking account of the views of the parents and community members. These services will include parenting and family support, primary and specialist health services, high quality play and child care facilities and outreach services.

While there are some important curricular issues still to be resolved about the most effective types of educational programmes and provision for very young socially disadvantaged children within the British context (see Chapter 8), there is little doubt that the active support of the children's parents or care-givers for such programmes will be essential, together with the provision of high quality training of all early years educators. These elements will help to ensure that the early educational disadvantages commonly experienced by vulnerable children at the threshold of their statutory schooling are eliminated.

Future Developments

Within this volume several possible developments in education are outlined, some of which are alternatives. Each possibility raises important issues in relation to educationally disadvantaged pupils. In Chapter 11 Sofer predicts that current uncertainties regarding the role of LEAs are likely to continue but, in the longer term, their powers and responsibilities may be taken over by other agencies. Recent Government pronouncements offer some support for this prediction, at least as far as 'failing' LEAs are concerned. For example, given his new powers under the School Standards and Framework Act, the Education and Employment Secretary has publicly advertised for private companies and other oragnizations and consortia to take on the education services of failing councils. It is even envisaged that a private company could take over the entire functions of an authority rather than specific services (TES, 1999b). A further possibility is that an EAZ forum could take over from a failing LEA (TES, 1999c). Such developments raise serious questions regarding the place of local democracy and the needs and interests of the disadvantaged, as Sofer points out.

Private Enterprise

The nature of the role and contribution of private enterprise to publicly funded educational services is a major issue which is now coming to the fore in Britain although it has figured in debates on education and disadvantage in the USA for some time. For example in that country the 'with-profit' Edison organization holds contracts to run all aspects of education in selected schools (Riley et al., 1998). As Riley et al. point out, '... the possible contracting of a profit making private organisation such as Edison presents a challenge to the EAZ concept, to patterns of school governance and local accountability, and to established educational institutions and orthodoxies in this country' (Riley et al., 1998, p. 15).

The evidence presented by some of the authors in the present volume is that market forces operating within the educational systems of England and Wales, particularly with regard to school admissions, school performance tables and school exclusions, have tended to compound the disadvantages of vulnerable children and young people. However, Davie argues in his Foreword that it would be unwise to throw out the baby with the bath water by totally rejecting the contribution of a market forces ideology to public education. Both the previous and present Governments have recognized and accepted the principle of this contribution but perhaps the debate should focus more upon the terms, conditions and frameworks within which private enterprise should be permitted to operate. In their report on educational disadvantage in Scotland Nisbet and Watt (1994) claim that the contribution which we should look for from the private sector includes funding, to supplement shortages within public funding, and also expertise in management, where ' ... a proper concern for market forces will keep development on the right lines, instead of being directed by liberal ideology' (Nisbet and Watt, 1994, p. 44). They argue that market forces should be given a more important place in settling all issues in education, resulting in greater efficiency and, ultimately, to prosperity, to the benefit of all, including the disadvantaged. They also contend that, while, at first sight, a private enterprise philosophy seems incongruent with the philosophy of caring which shaped the creation of the welfare state, it can be accommodated within the principle of 'interdependence', under which market forces, collaborative working among public, private and voluntary sectors and a caring attitude can be harnessed.

Active, Self-Motivated Learning

The nature and quality of children's learning is a vital issue. In his discussion of lifelong learning MacBeath (Chapter 15) argues that a shorter school day with more opportunity for study support, mentoring, coaching and community projects may prove to be more effective, especially with educationally at risk students, than a traditional approach to school learning. He sees study support as a testing ground for new approaches to learning in which teachers will have a less didactic role than teaching in the traditional sense. His views seem to have particular application to secondary education, given the stronger child-centred orientation of primary education, at least in its more progressive form. They can be closely linked with the findings reported by Sylva (Chapter 8) concerning the benefits of high quality early childhood education, which include not only cognitive gains, but positive self-esteem and self-concept as a learner, a disposition to learn in which motivation is centred upon mastery rather than performance, and, not least, positive social commitment. Combining the views of both writers one might envisage an educational system in which highly motivated young learners would enter the statutory school system that was highly pupil oriented, according them increasingly more responsibility for their own learning within an institution which provided interfaces with learning opportunities within the local community, the world of work and the global electronic network. Such a development, combined with the greater influence of students' views and aspirations within the curriculum and within school organization, as advocated in Chapter 9, would most powerfully counter the disaffection with traditional school learning and underachievement that currently characterizes many socially and educationally disadvantaged pupils.

The Contribution of Research

In a discussion of the relevance and contribution of European research to the education of disadvantaged pupils Evans (1997) concludes that if the research questions emanate from educational policy makers themselves they will take notice of the findings; if not they are less likely to do so. In this connection it is encouraging that the present British Government appears to adopt a positive view of the potential contribution of well conducted research in education. It recently announced an action plan designed to increase the impact of educational research upon educational policy and practice which includes better public funding and co-ordination of research projects, and more active involvement of policy makers, including LEAs and teachers, in commissioning, steering and disseminating research (TES, 1998f). While there may be some reservation about the size of the proposed co-ordinated research budget and the composition and role of the research forum charged with co-ordinating these reforms this is a welcome step in the right direction. In the present volume the contributing authors draw heavily upon relevant research findings, including their own work, in their discussions of aspects of educational policy and practice in regard to the disadvantaged. The Effective Pre-School Provision in which Sylva is involved (Chapter 8) is a good example of a DfEE-funded project specifically designed to inform and guide educational policy and practice. In some instances contributors have pointed to the need for further research to assist in the implementation of Government policy. For example Mortimore and Whitty (Chapter 10) conclude that research efforts to develop reliable and valid statistical methods for evaluating school academic performance measures so as to take account of their social intakes, the so-called 'value added' measures, are still far from achieving success.

Looking ahead the publicly funded Economic and Social Research Council (ESRC) has recently launched three major projects which are likely to feed into national social, economic and educational policy and practice affecting the disadvantaged. The first of these is the establishment of a new ESRC Research Centre for the Analysis of Social Exclusion (CASE) which will focus on three key dimensions of social exclusion, namely: the economy and incomes; families and family change; and areas and neighbourhoods. The second is a Youth, Citizenship and Social Change Research Programme which aims to explore the issues and implications raised by new social policies ranging from the introduction of student grants to the virtual exclusion of young people from state benefits. This will include a study of teenagers at risk in their transition to adulthood. The third is a new programme designed to increase understanding of the factors which underpin and create effective teaching and learning at all levels from pre-school to higher education and lifelong learning. One of its aims will be to help teachers to make better use of research in order to improve their teaching.

Concluding Statement

This book focuses on the educational and other problems facing disadvantaged or at risk children and the challenges facing schools and other institutions and services in trying to meet their needs, together with some possible solutions to them. It is written at a time when national interest in Britain in the problems of disadvantage stemming from poverty and class have re-emerged after years of neglect, and when a British Government is in power with an explicit policy agenda for tackling poverty and social exclusion at their roots. It has launched a wide range of educational initiatives linked to this aim, some of which are co-ordinated with other agencies such as the social and health services. Its future success in eradicating serious and widespread poverty will largely depend on the effectiveness of its economic, social and fiscal policies, as well as global economic factors. The success of its educational policy initiatives will depend not only upon the eradication or amelioration of poverty, but also on the way in which these initiatives are sustained and developed so as to take account of the issues and recommendations presented by the contributors to this book.

References

Cox, T. and Jones, G. (1983) *Disadvantaged 11-Year-Olds*, Oxford, Pergamon Press.
Day, C., van Ween, D. and Walraven, G. (eds) (1997) *Children and Youth at Risk and Urban Education: Research policy and practice*, Belgium, EERA and Garant Publishers.
Department for Education and Employment (DfEE) (1997) *Education Action Zones: An introduction*, London, DfEE.
Evans, P. (1997) 'Discussion of the papers: an international perspective', in Day, C., Ween, D. van and Walraven, G. (eds) *Children and Youth at Risk and Urban Education: Research policy and practice*, Belgium, EERA and Garant Publishers.
Her Majesty's Government (1998) *The Government's Annual Report, 1997–98*, CM 3969, London, The Stationery Office.
Kellaghan, T., Weir, S., hUallacháin, S.Ó. and Morgan, M. (1995) *Educational Disadvantage in Ireland. Combat Agency Report number 20*, Dublin, Department of Education.
Nisbet, J. and Watt, J. (1994) *Educational Disadvantage in Scotland: A 1990s perspective*, Edinburgh, Scottish Community Education Council.
Organization for Economic Co-operation and Development (OECD) (1996) *Successful Services for Our Children and Families at Risk*, Paris, OECD.
Pilling, D. (1990) *Escape from Disadvantage*, London, Falmer Press.
Riley, K., Watling, R., Rowles, D. and Hopkins, D. (1998) *Education Action Zones: Some lessons learned from the first wave of applications*, Education Network (unpublished).
Saunders, P. (1997) 'Is Britain a meritocracy?', in Cosin, B. and Hales, M. (eds) *Families, Education and Social Differences*, London, Routledge.
Silver, H. and Silver, P. (1991) *An Educational War on Poverty: American and British policy making 1960–1980*, Cambridge, Cambridge University Press.
Sure Start Unit (1998) *Sure Start News*, 19 November, London, Sure Start Unit.
Sylva, K. (1997) 'The early years curriculum: evidence based approaches', in *Developing the Primary School Curriculum: The next steps*, London, School Curriculum and Assessment Authority (SCAA).
Times Educational Supplement (TES) (1998a) 13 November, p. 23.
Times Educational Supplement (TES) (1998b) 11 December, p. 27.
Times Educational Supplement (TES) (1998c) 2 October, p. 1.
Times Educational Supplement (TES) (1998d) 4 December, p. 27.
Times Educational Supplement (TES) (1998e) 4 December, p. 12.
Times Educational Supplement (TES) (1998f) 13 November, p. 18.
Times Educational Supplement (TES) (1999a) 1 January, p. 8.
Times Educational Supplement (TES) (1999b) 15 January, p. 1.
Times Educational Supplement (TES) (1999c) 15 January, p. 9.

Notes on Contributors

Tim Carroll is a Senior Lecturer in the School of Psychology at the University of Wales Cardiff, where he directs the Master's training course for educational psychologists in Wales. Earlier in his career he taught in schools and served as an LEA educational psychologist. Dr Carroll has been researching pupil absenteeism since 1968 and his publications include an edited book, a co-authored book, chapters in books and articles in national and international journals. He has also acted as consultant on the subject to the Organization for Economic Co-operation and Development (OECD) in Paris. He is a Fellow of the British Psychological Society.

Maurice Chazan is Emeritus Professor of Education at the University of Wales Swansea. Following work as a teacher and an educational psychologist he moved to Swansea in 1960, where he was involved particularly in courses in educational psychology and special education courses in the Department of Education. He was co-director of the Schools Council Research and Development Project in Compensatory Education at the University from 1967 to 1972. He has carried out research and written extensively on educational disadvantage and emotional/behavioural difficulties. He is a Fellow of the British Psychological Society.

Theo Cox is an Honorary Departmental Research Fellow in the Department of Education of the University of Wales Swansea. After teaching in primary and secondary schools and working as an educational psychologist for an LEA he became a Lecturer in Educational Psychology at the University of Wales and also served as Senior Research Officer to the Schools Council Research and Development Project in Compensatory Education at the University of Wales, Swansea. Dr Cox's research interests have centred on educationally disadvantaged children. He is co-author of *Disadvantaged 11-Year-Olds* (Pergamon, 1983) and he has written chapters in books and research articles on this topic, as well as directing two funded research projects on disadvantage. More recently he has published two books (one co-authored, one edited) on the National Curriculum and primary (early years) education. He is a Fellow of the British Psychological Society.

Ronald Davie, formerly Professor of Educational Psychology in Cardiff and subsequently Director of the National Children's Bureau, now works largely as an independent child psychologist. He also holds a number of honorary academic posts. Most recently, Cheltenham and Gloucester College of Higher Education has appointed him to a Visiting Chair with a research focus. Apart from his strong inter-disciplinary orientation, he is perhaps best known for his work in the area of special educational needs and child advocacy and, earlier, as Co-Director of the National Child development Study, many of whose publications have highlighted educational disadvantage.

Peter Evans graduated in psychology from the University of London and completed his Ph.D in education at the University of Manchester. After a period teaching at the University of London Institute of Education he moved to the Organization for Economic Co-operation and Development (OECD) in Paris where, at the Centre for Educational Research and Innovation (CERI), he has responsibility for work in education on disabled and disadvantaged children. Professor Evans has published over twenty books and has written many chapters and journal articles.

Irvine S. Gersch is Principal Educational Psychologist for the London Borough of Waltham Forest. He has published extensively in the fields of pupil involvement, school systems, management, teacher support groups and behaviour management. He has co-edited a book on dealing with disruptive behaviour and undertaken research in the field of effective leadership. Dr Gersch was, until recently, Chairperson of the British Psychological Society Training Committee for Educational Psychology. He is a Fellow of the British Psychological Society. He is a member of the Government's Advisory Group on the Future Role and Training of Educational Psychologists.

Carl A. Grant is Hoefs-Bascom Professor of Teacher Education in the Department of Curriculum and Instruction, as well as Professor in the Department of Afro-American Studies at the University of Wisconsin-Madison. In 1997 he received the Distinguished Achievement Award from the School of Education at the University of Wisconsin. He has written or edited 17 books and monographs on multicultural education and teacher education, including *Research and Multicultural Education*, *Making Choices for Multicultural Education* with Christine E. Sleeter, and *Educating for Diversity*. A former classroom teacher and administrator, Grant was a Fulbright Scholar in England, researching multicultural education. In 1993 he was elected President of the National Association for Multicultural Education (NAME). He was elected as 'One of the 70 Leaders in Teacher Education' by the Association of Teacher Educators in 1990.

Eve Gregory is Professor of Language and Culture in Education, Goldsmiths College, University of London, where she works with students on under-graduate, postgraduate and research degrees. She has directed research projects funded by the Paul Hamlyn Foundation and the Economic and Social Research Council (ESRC) investigating children's out-of-school reading and the transfer of cognitive strategies between home and school. In 1997 she was awarded a Leverhulme Fellowship arising from this work. Her recent books include, *Making Sense of a New World: Learning to read in a second language* (1996), *One Child, Many Worlds: Early learning in multicultural communitites* (1997) and *City Literacies: Learning to read across languages and cultures* (forthcoming).

Sonia Jackson is Professor of Applied Social Studies at the University of Wales Swansea, Chair of Children in Wales and a Trustee of Who Cares? and the National Children's Bureau. She started her career as a clinical psychologist and later worked as an educational advisor and teacher before obtaining her social work qualification from the London School of Economics. She worked with the Department of Health team to develop the 'Looking After Children – Good Parenting, Good Outcomes' system and has directed research studies on early years care and education, child protection, and the health of looked-after children. Her interest in the education of children in care goes back fifteen years and she has published many articles and books on the subject.

Helen Lucey is a Senior Research Fellow in the Department of Education at King's College London. She has researched and published widely on the topic of gender and gender-related issues. Together with Valerie Walkerdine she co-authored *Democracy in the Kitchen: Regulating mothers and socialising daughters* (Virago, 1989). She is currently researching children's experiences and perceptions of the transition to secondary school.

John MacBeath is Director of the Quality in Education Centre at the University of Strathclyde. Over the past six years he has been involved in research and consultancy for a wide range of bodies, including the Scottish Office Education and Industry Department, the Prince's Trust, OECD, UNESCO, UNICEF and the European Commission. Much of his work in the last five years has been in the area of school self-evaluation, develop-ment planning and school improvement. Professor MacBeath has worked closely with national governments, institutions and education authorities throughout the world. In June 1997 he was appointed as a member of the Government's Task Force on Standards, chaired by the Secretary of State for Education, and, in July 1997, he was also appointed to the Action group on Standards, chaired by the Minister of Education for Scotland. He was awarded the OBE for services to education in June 1997.

Peter Mortimore has been Director of the University of London Institute of Education since 1994. During his earlier career he taught as a secondary school teacher in inner city schools and also worked as an HM Inspector and as an LEA administrator. He subsequently served as Director of Research and Statistics for the former Inner London Education Authority and, later, as Director of the School of Education at the University of Lancaster. Professor Mortimore is recognized internationally as a researcher, lecturer and consultant, particularly on school effectiveness and school improvement, and his collected works on school improvement were published in 1998 under the title *The Road to Improvement* (Swets). He was co-author of *Fifteen Thousand Hours* and *School Matters* and other books, and has written widely on other educational topics. Funded research projects with which he is currently involved include studies of school improvement, pupil grouping in schools and class size. He was awarded an OBE in 1993 for services to education.

Anne Sofer was the Director of Education in the London Borough of Tower Hamlets from 1989 to 1997. Before that she was involved in education as a teacher, parent, governor, member of the former Inner London Education Authority and Chair of its Schools Sub-Committee, political adviser and columnist. Since retiring from Tower Hamlets she has undertaken a number of assignments associated with inner city education, notably the establishment of the London Accord, a new organization for mobilizing business support for raising levels of achievement in the most disadvantaged schools, and membership of the DfEE-appointed Hackney Improvement Team. She is Vice Chair of the National Children's Bureau and a trustee of the Nuffield Foundation.

Kathy Sylva is Professor of Educational Psychology at the University of Oxford and a Fellow of Jesus College. After earning a Ph.D at Harvard University she moved to Oxford where she taught psychology while serving as a member of the Oxford Preschool Group. With Teresa Smith and Elizabeth Moore she evaluated the High/Scope Preschool programme. She moved to London University in 1990 to undertake research on assessment and curriculum in primary schools and, in 1997 she returned to Oxford's Department of Educational Studies. She currently co-leads three large research projects, including 'Effective Provision of Preschool Education', which is a national study investigating the characteristics of effective early childhood centres. Her books include *Childwatching at Playgroup and Nursery School*, which broke new ground by questioning an unbridled 'free play' ideology, and, more recently, with Jane Hurry, *Early Intervention in Children with Reading Difficulties*.

Sally Tomlinson is Emeritus Professor in Education at Goldsmiths College, University of London and a Research Associate in the Department of Educational Studies, University of Oxford. She has written and researched extensively in the areas of educational policy, special education and the education of ethnic minorities. Recent relevant publications include *Ethnic Relations and Schooling: Policy and practice in the 1990s*, edited with Maurice Craft (Athlone Press, 1995).

Valerie Walkerdine is Foundation Professor in Critical Psychology at the University of Western Sydney Nepean, Australia. Her publications include *The Mastery of Reason* (Routledge, 1998), *Schoolgirl Fictions* (Verso, 1990) and *Daddy's Girl* (Macmillan, 1997). She was also co-author and editor of *Changing the Subject* (Methuen, 1984).

Geoff Whitty is the Karl Mannheim Professor of Sociology of Education and Dean of Research at the Institute of Education, University of London. He taught in secondary schools before lecturing in education at Bath University and King's College London. In 1985 he became Dean and Professor of Education at Bristol Polytechnic and, from 1990–1992, he was Professor of Policy and Management in Education at Goldsmiths College, University of London. His main areas of research and scholarship are the sociology of education, education policy and urban education. He has directed ESRC-funded research projects on the impact of recent education policies such as the assisted places scheme, city technology colleges and changes in initial teacher education. His most recent book (with Sally Power and David Halpin) is *Devolution and Choice in Education* (Open University Press, 1998).

LaVonne J. Williams is a graduate student in the Department of Curriculum and Instruction at the University of Wisconsin-Madison. She has taught diverse student populations in two large urban settings. Her area of research and scholarship is teacher education and curriculum and instruction for multicultural populations.

Name Index

Subject Index